YOUR FIRST
LEADERSHIP
JOB

YOUR FIRST
LEADERSHIP
JOB

How Catalyst Leaders Bring Out
the Best in Others

TACY M. BYHAM &
RICHARD S. WELLINS

WILEY

Dedication

I dedicate this book to my wonderful family.

Mom and Dad, as a little girl you challenged me to experiment, encouraged me to step up to new experiences, instilled curiosity in me, and showed me the world beyond Western Pennsylvania. You gave me wings to fly to any career that captured my attention—mathematician, computer scientist, arts business manager, singer—and I chose to come home. Dad, I am proud to be walking in your footsteps, and I look forward to building the Bill Byham legacy into the DDI of the next 45 years. And, Mom, I learned a tremendous amount by your side as you continue to speak with your heart and pride to inspire volunteers and community leaders. You both have been absolutely the best leadership models for me, and I am grateful to be a reflection of the two of you.

To my son, Spencer—you have grown into such a magnificent young man. Every day you make me grateful for a sense of humor, storytelling skills, and hugs before bed. You are presently 14 years old (or 3½ in leap years), and who knows where you may find yourself in the future. I can tell you that I can't wait to see you take your first steps into leadership. And I hope you'll turn to this book for advice when you get there.

Tacy

It's been a decade since my last book, mainly because I couldn't find one I really wanted to write. This is one I really did.

I would like to dedicate it to my mom and in memory of my dad. While perhaps not knowing about it consciously, they were teaching me leadership lessons every day.

When this book is published, I will have just finished my thirty-sixth year at DDI. So, I also want to dedicate it to my two and only bosses—Bill Byham and Bob Rogers. Not only were they guides and mentors, but they also provided me with the freedom to learn, grow, and contribute. I consider myself very lucky, indeed.

Rich

Contents

Foreword xi

Preface xiii

Part 1: Catalyst Leadership 1

1. Now You're a Leader 3
   The Journey Begins

2. Boss or Catalyst? 9
   What Makes a Great Leader?

3. Navigating the Transition to Leadership 17
   The Mind-Set You Need to Succeed

4. Your Leadership Brand, Part 1 28
   Be Authentic

5. Your Leadership Brand, Part 2 35
   Bring Out the Best in People and Be Receptive to Feedback

6. Leadership Is a Conversation, Part 1 46
   How to Make People Feel Heard, Valued, and Motivated

7. Leadership Is a Conversation, Part 2 66
   How to Build Trust and Ownership

8. Your Five-Step Conversation Road Map 75
   Taking a Practical Approach to Get Results

9. Nothing Else Matters Unless You Get Results 87
   How to Execute with Focus, Measurement, and Accountability

Part 2: Mastery and Leadership Skills 113

10. Hiring and Selecting the Best 115
    Behavior Predicts Behavior

11. What Your Boss Really Wants from You 130
    Become an Adviser

12. Engagement and Retention 135
    Creating the Environment to Energize People

13. Meetings 149
    Make Them Count!

14. Coaching 161
    Learning from Success

15. Feedback Fundamentals 173
    Specific, Timely, and Balanced

16. Handling Difficult Employee Situations 181
    Focus on the Behavior, Not the Person

17. Delegation 191
    Be a Delegator, Not a Dumper

18. Performance Management 201
    An Ongoing Cycle, Not an Event

19. You and Your Network 209
    Nurture Your Business Relationships

20. Influence 221
    Look Up, Down, and Across

21. A Woman's First Leadership Job 229
    Own the Moment

22. Leadership Changes the World 241
    The Difference Is You

Part 3: Bonus Chapters and Tools 245
    (available online at the DDI microsite)

Citations 247

Acknowledgments 253

About DDI 255

About the Author 256

Index 259

Foreword

Leadership makes a difference.

You might not know that now. But you will.

I've been in banking my entire career, primarily with Fifth Third Bancorp, which operates in a dozen states in the Midwest and Southeast. Banking is an interesting business for many reasons, but one of them is this: We don't make anything. Our product is exactly like our competitors! We borrow it for the most part, and it all looks the same. It's green, rectangular, and has the same relative value on a given day. In order to stand out in a crowded field, the focus needs to be on how we deliver that value—100 percent through our people.

I believe that leadership happens all around you. It happens in the tone you set and in the many, many conversations you have to accomplish one simple, but complex thing—bring people into the vision of the outcome you need.

But most people don't think about those things until they get their first leadership job. You're good at being an expert, and then you get promoted for your expertise into a completely different job. And so you experiment, because no one ever tells you—except for DDI—the right or wrong way to get the most commitment from the people around you.

Let me rewind the clock a bit. My first big leadership job was what my organization called a "broadening" responsibility—an assignment that addresses a challenge a company is having and that also helps a leader grow and develop. One day I was called in to see my boss's boss, the Vice Chairman, and I found myself being asked to take on a division in which I had no expertise. None. I was being asked to leave my job in human resources to run operations for the much larger holding company. And I would be leading folks who were highly technical, very proficient, and very experienced. I was in my mid-thirties, with three kids under 10 at home. My new reports were, in many cases, 20 years older. It was a challenging division in need of some significant change and facing big new performance goals.

I talked to some people who knew more about the challenges facing the operations division. I was worried, but I took the job. I knew going in that I didn't have a quarter of the knowledge of the people who had been there for years. And, I was going to need all of them to teach me.

Foreword
cont'd

That was the moment I knew I needed to rely on leadership.

We did a number of things, all of them focused on gaining people's trust. We began something new, what is now commonly called "one down" or "two downs." We would regularly gather in large groups (some of the teams had 15 or 20 people), and I would encourage managers to talk about what they had accomplished. They could, in essence, brag to me. And then I would use those accomplishments to talk about what we could do if we all had the same vision. It sounds simple, but they were powerful moments. These conversations supplied the backbone for the kind of trust, vision-building, and engagement that, over time, helped everyone see how we could be recognized in the organization for the magnitude of the changes we were contemplating. I created a parade and gave them the opportunity to jump in front of it.

In the end, we accomplished one of the most significant changes in our company's history. We centralized operations, cut costs to the tune of 40 to 50 percent, improved service-level agreements and delivery, and boosted customer satisfaction.

So, now it's your turn. What will you do with the opportunity you've just been given?

I learned the concept of catalyst leadership from DDI early in my career, and this book will help you learn it too. You'll find out how catalysts can ignite a flame in others, gain their commitment, and drive productivity. Now, I've never met a perfect supervisor. I've never been one. Leadership takes work. But, the upside is tremendous—helping people achieve their goals and dreams.

We all approach leadership from different angles. But if you focus on the goal of catalyst leadership and put it in practice every day, then you'll bring out the best in others in surprising ways. You'll bring it about in yourself as well. And you'll love what you do.

Kevin T. Kabat

Vice Chairman and CEO at Fifth Third Bancorp

Preface

When we decided to write this book, we wanted to look at leadership through a fresh lens. After all, the last time we did a Google search, there were 392,000,000 entries for leadership books—double the number of cookbooks! There are leadership books written by or about the world's greatest thinkers (Confucius, Machiavelli, and Gandhi). And thousands of books on leadership have been published by dozens of management experts (Peter Drucker, John Kotter, Tom Peters, and Jim Collins, to name a few). All offer great stories, opinions, and practices of what constitutes the DNA of great leadership.

Our book, however, differs from all the rest in three respects.

1. **It has a singular mission:** to give you the practical advice and tools to succeed as a first-time, first-line leader. The first section features nine chapters that will help you better understand what it takes to become an awesome leader—one we call a catalyst who sparks action in others. And it focuses on a set of fundamental skills—we call them *interaction skills*—that will serve as the foundation for every one of the dozens of conversations you'll have with others every day. These are skills you can use, not only in the workplace, but also at home and in your community. The second section provides advice on a host of diverse, vital skills—we call them *mastery and leadership skills*—that you'll need to call upon in your new role. These include coaching, selecting new employees, and promoting a culture of engagement, among others.

2. **The content of this book is based on unparalleled experience.** For the past four decades, our company, DDI (Development Dimensions International), has helped clients *develop* over 250,000 leaders every year, in 26 countries, across thousands of organizations. Nothing we say in this book is based on whim or theory. It comes from real-time experience—a lot of it.

3. **We carry our experience one step further to evidence**. DDI has helped hundreds of clients demonstrate the relationship between our leadership practices and principles with metrics that matter: improved skills, higher engagement, better safety records, and gains in productivity. We don't rest on our laurels; *we rest on our proof*.

Whether you read our book in detail or focus on those chapters that are the most relevant for you, we'll have accomplished our goal if you use three or four pieces of the advice we've provided. You know, in many ways you can look at this book as a hybrid between a typical leadership book and a cookbook. We provide the kitchen-tested recipes, but it's up to you to do the cooking.

Tacy and *Rich*

Part 1: Catalyst Leadership

Whether you are new to the role or have some experience with it, the road to being an effective leader is rife with challenges and joys. *Catalyst* leaders represent the gold standard—energetic, supportive, forward-thinking mentors who spark action in others. The first part of this book presents a clear picture of what catalyst leadership is really about. There are dozens of tips to make your journey as smooth as possible.

We also introduce the concept of *leadership brand*. Just like a company's brand makes it a distinct entity, your brand can cement your standing as an effective leader. And, there are clearly identifiable practices associated with your leadership brand that separate truly effective leaders from average or poor ones. So, in this section of the book we'll help you create a new leadership mind-set and get results for you and your team. Additionally, we provide guidance on how you can flawlessly execute in the face of competing priorities.

Finally, we share some secrets for making every interaction a successful one. As a leader, you have dozens of conversations with others every single day. Your ability to connect with them—by making people feel valued, heard, motivated, trusted, and involved—will go a long way toward making you a perfect leader!

Great leadership takes place every day, in the smallest of ways.

1

NOW YOU'RE A LEADER
The Journey Begins

So, now you're in charge.

When you accepted your first leadership job—or even seriously considered putting your hat in the ring—you took one of the most important and courageous steps in your career. You're a boss! You're going places.

How's it going? Are you sure? How do you know?

Chances are, you're perched precariously on an emotional range from "awkward excitement" to "abject terror" and back again, with a constant baseline of "stressed." This shouldn't come as a surprise; you have a lot to prove. (Or, if you've been in the position for a while, you might have a lot to repair.) For over 45 years, our firm, DDI, has been an innovator in the field of talent management, which is a fancy way of saying that we help companies transform the way they hire, promote, and develop leaders. This book is based on what we've learned from developing more than eight million frontline leaders over four decades, in virtually every country and industry around the world. First-time leaders who transition well are more able to make a positive, lasting impact on their teams, families, and careers. Our approach helps people become engaged and more productive more quickly.

Speaking of stress, our research shows that a transition to a leadership position is among life's most challenging adjustments, ranking somewhere between personal illness and managing teenagers. In fact, only one in three leaders in our first transitional study felt they were effective in handling transitional challenges.[1] For first-timers, the stress can be particularly acute. You are taking on not only a new type of role, but also one that exists in a business environment defined by fast-moving challenges: volatility, uncertainty, complexity, and ambiguity. And you're in a unique position where your performance—or lack thereof—will determine whether your team will thrive or stall (along with your career). Are you as good as you need to be? Do you know what it means to get the best work from the people on your team? Will they hate you on sight? How will you determine if you're on track before it's too late?

The transition you're experiencing is profound enough for us to make a bold claim: Nobody comes to his first leadership position knowing everything he needs to know to succeed. When you get into truly unfamiliar emotional territory, your instinct might be to throw up your hands and try to do everything yourself. Perhaps you'll micromanage your team, take critical assignments away from direct reports as deadlines loom, or fail to give the kind of feedback that will help your team members do their jobs.

But let us make another bold claim: You'll find few greater rewards in your career than on the leadership journey you're about to begin. What you learn will transform the rest of your life in many wonderful ways. There are many reasons for this, not the least of which is what you'll discover about your own ability to grow and be effective in the world. We believe that over time, the skills you'll learn can help you communicate more clearly with the people you love, become a more active member of your community, and make a difference for the causes you care about. This is a journey that leads to a happier life.

When I first got the job, there was a lot of pressure, Karen told us. She became a leader by surprise and default when her own supervisor took ill and needed an extended leave. Karen was an expert telecommunications engineer, but she suddenly had 30 more-senior people to manage and a big project to finish. *I could tell that there was a lot of skepticism about me. And there already had been many failures in the project, like when a contractor failed to deliver.* But Karen was able to find effective ways to get the work done—on time!—through the people around her, and has earned the respect of her peers. *It has been the most gratifying thing! I was able to help them work well, and I still felt like myself. And we've been able to deliver a lot, and move the project to the next level. And now the whole company knows who our team is.* Best of all, she now looks at her life differently. *I learned I could be a real leader. I can make a contribution in lots of places.*

Joe, a supervisor in a landscaping business, learned that deep satisfaction comes from being a key part of helping others reach their true potential. *The very thing that is satisfying to me is watching the guys under me grow,* he said. Joe had been unable to find a job in teaching, and instead worked his way up in a national landscaping company. Many of his direct reports were untrained, non-native English speakers, and their work could be a gateway to better things for them. That's when he realized that he had a role to play in their lives. *I saw the other supervisors, and all they want to do is show up every day, do the work, and go home.* But Joe saw an opportunity to share what he knew about leadership and business and to develop his team in a deeper way. *I got dirty with them in the field, worked with them side by side. They began to trust me. And now I'm in a position to really watch them develop. Now I see that leadership goes back to the very reason I was interested in teaching in the first place.*

The real opportunity of leadership, as we see it, is a deeply human one. But precisely because humans are involved, lots of things can go wrong. As an example of the type of challenge you may encounter in your first leadership role, meet John, 42, an urban planner. *I got ambushed!* he says of his most problematic direct report. John ran a loosely knit team of eight, but it was one young engineer who derailed him. And he didn't see it coming. *She gave me no feedback of any kind. And then called me the worst boss in the world.* It was John's first attempt at leading a team—something he knew pretty well. Or, so he thought. He'd worked well as an individual contributor on interdisciplinary teams, and like most people, had strong feelings about what a leader should and shouldn't do.

At first he was hands-off, figuring that everyone liked to work independently. *I don't like working for people who are looking over my back all the time. So my approach was "you go do your thing, and I'll come to you when there's a problem."* When he felt the need to give input, *I came in and took over, and it seemed like micromanaging. But nobody said anything to me.* Until his six-month performance review. *I was completely shocked when my boss told me what she* [the young engineer] *had said.* Her complaints: John didn't set priorities, didn't pay attention to her work, took projects away from her with no explanation, and focused only on his own work. John realized too late that his hands-off style had backfired. And waiting for her to tell him what she needed out of a boss? *I was told that because I was more senior, I should have known better. And I think that's right.*

In our experience, it takes about 6 to 12 months for a new leader to hit stride or hit the skids. And that's exactly what happened to John. And once a major problem occurs, it might be hard to find the advocates you'll need to turn things around.

Q: The first time you managed people (not just a project) the emotion you felt was . . . ? #leadership

@nilofer awkwardness

@TonyTSheng terror that i would be revealed as not knowing what i was doing. Which i didn't. lol

@Mallory_C nervous that I would royally screw it up and be that awful, clue-less boss—always want it to be a productive experience.

@BigM5678 Overwhelmed. Many years passed before I could delegate w/o feeling I should be doing it myself or it's not going to be right.

This book is targeted to what we believe is the most critical role in any organization, the frontline leader. You're more important than you might think! And now, you're in a unique position to positively impact your entire company by working productively not only with your team, but also with other supervisors, peers in other departments, customers—everyone.

We can help you answer important questions about your ability to lead before you misstep. We can help you experience the joy of leadership sooner by managing the real and powerful human emotions that can block your success. And we'll show you how to master the new skills leaders need to work effectively, such as coaching others, engaging people, delegating, tapping into your new network, hiring, and even running a meeting.

We wrote this book to help you master your new leadership role more quickly, while avoiding some of the headaches and heartaches many people experience. And for those of you who may have already made some key mistakes, we can help you put things back on track.

"Frontline," "First-Time"—What's in a Label?

Throughout this book, we use the terms *frontline* leaders and *first-time* leaders interchangeably. First-time is fairly straightforward, referring to people either in their first leadership job, or those pondering a move into one. Frontline is more about the level of leadership. A frontline leader directly manages individual contributors. This leaves out higher-level employees, like middle managers or senior executives, who manage other leaders. Other terms for frontline leaders include *supervisor, team leader, foreman,* or *manager.*

How Is This Book Different from Other Leadership Books?

This book isn't based on one person's theory, a cobbled-together dataset, or an inspiring true story of running one campaign or landing a plane under difficult circumstances. (Some of these books are terrific, and we love them. They're just not what you need right now.) Instead, we're giving you specific, actionable information about what to do and how to do it, based it on a combination of hands-on experience and decades of solid research.

We include what we've learned from helping companies make thousands of frontline leadership selection and promotion decisions each year. We tell you about the competencies and attributes that lead to successful frontline leadership performance based on extensive job analyses we've conducted with hundreds of organizations—and how to develop them within yourself, starting today. And perhaps, most of all, when we call something a best practice, that claim is backed by dozens of research studies that demonstrate the impact of that practice on organizational performance.

At DDI, we believe that better leadership is far more science than art. Yet, it is based in a deep respect for and understanding of the people side of leadership. We believe that people can transform their relationships in work and life by modifying their behavior in simple, clear, and measurable ways. We've trained and sat with hundreds of new leaders just like you and personally shared the advice that's in this book. You'll hear some of their stories in these pages.

Although you can open this book at any point and find immediate solutions to problems you may be experiencing, we hope you first spend some quality time on the first section. These nine chapters distill DDI's work on early leadership and provide the best foundation for starting your leadership journey.

The second section is a deeper dive into some of the key skills you'll need to master in order to succeed. These mastery and leadership skills chapters can be read sequentially, or you can jump to the chapter that best meets your current need. Expect short, specialized content to help you tackle the nuts and bolts of mastering your new position. You'll also find checklists and discussion guides that you can use immediately in your working life. Revisit them often. And through our "Your First Leadership Job" microsite, we offer links to bonus chapters, online resources, content, and communities that can help you connect with other leaders in transition. You'll want to bookmark this site and return to it frequently:

www.YourFirstLeadershipJob.com

The book also includes exercises, quizzes, diagnostics, and other interactive tools in every chapter. We encourage you to explore them. Designed by organizational psychologists, they've been proven effective over the years. Use them and you'll be more successful . . . and find your job more enjoyable.

In addition to the research cited throughout this book, you'll meet real people who have shared their experiences as first-time leaders. Each story conveys a lesson, insight, success story, or cautionary tale. (We've changed names and masked companies to encourage candor.) We've also queried people via Facebook, LinkedIn, Twitter, and Quora, looking for stories and inspiration from their own leadership journeys. You'll find results from our questions and surveys throughout the book.

If you have one takeaway from this book, it should be this: Great leadership takes place every day, in the smallest of ways. It is reflected first and foremost in your conversations, the way you influence others, and how you interact with the people on your team and in your network. But the first step in your leadership journey is to think of yourself not as a boss, but as someone who can and should ignite a chain reaction of effectiveness that positively impacts direct reports, customers, vendors, peers, and supervisors alike. Your journey starts with a very specific kind of spark.

> A catalyst leader is someone
> who ignites action in others.

2 BOSS OR CATALYST?
What Makes a Great Leader?

Your New Job: Catalyst Leader

The term *boss* has taken a real beating both in work and popular culture. In movies the boss tends to be a ruthless gangster or amoral chieftain. In digital gaming, the boss is the last, biggest, and most horrific in a series of monsters that must be defeated. But in the workplace, now it's you. And you've got an image problem. Search for "Bad Boss" on Google and find over 36 million entries. Headlines include "Ten Things Only Bad Bosses Say," "What Makes a Bad Boss Bad," or, our favorite, "How to Survive 13 Types of Dysfunctional, Disrespectful and Dishonest Little Dictators." There are even multiple websites for bad bosses. One, BadBosses.com, shows a photo of a person with the head of a wolf. Needless to say, you don't want to become the wolf in your office.

Consider Marian, a marketing and social media specialist and writer in a communications department at a midsized university. She had the classic bad boss: didn't communicate, failed to set team goals, missed deadlines, and played poorly with his peers in other departments. His inefficiency gave the department a bad reputation throughout the whole campus.

When Marian's boss was abruptly fired, the team was shocked. *We had no idea he was so unpopular outside of our team,* she said. But when Marian was tapped as his interim replacement, there was a catch: He had negotiated to stay on for six months and was refusing to announce Marian's new job or even train her for it.

And all of this remained a secret. *He told me that he didn't want to be seen as a lame duck, but it got really awkward,* she said. As the months ticked by and no replacement was announced, the team became more and more anxious about the future and other departments began to openly revolt. To make matters worse, the not-yet-exiting chief had run projects aground across the university and had badly alienated senior leadership. Nasty surprises abounded. Marian, who was a half-time employee about to run a team of 11, had no idea what to do. *This is his legacy,* Marian said. *And I was afraid that I wouldn't be able to turn it around.* (For more on how Marian used her new network to revive her demoralized team, see Chapter 19 on networking.)

When we train frontline leaders, we use a different word that paints a far more positive picture than describing a leader as an irresponsible or horrific boss: *catalyst.* Much like an ingredient that induces a chemical reaction, a catalyst leader is someone who ignites action in others. That ignition might jump-start a change in an inefficient process, spawn a new idea for a new product, or, most important, effect change in others.

Both our research and observations show dramatic differences between poor and even average leaders and those we would label catalyst leaders. The latter have a knack for building engagement, involving others, and capitalizing on people's strengths and diverse viewpoints. And, they rarely blame others. Rather, they accept accountability to deliver on expectations.

Figure 2.1 illustrates what being a catalyst leader is all about.

FIG 2.1 Catalyst Leader

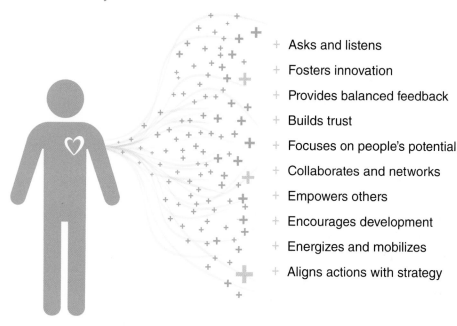

- Asks and listens
- Fosters innovation
- Provides balanced feedback
- Builds trust
- Focuses on people's potential
- Collaborates and networks
- Empowers others
- Encourages development
- Energizes and mobilizes
- Aligns actions with strategy

Whether you're a new leader or have a few years of experience, becoming a catalyst leader is hard work. It doesn't happen overnight. The common characteristic in great catalysts is their passion to become better leaders. They're constantly building their leadership skills. They're also introspective—looking in the mirror every day and asking what they could do to become better leaders.

What do great leadership and sushi have in common? Rich Wellins offers a powerful way to reframe how we think about leadership at our microsite.

Tool 2.1 is a self-assessment of your current proficiency as a catalyst leader. It will allow you to pinpoint strengths and areas you might want to work on.

TOOL **2.1**

Catalyst Leader Self-Assessment

Catalyst leaders find opportunities to ignite action in others. Are you a catalyst leader? To find out, first circle the number for each item that represents your current behavior. Next, add the numbers to determine your catalyst index. Finally, in the column to the right, check (✓) the three boxes opposite the behaviors you want to focus on.

DEMONSTRATES inconsistently:						DEMONSTRATES consistently:	
Tell and assume	1	2	3	4	5	Ask, listen, and learn	❏
Direct and prescribe	1	2	3	4	5	Guide, facilitate, steer	❏
Identify problems and mandate solutions	1	2	3	4	5	Help others recognize and solve problem	❏
Criticize	1	2	3	4	5	Provide balanced feedback	❏
Have all the answers	1	2	3	4	5	Ask for ideas	❏
Withhold information and feelings	1	2	3	4	5	Share thoughts, feelings, and rationale	❏
Threaten, intimidate, paralyze	1	2	3	4	5	Trust, build commitment, mobilize	❏
Focus on people's limitations	1	2	3	4	5	Focus on people's potential	❏
Encourage others' dependence	1	2	3	4	5	Foster interdependence	❏
Maintain the status quo	1	2	3	4	5	Encourage creativity and innovation	❏
Do it all alone	1	2	3	4	5	Support development of others	❏
Have a self-centered outlook	1	2	3	4	5	Have a team-centered outlook	❏
Take over and control	1	2	3	4	5	Provide support without removing responsibility	❏

Your catalyst index: _____ **(total of the scores above)**

50–65 You already are a catalyst leader, but you can still improve by selecting a few behaviors to work on.

30–49 You have a good start. Choose three areas you really want to work at.

13–29 As a newer leader, you have multiple opportunities for improvement.

What Enables Frontline Leadership Success: A Deeper Look

Over the past four decades, DDI has conducted hundreds of job analyses in just about every industry and all over the world. Many of these were aimed at frontline leadership roles and involved conducting interviews with the leaders and their managers to gather information on factors that differentiate average from truly outstanding performance. The data, once consolidated, is transformed into what we call a Success Profile[SM]. Our clients then use their success profiles as part of their selection, promotion, performance appraisal, and development programs. As shown in Figure 2.2, there are four components to a success profile for a frontline leader.

FIG 2.2 Success Profile

1. **Organizational knowledge**—What a person knows. *(e.g., company products/services)*

2. **Experience**—What a person has done in the past. *(e.g., served on a special project team)*

3. **Competencies**—What a person is capable of. *(i.e., groups of like skills and behaviors such as coaching or decision making)*

4. **Personal Attributes**—Who a person is, or personality. *(e.g., personality characteristics such as a strong learning orientation)*

In Tool 2.2, you'll find many of these frontline leader "success factors." Look at this tool as a compass to point you in the right direction. If you're considering a leadership position for the first time, you might ask yourself how you stack up against the profile. If you're already a leader, you can use the tool to guide your growth and development. Pick a few elements that might not be as strong as you'd like and incorporate them into your development plans. But, just as important, choose some strengths and use them to your advantage.

One friendly word of caution: You can acquire knowledge, and you can seek experience. You can adjust some behaviors. But personality elements are much tougher to change. For example, a high degree of arrogance—which is another way of saying overconfidence—is likely to derail your career. And you won't find a training course to make yourself less arrogant. Leaders normally don't go astray because they lack skills. More often than not, it's a personality mismatch. (We'll discuss this further in the Mastery chapters on selection and retention.) So, pay close attention to these factors when considering a move into leadership and be honest with yourself. Many former leaders have said that they gladly returned to a team member role. That can be a smart decision for many!

Frontline Leadership Success Profile

Write an "S" in each box that represents a strength. Write a "D" in each box that represents a development need for you.

KNOWLEDGE	COMPETENCIES
❑ In-depth knowledge of your company's products, services, and customers ❑ Understanding of how your team fits into the overall organization ❑ Familiar with various company policies/processes ❑ Business acumen, including understanding company strategy, competition, supply chain, financial metrics ❑ Knowledge of your chosen field *(e.g., finance, marketing, IT)*	❑ Building trust ❑ Delegating responsibility ❑ Planning and organizing ❑ Selecting talent ❑ Facilitating change ❑ Decision making ❑ Coaching ❑ Fostering innovation ❑ Building a successful team ❑ Creating networks
EXPERIENCE	PERSONAL ATTRIBUTES
❑ Leading a cross-functional or special team ❑ Providing feedback to others ❑ Coaching/Mentoring ❑ Planning and managing complex projects ❑ Working closely with internal/external customers ❑ Making difficult decisions ❑ Having functional experience in one or more disciplines *(e.g., sales, IT, R&D)* ❑ Navigating organization politics	Enablers: ❑ Enjoys being with other people ❑ Desire to continually learn ❑ High achievement orientation/driver for results ❑ Sensitive to the needs/concerns of others Derailers: ❑ Always seeking praise and approval from others ❑ Overly self-confident, dismissive of others' ideas ❑ Inability to read others' intentions ❑ Indecisive, can't make decisions ❑ Micromanaging/Controlling others ❑ Difficulty controlling emotions

The Bottom Line

The journey to being an excellent leader is a long one, and the road can be rough. However, the rewards along the way can be very satisfying if you've chosen to be a leader for the right reasons. A few years back, we asked over 1,200 employees around the world what they thought about their managers. One question we asked was, *What differentiates the best boss from the worst boss you ever worked for?* Sadly, only 22 percent of employees feel they are currently working for their best boss ever. As you might expect, they rated their best bosses as two to three times more likely to use catalyst behaviors. Nearly 68 percent of employees who are currently working for their worst managers ever are looking at leaving. And, more surprisingly, only 11 percent of employees working for their worst boss ever are motivated to "give their best." Compare that to the employees working for their best boss. The percentage jumps to 98![1]

In another piece of research, we asked employees how much more productive they could be if they went back to work for their best-ever boss. One in four said they would be anywhere from 40 to 60 percent more productive.[2]

Reflection Points Explained

Throughout this book we'll be prompting you to think about where you are on your leadership journey. If you keep a journal in any form—Moleskine®, Evernote, digital recorder, whatever—consider memorializing your thoughts. Use these reflections to chart your progress, clarify next steps, and examine the emotions that might be undermining your effectiveness. Use your observations to help you gather useful feedback from trusted sources, and share meaningfully with others online and in real time. They'll also make excellent fodder for your best-selling memoir when you become a Big Shot.

What makes you most anxious when you review Tool 2.2? Look at the boxes you marked with a "D" (development need). Are your concerns valid? Choose one or two items as a monthly To-Learn list. Consider consulting with a trusted member of your network for advice and feedback.

Then, look at the boxes you marked with an "S" (strength). Which of these can you leverage?

What will your list look like in six months? In 12 months?

*Before you are a leader,
success is all about growing
yourself. When you become a
leader, success is all about
growing others.*

– Jack Welch

3 NAVIGATING THE TRANSITION TO LEADERSHIP
The Mind-Set You Need to Succeed

When Mary described how she felt about her first leadership job, she repeatedly used the same term: "off-center."

Occasionally, she adjusted it to "totally off-center" or "completely off-center." But the outcome was the same. Mary's first eight months as a leader made her realize how unprepared she was. She had moved from a production job to a sales function, with no prior sales experience, and she was managing others for the first time. An all-male team of 12! A female leader was a rarity in the male-dominated culture of chemical engineering, though Mary didn't have time to enjoy the sound of the glass ceiling shattering. Instead, she found herself eye-to-eye with an unhappy rival. One of her new team members had been groomed for the job she now had, and was none too happy about losing out. To make matters worse, the previous boss had been beloved by the team. How could Mary possibly fill his shoes? That dizzy, off-center feeling was her constant awareness of being in a totally unfamiliar landscape without the tools to navigate clear.

In Chapter 1 we mentioned our research on the stress associated with transition to a leadership role. Remember? Stress levels ranked somewhere between personal illness and raising a teenager. Do any of Mary's stressors sound familiar? Almost all leaders we interviewed found their first few months full of what we call transitional challenges. What are yours?

Think about the first time you told friends about getting (or wanting) your new leadership job. What was appealing to you? What did you think it would mean for your career? Did you talk about perks or power? Competing with others? Getting away from people or job functions you didn't like? Be honest: What's really driving you?

Later in this chapter we'll dig deeper into transitional challenges, but let's start with your decision to become a leader in the first place. Maybe you struggled to decide if it was worth giving up a job you were good at—and maybe even loved—for an uncertain role rife with new risks. Typically, there are two circumstances surrounding this decision. The first is voluntary—you identified an opportunity and went for it. If this describes you, then your challenge is to make sure your leadership heart is in the right place. Examine your motivations. Did you make the leap for more power, money, or fringe benefits? If so, you could find yourself unhappy. Although there may be material rewards associated with a promotion, leadership is about giving up power. A good leader dedicates himself to seeing his team grow and making a difference to his organization. If you aren't prepared to do a leader's work, then no money will ever be enough.

Then there's the other scenario: You might have been asked to fill a leadership gap. Stepping up in this way can make you feel off-center for entirely different reasons. Maybe you felt pressured—worried that refusal to step up would signal a lack of ambition or dedication. Or, maybe you were afraid that you'd be passed over for special assignments or future promotions if you waved off the opportunity or changed your mind later. These are all valid concerns.

But consider one simple fact before you say "yes" to a leadership job thrust upon you. In our leadership transitions study,[1] we asked over 600 participants whether they voluntarily chose to take a leadership position or were pressured into it. Then we asked how it worked out. The people who caved to the pressure eventually *did* make a decision . . . to head for the door!

Our study showed that these people were three times more likely to be dissatisfied and twice as likely to consider quitting as those who voluntarily sought out the position. That's strong evidence that you should think more about your true career goals than the social pressure of your company environment when you leap into leadership.

What's in a Question?

So, are you ready? Let's unpack the question first. What you really need to ask yourself now is whether you have the *mind-set* or *potential* to lead. What's the difference? As we discussed in Chapter 1, leadership is a career journey that can span years. No one we have ever encountered had all the needed skills, experience, and knowledge when he stepped into his new positions. Good leaders are learning to lead every day. What you need to ask yourself is this: *Do I have the potential to become a good leader over time?*

Leaders aren't born; they are made. And they are made just like anything else, through hard work.

—**Vince Lombardi,**
American professional
football coach

Consider Jack, who was an excellent technical specialist. He loved working with clients and was very, very successful. His outstanding reputation soon earned him an offer to lead a small team. He accepted the position and immediately hated it. Although he gave it some time, he asked for his old job back about a year later. Recognizing his talents, the company gladly returned him to his previous role, where he has been happy and highly engaged ever since.

Jack was smart to understand his own strengths and abilities. And smarter still to make sure that his skills stayed sharp so he could maintain his value to the company. But Jack was smart in yet another way: He knew his own leadership heart. Being a leader simply wasn't a role he enjoyed. And he learned that there is more than one way to grow and to succeed. Jack could have benefitted by using Tool 3.1 to reflect on his leadership mind-set.

TOOL 3.1

Assessing Your Leadership Mind-Set

In our work with clients, we've developed a set of potential factors that predict the probability of a leader's success. We've condensed those factors into seven clusters of questions to consider as you choose to assume a leadership position . . . or not!

Use this tool to consider your own strengths and motivations. We suggest that you revisit these questions often as your leadership journey progresses. Consider using them as conversation starters with people in your network.

1. Are you really motivated to lead? Do you have an upward ambition to expand your sphere of influence in the organization?

2. As you interact with others, do you inspire performance and morale? Do you believe in the strengths of others? Do others look up to you as a leader, even informally?

3. Are you able to show confidence without being seen as a know-it-all? Do people trust you? Are you willing to be accountable for your own actions?

4. Are you open to constructive criticism? Do you seek feedback from others? Do you have insight into your own strengths and weaknesses?

5. Do you learn from past mistakes and success? Do you desire to learn new things? Seek out different experiences?

6. Do you have a sense of urgency? A desire to get things done? Do you rebound quickly from a setback and continue to pursue your desired goal?

7. Can you respond effectively to unclear or ambiguous situations? Can you see things in shades of gray rather than black and white? Can you adjust quickly to new situations and people?

What Do We Really Mean by "Transition"?

A transition, of course, is a change from doing one thing to doing something new and different. In today's workplace, transitions come in all forms and shapes. It can mean relocating to a new country, moving to a new business unit, or leaving one company for another. All of these transitions come with an abundance of new challenges, excitement, and anxiety. Although you might have experienced many changes at work before now, we're spending extra time on your decision to move into a first-time, frontline leadership role because it is so specific and unique. And transitional challenges don't disappear after your first two or three months. It can take one or more years to get used to your new role.

To give you a glimpse of the big picture, many organizations are using a model DDI introduced over a decade ago called the Leadership Pipeline. The pipeline analogy fits, because the objective is to ensure a ready-now cadre of leaders to move from one level to the next. Figure 3.1 represents a typical pipeline with four levels. Each move from one level to the next is labeled a *transition* or *turn*. Most of you reading this book will be making the transition from individual contributor (team member) to people leader (frontline).

FIG 3.1 Leadership Pipeline

Making the Jump Up

Each transition carries a unique set of challenges and differs in terms of accountability, decisions, number of direct reports, and so on. When we asked leaders in our study what was most difficult about their transitions, dealing with ambiguity topped the list.[2] The percentages add to >100 percent as leaders selected their top three.

41% Dealing with ambiguity and uncertainty

38%   Getting work done through others

35%   Navigating organizational politics

34%   Engaging and inspiring employees

32%   Creating a new network

In our opening story, Mary was facing a stressful transition. Let's take a closer look at some of the challenges you'll be facing as you make a transition into a frontline position.

1. **Shifting your mind-set from working as an individual contributor to getting work done through others.** As a leader, your pride, passion, and engagement must come from what your team does—not what you do personally. This challenge is especially difficult for people in highly complex or technical roles. We interviewed a senior-level legal counsel who was in his job for over 15 years. He was chosen to lead a large team responsible for legal, human resources, and a host of other critical administrative processes. His biggest difficulty, especially with his legal staff, was to fight the inclination to do the work himself, rather than delegate. You can't do your old job and learn to lead at the same time. And, it's a turnoff for those who work for you.

2. **Earning your right to lead.** Even though you were chosen because of a perceived competence to lead, others might not see it that way. In many cases, there will be people on your team who were peers in your previous role. Imagine the difficulty of giving performance feedback to someone you were close to at work and perhaps outside of work. (And, even if you aren't leading former peers, some on your team will feel they were passed over for the job and ended up stuck with you.)

3. **Developing a wider, broader network.** Your ability to succeed as a leader will rely on your ability to not only engage and influence your team members, but also to form positive working relationships up, down, within, and outside your organization. Networking, which we discuss in greater detail in the Mastery section, is key to getting the job done. It means forming beneficial, positive relationships with your manager and peers as well as your suppliers and customers. Networking also provides an effective means for learning from and getting support from others. Interestingly, when we asked leaders who was most useful for them in making a leadership transition, colleagues and peers outranked one's own manager by a factor of slightly more than two.[3] Effective networking is a give-and-take game. Your influence will expand if you're looking for ways to add value for others, not just for yourself.

When Dale moved to his new position, he had a networking challenge: His delivery team had a bad reputation with the sales organization. Sales always went to other delivery teams to get their work done! Dale immediately reached out to key members of the sales organization to hear their concerns, needs, and suggestions, all of which helped turn his team's reputation around. He stays in touch with the sales leaders, and his team is now in high demand. But, he told us, it took him nearly a year and a half to turn things around. And he didn't feel truly comfortable in his new role until he did.

4. **Translating strategy into action.** While your new role will have strategic components, you'll spend much of your time executing your organization's key objectives. In Chapter 9, we discuss your role in execution. While you might be asked to support a new product or implement a new IT system, you might not be the one who developed the product or chose the system. Your job will be to introduce and gain commitment to change, establish accountabilities, and coach and support others. This is much more easily done when the new direction or strategy is seen as the right thing to do. It's much more difficult to execute an unpopular action that will meet resistance or that you don't agree with.

Remember, you're part of the organization's leadership team now. You have two choices if you don't like a decision being made by upper management: Either live with it or try to influence it. See Chapter 20 ("Influence") to learn more.

This is no small point. And we need to be honest with you: As a first-time leader, you may have limited influence over top-line decisions. But once the light turns green on a decision, you need to show your full support and share that with your team without flinching. Nothing can be more damaging to your credibility than to go to your team and say, *I need your help in executing our new XYZ initiative. I know it will be tough, and I personally don't support it, but. . . .* You'll find the next chapter essential reading for handling these and other thorny situations.

Getting Ready: Fast Track

We've established that a transition to leadership can be stressful. And that you're ready to step up to the next level. Now it's time to dig in to address your many new challenges. This will give you a significant head start as a new leader.

The first step in fast-tracking your success is to confirm that your understanding of your role aligns with the organization's expectations. This will require a bit of detective work as you'll need to speak to other people. This might feel like an overwhelming task in your early days, particularly if you're an introvert. But the conversations you have now not only will save you a lot of heartache later, but they'll also help you build your all-important new network. Be sure to take good notes.

These are the getting-to-know-you conversations that will help you understand the organization's culture—how it operates informally and formally. To be most receptive, you'll need to reduce the noise of compounding requests, emails, redundant meetings, and seemingly pointless activities. In other words, learn to separate what you "must have" from "would be nice to have."

You know how I found out there were no meetings on Fridays? I called my first meeting on Friday morning and nobody showed. You know how I knew I had a culture problem? When nobody bothered to tell me that there were no meetings on Friday.

—Heidi

But there's a bigger opportunity for you here. You'll be able to avoid falling back on any potentially unproductive coping habits—avoidance, micromanaging, confrontation, and so on—as your leadership journey becomes more unfamiliar and stressful. (Think of it as personality insurance.)

Bottom line: The conversations you have now will help you find the answers you'll need when you wade into unfamiliar territory.

Reach Out to Stakeholders

To begin your conversations, reach out to three key stakeholder groups. We've provided some sample questions to get you started, but feel free to add your own:

Your manager. She can help you understand how your group supports the broader business strategies. She also can spell out your priorities and her expectations.

Example: *I'd love to hear how you think my team fits into the overall company. What has worked in the past? What's missing now? What mistakes have past leaders made that I can learn from?*

Other leaders. Your fellow managers can help with your transition by sharing standard operating practices (written and unwritten). They also can provide insights based on their working relationship with your manager.

Example: *Can you advise me as to what type of information you regularly receive about our department? For example, what metrics does Finance regularly report on? And, what advice would you have for working with my new boss?*

Your team. Your direct reports can teach you about their current unwritten rules of operation (e.g., preferred communication methods, team traditions, when they have pizza lunches, and so on), their expectations for you, and what's gone wrong (or well) in the past.

Example: *You've been terrific about listening to my ideas, but now I'd love to hear from you. As far as how the team operates, what's been working for you? What do you wish you could change? How can I work with you to make sure the team has what it needs?*

Tool 3.2 is a detailed checklist we've given to thousands of leaders over the years. Use it to help you craft your initial conversations with your new colleagues. But don't stop there—keep a running list of things you notice about yourself, the organization, and individuals during your first few months on the job. (Remember that two-hour weekly reflection time?) Turn those observations into new lists of questions and periodically take them to your new network of team members, managers, peers, and human resources.

TOOL 3.2

What Do I Need to Know?

1. Read the questions below and check those to which you don't know the answer.

2. Identify the three most important items you checked, numbering them in order of importance 1, 2, and 3.

3. Seek answers to your three questions from sources such as your team, your manager, human resources, and other leaders.

Interactions with Others
(My Team Members, Colleagues, and Manager)

❑ How do individuals prefer that I communicate with them (face-to-face, phone, email, etc.)?

❑ What kind of information will I be receiving that I didn't receive before (higher-level information, human resources, other email distribution lists, etc.)?

❑ What information do my team members, other leaders, and my own leader need from me?

❑ What support can I expect from my manager, my colleagues, and my team?

❑ Who can advise me on meeting the challenges of being a new leader?

❑ Other:

My Responsibilities
Should my priorities be:

❑ Administrative?

❑ Managing/Leading my team?

❑ Doing project work?

❑ Coaching/Developing others?

❑ Planning and organizing?

❑ Making decisions?

❑ Managing/Monitoring a budget?

❑ Sharing information, both up and down?

❑ What are the limits of my authority?

❑ What training and resources are available to me?

❑ Other:

My Manager's Expectations

❑ What results does my manager need from me in the next three months? Six months? Year?

❑ What am I being held accountable for?

❑ How should we monitor my progress?

❑ What kind of information do I need to give my manager, and how often?

❑ Considering all that I need to do, what are my manager's priorities for me?

❑ Other:

Organizational Issues

❑ Where is the organization going (its strategic direction)?

❑ What is the organization's three-year plan? Five-year plan?

❑ How does my group support those plans?

❑ What recent or impending organizational changes will affect my group?

❑ What do I need to know about the culture of the organization or of my department?

❑ Other:

Your First Six Months

We hope this chapter has helped you affirm a decision about leadership that works for you and your significant others. You can now dig in to this book with fresh eyes, looking for the most relevant information as you begin to pick up the pace and start moving faster and more confidently forward. And if you've confirmed leadership isn't for you? Congratulate yourself on a good decision and dedicate yourself to building the skills you'll need to continue to grow as an individual contributor. But do us one favor: Find a colleague with potential and a curiosity about leadership and give her the gift of this book. Tell her you believe in her. Your network will thank you for your generosity. (And so do your authors.)

On the microsite, you'll find an extensive checklist of the key activities new leaders should strive to accomplish in their first six months. Take a moment to review it before you continue reading. This tool will help you make your transition a smooth one, so you'll want to read with these ends in mind.

Reflection Point

Q: Who believed in you before you believed in yourself?

Q: Who in your life (or on your team) needs you to believe in them?

It takes 20 "attaboys" to overcome that one "oh, @#$%!"
moment. And sometimes that
doesn't even help.

4 YOUR LEADERSHIP BRAND, PART 1
Be Authentic

It was the shriek heard around the world. Or so it felt.

Tanya worked in supply-chain management for an aeronautics manufacturer. As an individual contributor, she excelled in her job and had a real knack for antic-ipating problems. *I felt I could "see around corners" and really improve things*, she said. So, when she was promoted to her first leadership role and relocated to Florida—an added perk!—she felt both proud and ready. It was her time.

On day one Tanya met with her team—a seasoned group of contributors, many of whom were more senior than she. Tanya embraced the moment with confi-dence. She talked about how excited and privileged she felt to lead them and acknowledged their unique role in the organization. So far, so good. She came prepared with fresh ideas based on what she had seen implemented in other parts of the company and that she believed could improve her team's operation immediately by driving efficiencies, eliminating errors, and, most importantly, reducing last-minute stressors. *They were smiling, nodding, and asking great ques-tions*, she recalled.

Then it was her turn to listen.

The team took turns reporting on projects, accomplishments, and bottlenecks. It all went smoothly. Then, an associate handed out the team's monthly dash-board, a common report that had been distributed to the Operations Team earlier that day. When Tanya saw the report, she panicked. *WHAT?*

And in that single moment, Tanya damaged everything she'd worked for.

Her shriek jolted the team out of their collective happy place and into a defensive crouch. *This report just went to MY boss? Who else on our team read this over?* she demanded.

I was worried about the impression that Operations would have of me. And I said that to them, she said. *I complained about the grammar, the graphs, the formatting, and the data. Everything.* She yelled at the associate for letting the document go out the door. The group sat in shocked silence as Tanya continued to berate them. When she shared this story in a leadership training session—between deep gulps and behind face palms—it was eight years later. But the pain of her mistake was still fresh. *I was labeled as a hothead and a perfectionist by everyone on the team,* she said. Probably worse things were said, she thought. There isn't a breakup song for moments like this, but there should be. *It was a train wreck.* Her sullied reputation followed her for years.

Make a Good First (or Second) Impression: Your Leadership Brand

Most people will experience moments when they regret something they said, did, or failed to do. It's part of being human. But for a freshly minted leader, those human moments can accumulate quickly and do real damage if you're not careful. In Chapter 3, we introduced you to one of the many reasons why: It's easy to underestimate how profound the transition is from individual contributor to leader. Like Tanya, you're probably approaching the first encounters with your new team with a sense of anxious anticipation and armed with a mental checklist of the unique value you have always brought to your work. As your new team looks to you for the first time, they are understandably worried about how that value will make things harder for *them*.

The people who now report to you will form an early judgment about your leadership capabilities that will define your reputation in ways that may not serve you well, particularly when you're also mastering the full scope of your new job. Consider the simple truth that consumers face: If their experience with a product is not good, they won't use it again. And they'll most likely complain about it to other people. The dark cloud spawned by poor word of mouth can dampen a product's prospects in the marketplace for a long time. So, whether you're 30 seconds into your leadership job or have been in place a while and could use a reputational do-over, you'll need to develop and consistently operate within a broader framework of how you think about your new role. This chapter will help you do that. We'll introduce you to three attributes that will help you create a positive *leadership brand*—one that cultivates trust and truly reflects your authentic self.

What's in a Leadership Brand?

While there's no one perfect way to be a leader, there are clearly identifiable practices that set apart truly effective leaders from average or poor ones. Research[1] has shown that successful leaders demonstrate three key attributes— we call them *leadership differentiators*—that help them gain confidence and skill in leading a group. Embrace them and you will be successful out of the gate. They are:

- Be authentic.
- Bring out the best in people.
- Be receptive to feedback.

Clearly, these attributes are commendable for everyone, whatever their life's work. Good leaders eventually realize their true value—some earlier and some later—during their career. Research clearly shows that these differentiators can predict future success, as well. That's important information for you on two other fronts. While as a leader you'll be coaching others, you also might be in a position to help select future peers and team members. Look for these attributes in others. (We'll explore this in greater detail in the Mastery chapters on selection and coaching.) Even if you are not a leader yet, these skills will help you make your mark as an individual contributor and distinguish yourself as a strong candidate for advancement. And people will want to work with you more. Which is a good thing!

Each of us has experienced good and less-than-stellar leadership in our lives, whether from parents, from teachers, or at work. Because of these experiences, most people have thoughts about what they would do—or avoid doing—if they were to become a leader. Use Tool 4.1 to capture some examples of leadership that you might imitate or avoid, based on what you've experienced. Exploring these experiences helps to reveal what you value and allows you to polish your authentic voice.

Never Do/Always Do

When I thought about becoming a leader, I vowed that I would:

NEVER DO . . .	ALWAYS DO . . .

Think about it:

Why did you say you would never do that?
Were those actions hurtful? Did they affect morale or productivity?

Why did you say you would always do that?
How did it make others feel? What positive effects did it have on the group?

Spoiler alert: Thinking through this tool is necessary to complete the final exercise in the next chapter. Don't skip! It's important.

Be Authentic

If you're like most new leaders, you might have some convincing to do. Nancy was a recent participant in a DDI course for new managers and showed up with a fairly typical problem. She had been so focused on gaining the technical skills she needed to win a job leading a team of IT analysts, that she was surprised—and a little hurt—when they appeared less than thrilled to see her in charge. *I never estimated how hard it would be to manage people*, she told us.

Nancy made the transition from an individual contributor, where all she had to do was manage herself, to leading a core team of six, with an extended team of 30. To compound her challenge, many members of the extended team ranked higher than she did on the organization chart. *They're directors, but I'm only an engineer with no real title*, she explained. Also, she was the only woman on the team. *I couldn't get them to attend meetings or even return my calls. I kept thinking, "Why won't they listen to me? Will they ever work with me?" It scared me.* It wasn't personal—it was just that she was an unknown quantity in a highly competitive environment. *I realized I had to learn how to talk to people, to gain their trust. But then I realized I didn't know how.*

What Nancy experienced with her new group was not uncommon among new leaders. The team didn't really know her—she needed to gain their trust, and a big part of that is showing authenticity. What's authenticity, you ask?

Being authentic means that *your actions mirror what you believe* and feel, and that there is no contradiction between what you do and what you say.

You demonstrate authenticity when you:

- Do what's right, even in difficult situations.
- Treat people with respect.
- Promote trust among others.
- Keep promises and commitments.
- Admit mistakes.
- Give credit when it's due.
- Disclose by sharing your thoughts, feelings, and rationale, when appropriate.
- Display confidence but avoid arrogance.

Conversely, leaders who are inauthentic can have a debilitating effect on the teams they lead. These leaders tend to:

- Hoard information.
- Pit team members against each other or play favorites.
- Disregard team members who don't agree with them.
- Ignore tensions and workplace conflict.
- Blame others for their missteps.
- Take credit.
- Radically change their behavior to sound more leaderly.
- Pretend to know everything.

With these behaviors in mind, it should come as no surprise to learn that in our many focus groups with senior executives, the importance of authenticity in leaders received some of the most resounding affirmations—across cultures, industries, and professional sectors. Executives worry about how their leaders are perceived, and so should you. Why? Authenticity is fueled by integrity, which in turn fosters trust—the fundamental catalyst in the most-admired workplaces. Most-admired workplaces have happier, more engaged, productive, and creative employees. When people trust you, it's not just good for your reputation—it's good for business, too.

One of the hardest things I had to do was to tell people that we were not just eliminating their jobs, we were eliminating their entire lives. Manufacturing. Gone. And I needed them to keep working as hard for us as they were before until the transition was complete. They did it because they trusted me. We're family here. I listen. I tell people the truth. And they see me fight for them.

 —**Ursula Burns,** now CEO, Xerox, on the decision to save Xerox from bankruptcy in 2001 by eliminating the company's manufacturing unit. Some 40 percent of the workforce was laid off.[2]

Cultivating an Authentic You

Like Nancy and Tanya, you've inherited a group of people whose futures are now linked with yours. And they don't really trust you yet. There is only one way to overcome that—by interacting with them confidently, honestly, and openly. You'll show integrity through consistent, well-crafted, honest conversations and behaviors. And you'll stay real without disclosing inappropriately to build trust. This is what we mean by *authenticity*. But, crafting your leadership brand goes beyond being your authentic self. In Chapter 5 we'll explore the other two differentiators—bring out the best in people and be receptive to feedback.

Strong Ego or Big Ego? Do the Math

As a new leader it's smart to look to the future. Will the actions you've taken help your ego grow big or grow strong? Authentic leaders with strong egos show the courage and humility to admit mistakes. Indeed, the very admission of a mistake earns credibility with employees. People who exude authenticity are unafraid to disclose their feelings and are seen as confident without being arrogant. And they tend not to be attention seeking. In *Good to Great* (2001),[3] Jim Collins profiles 11 highly successful senior leaders with strong egos who are not household names. Nonetheless, their companies averaged returns 6.9 times greater than the market's—more than twice the performance rate of General Electric under legendary Jack Welch. In contrast, big egos seek the limelight, take credit, and engage in big talk. Donald Trump, whose companies have filed for bankruptcy four times, is considered by many people to be a big ego sort of leader.

Reflection Point

With shrieking Tanya from our opening story in mind, consider these three points:

1. What should Tanya have said to her team about her mistake?

2. Have you ever faced (or seen someone face) something similar? What worked about how you (or he) handled it? What didn't?

3. Where do you personally draw the line between authenticity and disclosing too much?

> Great leaders know that their success relies on the success of the people they lead.

5 YOUR LEADERSHIP BRAND, PART 2
Bring Out the Best in People and Be Receptive to Feedback

As you'll recall from Chapter 4, successful leaders demonstrate authenticity. In this chapter we'll discuss the other two key differentiators:

- Bring out the best in people.
- Be receptive to feedback.

Bring Out the Best in People

We've found that the best leaders have the innate ability to make everyone around them better. As you are new to leadership, we recommend adding Douglas McGregor's 1960 management classic, *The Human Side of Enterprise*,[1] to your reading list. It describes two types of leaders: Theory X and Theory Y. Theory X leaders are known as micromanagers who command and control. In contrast, Theory Y leaders believe that people deserve to be treated with dignity and respect, are honest, and can be trusted. Theory Ys are the bosses everybody wants to work for, and the ones who get the most promotions for their people. In times of crisis people tend to gravitate toward these individuals. They are easy to talk to, are receptive to feedback, and care about the people in their charge. And they show it.

Toward the end of the twentieth century, DDI founder Bill Byham penned a humorous fable about Theory X versus Theory Y leadership, titled *Zapp! The*

Lightning of Empowerment. It became one of the top-10 business books of the 1990s,[2] and its concepts about employee empowerment hold up very well in today's challenging work environment. Byham wrote that leaders who Zapp! others "provide responsibility, a sense of ownership, satisfaction in accomplishments, power over what and how things are done, recognition for their ideas, and the knowledge that they're important to the organization."[3] It's important to understand that this engagement in constant improvement cannot be imposed or forced on employees (in the book it's known as being "sapped"); it's only fully achieved by empowering them.

So, you can see, both McGregor's and Byham's observations have survived the test of time. Management tomes and business magazines correctly tout our current era as an age of collaboration—an optimistic time where solutions are crowd-sourced, opportunities are designed, and far-flung teams work together creatively at all hours of the day from every corner of the globe. While it is true that new technologies enable new ways of working together, it's also true that the type of leader who thrives in this environment—one who resists traditional command and control structure—has always existed. And it is precisely this type of person who will thrive as a leader today. Don't worry if you're not a natural at this; you can learn. One key is to ask smart questions and listen to the answers. In Chapters 6 and 7 we introduce five Key Principles to help you Zapp! your employees, as a catalyst leader.

As a new manager at a tool manufacturing facility in the United Kingdom, Carey suddenly had his hands full. He was responsible for a small team of designers, *and then also I had a bunch of guys in the tool room—about 22 tool makers. About 30 people all together.* But he had a much bigger problem than proving himself to his former design peers—the tools themselves. The system of catching and correcting problems as the work was handed off from design to fabrication and beyond wasn't working. The failure rate was too high. *From the concept of the product right through to when it landed in production, that whole process had to be looked at completely and remapped out,* Carey said. *So, I deleted the whole process.*

> Everything we do is about getting people to be more open, more creative, more courageous. It's empowering to be asked to look at what's possible, not told how to do it.
>
> — **Jack Dorsey,** cofounder, Twitter and Square

Carey then made the decision to team-source the solution. Anybody who touched a tool at any stage was involved in the entire process redesign. *I got them all together, to look at each product and walk through its life cycle.* They discussed various scenarios as a group. The changes they would have to make in the way they worked separately and together were significant enough to cause pushback if he wasn't careful. *We created a process with a checklist . . . and with each tool project, there's a checklist to go through for each phase. And it worked really well.* Carey, who had won a national apprentice competition as a teen and taken night classes in CAD to win his first tool-making job, understood that the people who designed the components were his best hope for designing a new way to work together. *I don't want it to sound like you're manipulating people, but if you involve the people early enough and they're involved in most of the decisions that they need to change, you're on a winning streak. They have a real input into the actual picture of what the outcome is going to look like. You kind of become co-owners of it.*

It takes win–win thinking to help others be the best they can be. Great leaders possess this outlook. They know that their own success relies on the success of the people they lead and that one of their chief responsibilities is to foster their team members' skills, abilities, interests, and efforts. It's never too early to establish this positive philosophy and put it into action.

To bring out the best in people:

- Encourage your team to try new things.
- Cultivate and optimize others' talents and capabilities.
- Take the time to find out what motivates your team and assign work in line with people's skills and interests.
- Compliment people on their efforts.
- Give people input on things that affect them.
- Trust in the strengths of others.
- Allow them to safely learn through failure, so they can take appropriate risks.
- Unite others toward common goals.

Schedule a One-on-One Meeting with Each Team Member

To help you bring out the best in your team, you need to get close and understand their skills, abilities, and motivations. These conversations are different from the ones we asked you to have in Chapter 3. Those were about *you*. These are about your *team*. Tool 5.1 will be helpful during these discussions.

It's a simple checklist we've given to thousands of new leaders to help them craft their first getting-to-know-you conversation with their direct reports. Let each team member know the purpose of the meeting in advance. Choose from the open-ended questions here to initiate a conversation. Don't cheat and add work-specific conversation in as well! Above all, signal that you're open to their questions about you.

- ❏ What do you enjoy doing most as part of your work? Why?

- ❏ What do you miss most about the jobs you've had in the past? Why?

- ❏ What things about your current job do you enjoy the least? Why?

- ❏ How do you cope with or relieve stress?

- ❏ To help you do your job, what could I change about:

    - ❏ Your work environment?

    - ❏ The content of your work?

    - ❏ How you get your work done?

- ❏ What form of recognition do you prefer or not prefer?

These getting-to-know-you conversations are incredibly useful. They demonstrate your commitment to listening and help people feel valued. Hey, you might even learn a thing or two! But more likely, they'll help you build a baseline of comfort and familiarity that will make your early months as a leader happier for everyone. Sure, you might find that a team member finds some of his responsibilities uninteresting or unmotivating. The more you understand the people you work with, the easier it is to help them be successful.

And you'll never know unless you ask.

Be Receptive to Feedback

Our first two differentiators focused on how best to interact with the people around you—by being authentic and bringing out the best in them. You help them succeed and you *share* feedback—both positive and developmental. But what about when the feedback is for you?

For this last differentiator, we'll explore how your team members and other workplace associates can reciprocate and bring out the best in you by *giving you feedback*.

Carolyn is a logistics manager for a nonprofit food bank and social services organization. Although she'd had food service experience and good management experience as a volunteer, Carolyn wasn't prepared for the more exacting nature of her new job, which required broad logistical planning and data-driven decision making. She went from the pantry into the frying pan pretty quickly. *I don't know much about spreadsheets*, she said. *I'm more of a people person.* Her supervisor, who had held her current job for five years, was both Type A (you know the type—highly ambitious, competitive, and prone to stress) and hands-off. He just shoved her into the deep end. *I just felt I was never going to learn this. It feels like a lot of responsibility when you know that there are going to be elderly people waiting in a line outside in the cold. I was worried about making mistakes.* When she did make a mistake—failing to deliver to a new site on time—it threw her team into chaos for about half an hour. *I think a few people were confused or a little annoyed, but I didn't sleep for like three days.*

Instead of retreating, Carolyn asked her boss and a few of her direct reports for feedback about the incident. *We talked all through it*, she said, *and got good, specific advice.* [My boss] *asked me to write it out—where I had made errors and what I would do to change them*, an exercise that helped her feel more connected to his vision for her job. But her forthcoming nature helped her in another unexpected way.

I was feeling pretty beaten down . . . one of my employees was walking out at the same time I was and turned around and said, "You know what? You're going to get it! It's a lot of stuff to learn; you're going to get it—you have it where it counts." The investment she made in being open and authentic had paid off. *That he could say something so supportive was really helpful at the time.*

Carolyn showed a powerful mix of traits that helped her through her rocky first days on the job: Resilience, mental toughness, humility, and the ability to face failure effectively and with grace. She's in good company. USA Olympic gymnastics coach Mary Lee Tracy has been quoted as saying that one characteristic distinguished her elite athletes from the rest: *Athletes are no different than other people in that they will make mistakes. What is so important and what I look for in future elite athletes is how they respond to failure. It's so important they don't continue to fail, but fail forward.*[4]

Leadership research also bears this out. One of the variables that over time has shown to predict leadership success is an individual's "receptivity to feedback."[5] Those who generally seek and use feedback from others and view mistakes as learning opportunities tend to be more successful in leadership roles. The *fail forward* concept should be adopted for all leaders. But it only works if you're willing to seek and accept the feedback of people who are in a position to evaluate your work.

Failing forward is when you continue to try new approaches and new solutions to solve an existing problem. You still may not achieve your desired results, but you're still moving forward, learning, and making progress toward solving the problem. Failure, on the other hand, is when you don't get the desired results because you quit trying or you continue to do the same thing over and over again.[6]

–Mary Lee Tracy,
USA Olympic Gymnastics Coach

First, Ask . . .

We know from experience that what we're asking you to do is harder than it sounds. Most leaders find seeking feedback to be pretty difficult. Nobody wants to show weakness, particularly in business. Part of it is personality based: Receptivity to feedback is learned early in life and can be difficult to develop as an adult if you don't make an effort. But seeking growth is not showing weakness. Leaders who are never wrong typically suffer the ripple effects of low morale and high-turnover (which *is* bad for business). And they keep making the same mistakes again and again, which can cause real problems for an organization.

But anyone can master the practice of seeking and using feedback. The first steps, of course, are up to you.

To show your receptivity to feedback:

- Ask for and use feedback about your leadership from multiple sources.
- Accept and act on developmental feedback.
- Acknowledge your shortcomings.
- Display humility.
- Hold yourself to high expectations.

Then, Widen the Circle

With feedback it's not a "less is more" but a "more is more" opportunity. The more perspectives you gather, the more likely you are to get the true message people are sending.

Consider asking:

- **Your manager** for perspective on how you're leading the team, how you're communicating back up to him, and how well you work with peers.
- **Your peers** to provide perspectives on your interdepartmental collaborations and insights from customers.
- **Your direct reports**, who can let you know if you're communicating your expectations clearly and appropriately seeking their input in your decision making.
- **Your customers** to share their perspectives on your and your team's performance.

To help you remember, we've built these touch points into the six-month checklist on the microsite.

Finally, Receive with Gratitude

Saying that you're open to receiving feedback is one thing. Actually welcoming it is another matter, especially if the feedback challenges you in unexpected ways. It can feel like very bad news. But you can train yourself to see feedback as the gift it truly is.

Let us paint a picture for you. Imagine one of your peers tapping you on the shoulder and saying, *I need to tell you something: It seems like you don't always see what's going on in your team. Or maybe you see it, but you're not doing anything about it.* That's not fun to hear. But, how to react is your choice. It can be natural to get defensive and say something like, *I absolutely know what's going on in my team. How dare you suggest otherwise?* What will your body language be? Arms closed, leaning away from your peer? Will you be scowling?

Leaders who are open to feedback begin by thanking the giver for sharing and then asking questions to gather the specifics. And these are the leaders who will succeed.

We hope not! The best response would be to accept this feedback and probe to really understand it. *Thank you for telling me that,* is a good place to start. Be aware that not everyone is skilled at delivering feedback, and many people leave out the specifics that paint the full picture and make it easier to accept. It's up to you to ask good questions to get more information that can help you use the gift you've just been given. Leaders who are open to feedback begin by thanking the giver for sharing and then asking questions to gather the specifics. And these are the leaders who will succeed.

Don't like feedback surprises? Try asking team members for feedback as a regular part of team or individual meetings. This signals that you're trying to build an environment of trust and continuous improvement. And acting on feedback is even better; it demonstrates that you have room for improvement, which makes you more approachable and human.

Seek to Lead

Researchers Jack Zenger and Joseph Folkman analyzed the feedback-seeking behavior of 51,896 leaders over three years.[7] They discovered that:

- **Leaders who seek more are viewed as stronger.** Leaders who actively sought feedback and looked for opportunities to improve were viewed as 86 percent effective. They topped the list. Leaders who fell lowest on the survey in terms of openness to feedback were rated as only 15 percent effective.

- **Feedback-seeking behaviors decline with age.** Most people seek more early in their career, but the tendency diminishes over time.

- **Senior leaders are less likely to ask for feedback.** Supervisors will seek feedback for improvement 64 percent of the time, while senior leaders seek it only 43 percent of the time.

In summary, feedback matters! Consistent failure to seek feedback on your brand can have a negative impact on your career. In a study of 462 leaders in a Fortune 500 company, 77 leaders, average age of 50, were asked to leave their organizations, after an average tenure of 18 years. An analysis of 360 degree feedback data collected 2 years prior to their dismissal found a significant difference on a measurement of the extent to which leaders made a constructive effort to change based on feedback from others.[8]

Your Leadership Brand = Your Leadership Legacy

In Chapter 4 we asked you to reflect on "things you said you'd never do" and "things you said you'd always do" when you became a leader. Because the choices you make every day shape your personal leadership brand, it's essential to think about how you might be limiting yourself before you start. But at the same time, you're building a leadership legacy. And you want to make sure it's one you can be really proud of.

A more traditional view of legacy is that it's something you leave behind when you're *gone*. We think about it a little differently: Your legacy is something you actively shape in the *present* so that you, your team, and the organization can capitalize on the benefits *now*. Think of it as your evolving, living brand. If that sounds poetic, it is meant to. This is the true craft of leadership, where you reveal the best in yourself and others over time, by mastering the interactions you have with others.

I saw the angel in the marble and carved until I set him free.

—attributed to **Michelangelo**

TOOL 5.2

Use Tool 5.2 before you head to the next chapter. What you'll learn there expands on the work you've done here—specifically where it relates to the rich array of conversations you'll be having with everyone in your work life. Sketching out your legacy first will help you make those conversations more rewarding, powerful, and authentic to you.

My Legacy, My Brand

Think about the legacy you want to build and how the differentiators might help you build that brand reputation. Your task in this activity is to craft a statement of what you wish to accomplish to help you be a more proactive leader. What would you like your team members to say about you? To do that:

- Think of how the three leadership differentiators will play a role in your legacy.

- Remember that while business results are important, the only way to achieve them is through people.

Here are some examples of what might be covered in a legacy statement:

- Creating an environment in which feedback is accepted and appreciated.

- Making people feel that their opinions and observations contributed to the team's success.

- Being willing to listen; making people feel valued.

- Trusting people to make decisions; treating people with respect.

And now, for inspiration, here are some sample legacy statements from global leaders we have interacted with over the past several years. As you can see, some leaders wrote a sentence or two while others wrote a full paragraph:

Sample 1: *I'm a result-driven leader, who consistently holds people and myself to a high standard. I look for opportunities to develop others to think independently then I value their effort and celebrate their success.*

TOOL 5.2 *cont'd*

Sample 2: *I am a leader who inspires trust through values-driven leadership and models a character of commitment, ownership, humility, and integrity. I will achieve this by:*

- *Demonstrating consistency and fairness in actions.*

- *Practicing what I preach.*

- *Being available.*

- *Sharing ... sharing ... sharing.*

Sample 3: *I'd like to describe my leadership brand as someone being authentic, being a talent advocate, as well as actively involved in the business. As an authentic leader, I like to come across as someone being sincere, genuine, and most importantly, having the passion and interest to be a leader. As a talent advocate, I am constantly looking for good talent, how to attract them, and how to develop them, but most importantly, how to help our associates to be successful in their career. To be actively involved in the business, I'm constantly learning about our competitive landscape here in China. To learn about the industry, but most importantly, to learn how to run a sustainable, profitable organization. So leadership, to me, is an ongoing learning journey. With that in mind I hope to constantly get your feedback on how I'm doing in these three key areas. Thank you very much.*

Your Turn

Write your legacy statement here: _____

_____

_____

_____

_____

_____

_____

_____

_____

> The best conversations—frequent, clear, authentic, and occasionally difficult—help colleagues feel understood, valued, trusted, and motivated.

6 LEADERSHIP IS A CONVERSATION, PART 1
How to Make People Feel Heard, Valued, and Motivated

Here's the beautiful little secret* about leadership: It's really about connecting with other human beings.

For some of you—the shy, the introverted, the impatient, or the just plain overwhelmed—this may come as an unwelcome surprise. But in fact, it's one of the best insights we can offer you. And, as we've promised throughout this book, there is real science behind having effective conversations that connect you with people in every part of your life. In fact, your success—in leadership and in life—will depend on the conversations you have with the people around you. Really.

How to Succeed by Becoming a Relationship Capitalist

In 2010, McKinsey & Company published important research that got our attention. The authors believe that the ability to master interactions between people—what we're calling *conversations*—has the potential to generate real competitive advantage for individuals and companies.[1] In fact, in honor of this, the authors aptly coined a new phrase—*relationship capital*—to describe the ability of workers at all levels to leverage their conversations.

*As opposed to a dirty little secret, this one is more than a shortcut. It's noble work!

To illustrate relationship capital in action, here's a snapshot of a typical day for Tacy:

- Make small talk with a neighbor about the construction down the road.
- Start work with her weekly "big three issues" staff meeting.
- Seek her boss's advice on pricing for an unusual proposal.
- Convey to a practice leader her concerns about an upcoming deadline.
- Participate in a conference call (over lunch!) with the campaign committee for a nonprofit theater company she is actively involved with.
- Meet and provide coaching on the innovation camp led by the technology and consulting teams.
- Stop in the hallway to advise a team member seeking restaurant recommendations for his upcoming trip to New York City.
- Return home and subtly (who are you kidding?) remind her teenager of his next-day schedule and check his homework—all while cooking dinner, of course.
- Chat with her brother, Carter, about parenting, friendships, and work challenges as they walk their dogs after dinner.

All of these conversations matter to the people who are having them. Some are scheduled; some happen spontaneously. And the ability to effortlessly maneuver through each can make or break you as a leader, a parent, or a friend.

DDI has conducted hundreds of studies on what constitutes successful leadership. We've come to understand what good leaders do: They foster innovation, coach for success, put customers' needs front and center, make good decisions, and develop future talent.

If these are the *whats* of good leaders, what are the *hows*? Across all of that research, one theme stands out: Little of what leaders do gets done alone. That's why we believe so strongly in the concept of leader as catalyst. No longer in the role of primary doer, decision maker, and problem solver, catalyst leaders shift their focus to being a coach, supporter, and adviser. To accomplish this, they engage in dozens of conversations every day—with employees, shareholders, peers, bosses, and customers.

And the best conversations—frequent, clear, authentic, and occasionally difficult—help their colleagues feel understood, valued, trusted, and motivated. Not coincidentally, these conversations are the keys to a truly engaged team, and if we may be so bold, the keys to a truly happy life both at and outside of work.

And make no mistake, the interactions that now so frequently occur in other formats—on email, text, phone, chat, and internal networks—are, at their very core, a type of conversation with a real human being on the other end.

This chapter introduces the skills you'll need to make the most of every opportunity to connect with the people in your life. With a little time, these skills will become second nature. And we promise that the rewards will be just as gratifying—and maybe even as surprising—as the following one.

> *I just wanted to write you a note to let you know of something that occurred after the class I participated in. I have a 15-year-old son who has numerous behavior problems that we have not been able to deal with. We were getting ready to create an intervention for him to save him from his destructive tendencies. The night I came home from your class, my wife and I were discussing the steps in the intervention with heavy hearts. As I opened my briefcase, the form we practiced in our leadership class lay on top. I pulled it out and completed each section as if I were talking to him. I focused on listening first and asking him how he felt. I recognized that I did not do that well in the past. I went to my son's room and started the dialogue. In the past two weeks, there have been more conversations than have occurred in our entire relationship. I know I was a difficult student, but I wanted you to know that this behavior has turned him around 100 percent. I have a new son, and there will be no intervention. I do believe that this can work.*
>
> —DDI Course Participant

Practical Needs and Personal Needs

The advice in the next two chapters is based on DDI's more than 45 years' experience assessing people, conducting workplace research, and designing development programs. We've identified the behaviors and skills that lead to effective conversations and relationship building. (Visit the "Your First Leadership Job" microsite for a full report on the science behind personal and practical needs.)

We've found there is a core set of essential skills that everyone must master to build relationships effectively and get work done. We've discovered that the process by which people embrace these skills transforms their lives. So many people become leaders because it was the next logical step in their career—more money, more prestige, glowing praise at family dinners. Many people know what they want to get from leadership, but not what they want to *give*. The skills described in the next two chapters allow you to *get* more from your role as a leader, but also have you *giving* more to others.

It starts with a simple truth: People come to work with both practical needs (to get work done) and personal needs (to be respected and valued). Your team is no different. And if you've been in your new job for more than a day or two, you've probably noticed that your direct reports are bringing you a steady stream of issues—many of them involving other people—for you to "fix." It's tempting to jump in and tackle the practical aspects of these issues. It feels more like what a true leader would do. No emotion, just solve the problem! But in fact, you must always consider the personal needs hand-in-hand with practical needs.

> People come to work with both practical needs (to get work done) and personal needs (to be respected and valued).

Think of it this way: *Practical needs* are the "route" you need to take to ensure that your interactions with people meet their intended destination. *Personal needs* can arise at any time while on route. Addressing them effectively can help you overcome roadblocks.

We address the practical side in Chapter 8, with the *Interaction Guidelines*. And to meet the personal needs of others, we introduce you here to the *Key Principles*. At first, they might sound pretty basic—like the good advice a parent or teacher might have given you. But they work wonders!

The five Key Principles aren't meant to be used sequentially; instead you'll use them as you need to—during any stage of a conversation. And as we dig a little deeper, you'll see that the Key Principles are true keys to unlocking the best in others and yourself.

The Key Principles

Purpose: To help meet people's personal needs.

ESTEEM Maintain or enhance self-esteem.

EMPATHY Listen and respond with empathy.

INVOLVEMENT Ask for help and encourage involvement.

SHARE Share thoughts, feelings, and rationale. *(to build trust)*

SUPPORT Provide support without removing responsibility. *(to build ownership)*

Maintain or Enhance Self-Esteem

When my manager told me that people on our team didn't like working with me, I was shocked. When I asked why, she said it was because I was aloof and didn't seem to want to work with other people. "We thought you were different," she said. "You're just not a generous person." Different? Not generous? What did that mean? I kept thinking, am I really like this? Am I really this person? This unlikeable, not-generous person? How can I keep working with these people? I felt like my life was over.

—Amy

Self-esteem has gotten a bad rap lately, a running joke on a generation that overprotects its young. (At least in some parts of the world.) In an environment where everyone gets a trophy for being on a team, as opposed to excelling, self-esteem has come to represent meaningless praise and a lack of discipline. In reality, it is one of the most important concepts to remember when working with other people.

In the preceding example, Amy describes some brutal feedback that crushed her self-esteem and sent her into downward cycle at work for months. It wasn't just that her memos were a little light on data or her presentation skills needed polish; it was that her personality was problematic. Sadly, that difficult feedback was totally avoidable.

Self-esteem simply refers to the way you think about yourself. Are you good enough? Are you a valuable person? Do people respect you? Do you make important contributions to your world? Are your essential qualities visible to others?

As a leader, you have a prime opportunity every time you interact with someone to impact the way they feel about themselves. It's one of the most powerful interpersonal skills you can use, and one of the most extraordinary gifts you can give to the people in your organization.

Note the "or" in our first Key Principle: "Maintain or enhance self-esteem." When you interact with people, you have two choices: Either maintain how people feel about themselves (that is, don't make them feel any worse) or boost that feeling. Many interactions allow you to acknowledge the good ideas that were shared or to appreciate the efforts that were made—and thereby enhance someone's self-esteem.

In other interactions, performance falls short and the situation doesn't call for a compliment or recognition, but instead a course correction. When someone walks away, they shouldn't feel worse about themselves than when they started the conversation. Diminishing someone by belittling them or making them feel that they are somehow personally insufficient for the job at hand—like Amy's manager did to her—can be hurtful and very difficult to bounce back from. And it's unnecessary. Even in these difficult times you can—and should at a minimum—maintain the other person's self-esteem.

As it turned out, ungenerous Amy is a smart person—Gen Y and fresh out of college. She had spent her life communicating from behind a smartphone and struggled with interactions in the office environment. So, she took action. She sought useful feedback from trusted colleagues on how to better communicate with teammates. She repaired the relationships with her peers and slowly regained her confidence. But it took her nearly a year to feel truly better, and another four to earn her next promotion. And she never trusted her manager again. Now that she's a manager herself, Amy says what a lot of people say: *I'll never treat anyone the way I was treated.* But it's a hard way to learn the lesson.

Getting Psyched

Remember your intro to psychology course? Self-esteem is the second highest need on Maslow's hierarchy.[*2] And it can be affected by any and all interactions you have with other people. The concept of self-esteem rose to popularity in the late 1960s, pioneered by psychotherapist Nathaniel Branden and psychologist Stanley Coopersmith. To date, approximately 536 studies, 769 articles, and 80 books have been written on the impact of self-esteem on work performance.

Some of the reported outcomes of high self-esteem include high levels of career and job satisfaction, improved motivation and engagement, high-quality work, better personal and professional relationships, and more innovation at work. Individuals who maintain or enhance others' self-esteem tend to be seen as highly effective and enjoy better team communication and less tension in the workplace. They also are likely to lead employees with higher job satisfaction and performance, greater loyalty, and interpersonal trust.

*Abraham Maslow (1943) created a hierarchy of needs for human motivation. Each basic/lower-level need must be satisfied before people move up to the next. Maslow's hierarchy starts with physiological needs (food, water, sleep) and moves to safety needs, then to love/belongingness, esteem, and self-actualization (full realization of potential) at the highest level.

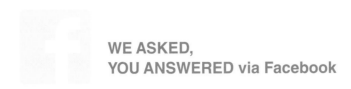

Dave Kipp—I had a boss who once told me: *"Kipp, you'll never get anywhere because you're not enough of an SOB."* The rest of my career has been about refuting that guy's premise.

How to Maintain Others' Self-Esteem

- **Focus on the facts, not the person.** People's sense of self-worth can be damaged if they feel you're attacking them personally or if they have to guess what you really mean. Saying, "Usually you're one of the most punctual people on our team, but in the last month, you've been late for team meetings," is more likely to maintain self-esteem than throwing out this comment in the staff meeting: "Do you have a problem with punctuality?" Obviously you're burning a few bridges with that second comment.

- **Respect and support others by not labeling them.** Labels can hurt—she's rude, he's insensitive, or that group is totally uncooperative. Labels can leave people feeling like their reputations are at stake and that they'll be tagged forever, no matter what they do. A critical leadership skill is to show a little respect and avoid labels.

- **Clarify motives by asking smart questions.** Guessing what might have caused a problem or difficulty is just that—guessing. Open-ended questions help you clarify motives. For example, asking, "What do you think has caused the delay?" is much superior to asking, "Are you purposely trying to sabotage this project?"—which is guaranteed to put the other person on the defensive.

So, if maintaining others' self-esteem is the minimum you should shoot for, what about enhancing it? Again, the answer is fairly straightforward: Share an authentic compliment. And yet, people tend to resist doing this.

When we ask first-time leaders taking our courses why they're reluctant to praise their direct reports, they typically come up with a pretty good list (see the next page). What's your excuse?

- "I'm too busy."
- "Because I'm always in problem-solving mode, running around trying to figure out what's wrong, what has to be fixed."
- "Because I don't want people to think I'm playing favorites."
- "No one ever gives *me* positive feedback!"
- "If I give somebody positive feedback when they do something, they'll slack off and think that's the required level of performance."
- "We expect a high degree of excellence in our company, so praise is unnecessary."

We get it! But we've also found that most leaders who resist this just don't know how, why, and when to deliver a compliment. And they fear that by bungling it, they'll come off as weak or inauthentic, or lose authority. None of that needs to be true.

Specific and Sincere

The technique behind delivering compliments, or as we say, enhancing self-esteem, is fairly simple. A compliment needs to be sincere—as in actually true and you really mean it—and specific. And research and our experience confirm that a compliment will not immediately turn someone into a slacker. Quite the opposite. In fact, complimentary feedback from a manager is motivating. Why? Because it reminds people that they have true value and that their contributions are important. That they are seen for who they are, and that they matter. And here's the biggest surprise of all: When you give a sincere compliment, you too will feel good. (Yes, we have empirical research suggesting that it's better to give than to receive compliments.[3]) And that will make you a better, calmer, more optimistic leader. And who wouldn't want to work for a person like that?

Reflection Point

 Who on your team needs to know what you truly think of them? Who in your life? What feedback or compliment can you give these people that would make a difference for them and maintain or enhance their self-esteem?

So, when should you compliment somebody? Of course, when she's improved measurably, hit a goal, resolved a difficult problem, or contributed something above and beyond during a time of real pressure. But sometimes—and this takes practice—you can deliver a compliment after observing something that would delight a person to know about herself. It can be random, but it has to be true. Here's the beauty of this kind of compliment: It lets the person know that you have a sense of who she is at a deeper level.

WE ASKED, YOU ANSWERED @Twitter and Facebook

Q: What was the best compliment you ever got from your manager?

FB Jennifer Fader Scott You make us all laugh even when things are bad.

@mrshanebennett a genuine thank you

FB Lori Wurm Weitzman The kids love you, trust you, and rely on you. We're lucky to have you.

FB Dimitry Elias Leger I underestimated you in the beginning.

@kevinmercuri Short, succinct email that read: "I'm really happy with your performance. . . . You are helping to grow this agency."

FB Robin Beers You are the best at what you do.

@iROKOHope He told me, and I quote: "Your job is impossible. Making me look like a human being. . . ."

FB Chris Allieri You are fearless in a room full of strangers. That's good.

@davidcuddy [An executive] stopped by to ask who wrote that. I thought he hated it so I said you did. It turns out he liked it. ROFL

FB Justin Holland You seem to be able to see around corners.

FB Hugh Weber You ask great questions.

Wasn't that a nice list? Of course, the challenge with Twitter is that we're confined to 144 characters and can't get the full story behind this praise. The reality is that enhancing self-esteem doesn't sound only like these short-and-sweet statements.

Short statements of praise feel good to receive, yet don't always generate the intended impact for two reasons. First, they can come off as trite. For example, Ellen told us that her manager's favorite descriptor was "awesome." He said it to everyone, every day, every week, about everything. So, even when it was intended as a compliment, this particular word felt insincere. Second, short-and-sweet compliments lack specificity. Being specific encourages people to continue offering their good ideas, lets them know exactly what they've done to contribute to the group's success, and motivates them to repeat those specific actions, when appropriate.

 **KEY TIPS:**

Maintain or Enhance Self-Esteem

To *maintain* self-esteem:

- Focus on facts.

- Respect and support others.

- Clarify motives.

To *enhance* self-esteem:

- Acknowledge good thinking and ideas.

- Recognize accomplishments.

- Express and show confidence.

- Be specific and sincere.

Good or Excellent?

Read the following pairs of statements from leaders. Choose the one in each pair that is the *more effective* use of the Esteem Key Principle.

Q1. **A.** Thanks for letting me know about this. I can't tell you how much this will help me correct the problem.

B. Because you told me about the problem and worked with me to correct it, we were able to avoid confusing others. Thanks for speaking up.

Q2. **A.** When you volunteered to conduct Monday's meeting, I was able to drive my grandmother to her doctor's appointment.

B. I'm glad I ran into you. I've been wanting to tell you how much I appreciated your help last Monday. Thanks!

ANSWER KEY: **Q1.** The correct answer is statement B. It gives specific reasons why the action helped with the problem; **Q2.** The correct answer is statement A. It states specifically why the support was appreciated.

Listen and Respond with Empathy

Think about the last time you were really upset and told a boss, manager, or colleague the whole story—in all its emotional and glorious (or not!) detail. When you finished, the person probably paused and said, *I know exactly how you feel.* What was your very first reaction to that? Was it *No. You don't?* The most common mistake people make is to use a phrase like, *I know how you feel* that sounds empathetic, but in fact means nothing. Many people compound the problem by adding their own story of woe—something vaguely similar—as if to prove they *really do know.*

But instead of making you feel better, they've just demonstrated that they haven't really heard you at all. Worse, it probably made you feel like you were being managed. In one fell swoop, they burned valuable time by turning the discussion away from you, and then pushed you farther away from them and a potential solution. Feel familiar?

Listening and responding with empathy, when applied in combination, are two of the most powerful skills you can master.

Listening and responding with empathy, when applied in combination, are two of the most powerful skills you can master. Why? When dealing with an emotional situation, these behaviors immediately reduce the tension and temperature in the room. And until things calm down, nothing productive can occur. But these are also two of the most challenging skills to learn. Emotions—of any kind—in the workplace tend to make people uncomfortable. *Intensity! Make it stop!* As a leader, your temptation may be to rush through the moment by telling people (1) that you get it, (2) not to feel the way they're feeling, and (3) what to do to remedy the problem as quickly as possible. (Perhaps you've noticed in your personal life that ordering an upset person to stop being so emotional doesn't work very well either.) To be successful, you'll need to manage your own discomfort and resist that temptation, because it won't work, and it will do nothing to build your relationship.

Here's how to frame an empathy conversation that will work:

1. Show that you recognize what the person is feeling by describing the emotion being expressed in front of you.

2. Show some empathy.

3. Ask a question about the situation.

Tacy Shares:

When my 14-year-old son, Spencer, started moping around our house, I could tell it wasn't just hormones. He was about to have final exams for the first time in his young life, and the lead-up to the big week wasn't going well. But he kept retreating from my efforts to cheer him up or help him prepare. I tried everything: *Buddy, what's going on?* (silence) *What's on your mind?* (silence) *What are you thinking?* (more silence) *How can I help?* I received another prolonged silence followed . . . finally . . . by a monotone, *"It's crazy right now."*

Staked to an entry point, I encouraged him, *Tell me about it,* and he did. With his eyes cast downward and still moping, he mumbled about how he had all these back-to-back tests that he'd never had to take before. And he said, *"Mom, I don't know how to do all of this at once."*

Then I offered, *I think you're scared and there's a lot of pressure. You've never had finals before. Is that about it?* Well, eureka! Breakthrough! His eyes then met mine, and he continued to open up, sharing that he felt overwhelmed and that others in class seemed so much further ahead of him. Simply using empathy to acknowledge and label the feeling he was experiencing enabled him to open up and look at the problem more rationally. It also enabled the two of us to break the ice and move through to problem solving together.

Empathy works as well in your job as it does at home. We've developed video scripts for many of our courses to model the art of recognition, empathy, and connection. Here's a snippet involving Steve, a leader who heads up a project team charged with updating the organization's outdated system. With the deadline looming, the project that had been sailing smoothly now has ratcheted up urgency and tension and eroded collaboration among team members. Alex, who reports to Steve, is having trouble balancing his workload.

Alex: *So I had to stay late that night. Then last Friday, Marcia comes to me for about the twentieth time that day. Interrupts me right in the middle of this complicated calculation. By that time, I'm telling you, Steve, I could've just . . .*

Steve: *Alex, I know you've been feeling the pressure, especially these last few weeks* [empathy]. *You know, people are beginning to sense that. In fact, some of us are not coming to see you with questions or suggestions because of that. And that's the reason I wanted to talk to you today.*

Alex: *About what? That I'm under stress, or that people have a problem with it?*

Steve: *Well, actually, both. Have a seat. You're really busy—I know that* [empathy]. *We're also at a critical stage in the project. Now, if we can't use your expertise when we need it—if you're not there for us—we can't meet our deadlines, and our schedules slip. And that can have an effect on the entire organization.*

Research shows: Leaders who demonstrate empathy with their employees are perceived to be better coaches.[4] Employees who believe their leaders are empathetic tend to be more engaged in their work and less fatigued, depressed, and anxious.[5]

Identify Facts and Feelings

There is a way to say, *I know exactly how you feel*, that people not only will accept as sincere but also will feel better about you because of it. There are two words that will remind you to do this: "Facts" and "feelings." When responding to someone with empathy, the first step is to reflect the facts you heard, quickly, so the person knows you've actually been listening.

An empathetic statement shows that you understand—though don't necessarily agree with—what a person is saying.

So, in the preceding scripted example, Steve saying, *Alex, I know you've been feeling the pressure, especially these last few weeks*, demonstrates that he was listening and understands Alex's predicament. It would have been a mistake for Steve to start with, *I know how you feel* or *I've been under similar pressure*, as that would have taken the focus away from Alex.

A key point to remember is that empathy is not the same as agreement. An empathetic statement shows that you understand—though don't necessarily agree with—what a person is saying.

Here's another example. Imagine you have a team member who feels out of the loop. An empathetic first response might be, *It must be annoying to think that people are purposely not including your group in the decision-making process.* You've given her a chance to share. In our experience, once people have had an opportunity to vent their emotions and are sure you understand, they can focus more easily on the topic at hand. They can begin developing ideas, solutions, and actions because they trust that you understand how the situation is affecting them.

Next, you want to show that you understand the emotion the person is expressing—and why. And for that, you'll continue to listen carefully and then label that feeling. Steve labeled Alex's emotions as pressured and busy.

Notably, empathy is not reserved only for negatively charged emotional times. When people are proud of an achievement or happy to have completed a difficult task, a leader's empathy statement allows them to bask in the moment. Again, identifying facts and feelings shows that you're listening and that you get it! And this builds relationships. So, for example, you could simply be one of many people to congratulate a colleague. Or, you can stand out by saying something like, *The look on your face says congratulations are in order. You must be pleased* [feeling] *by the how the sales presentation went* [fact]. *I'm confident we'll get the business!* [self-esteem]. A statement like this would go a long way toward solidifying a working relationship.

Can You Hear Me Now?

Listening can make the difference between landing or losing a job, achieving or missing an important deadline, or feeling like part of a team rather than a misfit. Yet, despite the fact that listening is one of the most important communication skills, it isn't always given its due. People seem to value speaking more!

> Listening can make the difference between landing or losing a job, achieving or missing an important deadline, or feeling like part of a team rather than a misfit.

One trap that leaders often fall into is listening just enough. That is, we listen until we know the answer, then interrupt and continue talking. Or, sometimes we listen and disagree with what's being said, so we offer an immediate rebuttal. This is listening to refute. Other times, we're so excited by the ideas being generated that we jump in to build on the idea and cut the other person off before he can finish his sentence and contribute all of his ideas.

When you tune in to what someone is saying, you're really listening to the feelings behind the words. You're listening with *empathy—understanding and being sensitive to others' thoughts, feelings, and experiences.*

The ability to *listen and respond with empathy* is a communication skill that can enhance your workplace and personal discussions. It can help you learn how others are feeling and let them know that you understand, even though you might not necessarily agree. It's the key to open dialogue and effective conversation.

KEY TIPS:

Listen and Respond with Empathy

- Respond to both facts and feelings.

- Defuse negative emotions.

- Empathize with positive feelings too.

Listen with the intensity that most people save for talking.

—**Lily Tomlin,** actress, comedian, writer, producer

QUIZ YOURSELF   Was That Empathy?

Read the following pairs of statements and decide whether they are effective or ineffective examples of the Empathy Key Principle.

Q1. All of you seem unsettled about the direction we're taking on this project.

        A. Effective   **B.** Ineffective

Q2. That's too bad, but I'm sure you'll work out how to reprioritize your schedule.

        A. Effective   **B.** Ineffective

Q3. You look really relaxed. You must have had a wonderful vacation.

        A. Effective   **B.** Ineffective

ANSWER KEY: **Q1. A:** Effective with a clear fact and feeling; **Q2. B:** Ineffective because the feeling was not labeled **Q3. A:** An effective example of empathy to label a positive emotion.

Ask for Help and Encourage Involvement

Memorize this phrase: *Absolutely, I'm happy to help. Tell me what you're thinking so far.* This, or some variation, is one of the fastest ways to get people involved in solving the day-to-day problems you'll be facing together. People have expectations about their jobs that go beyond a paycheck. They want:

- A say in how to do their work.
- To be involved in decisions that affect them.
- Input regarding changes they'll have to implement.
- To share in the solutions to their own problems.

As we detailed in Chapter 2, your job as a new leader is to get work done through others. The most effective way to do that is to spend less time expounding upon your ideas and what *you* think should be done (and expecting them to do it) and more time asking for *your team's* ideas and what they think. There are several tangible benefits to this approach. First, chances are they've got at least part of the answer figured out already. Second, when you ask people for input, it's another way of letting them know that you value their opinions, knowledge, and skills. Third, you get to see how smart they are and learn how their mind works. And fourth, human beings are almost always committed more to their own ideas.

This Key Principle helps you draw expertise and originality from the most important resources. Involving others can build a collaborative spirit that inspires people to put their best efforts into their work.

Seek More Than You Tell

Epictetus, the ancient Greek philosopher, is quoted as saying *We have two ears and one mouth, so we can listen twice as much as we speak.* In fact, research suggests that there is a real, measurable benchmark to shoot for in our everyday conversations. As a true professional, your role is to gather information, not give it out. A listening deficit can paralyze cross–unit collaboration, sink careers, and cause issues with productivity, trust, and engagement.

Instead of being an average leader who *tells* people what to do 70 percent of the time and seeks input just 30 percent, aspire to be like the most successful leaders, who seek input 70 percent of the time and tell only 30 percent.[6]

While this can feel counterintuitive at first, old habits might be the biggest stumbling block to involving others. Many of us are hardwired *not* to ask for help for any number of reasons: Because we think it makes us appear weak or we have to be a superhero. Because we think people will say no or that we have to do everything ourselves. Whatever the reason, commit yourself to change the way you approach people—first ask others to contribute and turn telling into seeking. Involving questions are open-ended and look like this:

- *Given your experience, where do you think we should start?*
- *What ideas do you have?*
- *How can we do this better?*
- *What can we do?*
- *How do you think the plan will work for you?*

Learn Now or Pay Later

DDI has assessed hundreds of thousands of leaders around the world on their use of the five Key Principles in common interaction situations. It's critical to point out that the data is not based on survey responses, but on *observations of actual leadership behavior*.

An analysis of these frontline and senior-level assessments reveals a number of common mistakes that people make during interactions. While people may demonstrate real strength in one area, it is the *combination* of elements that makes the difference. Behaviors used together lead to effective and productive interactions in the workplace. And this data suggests plenty of room for improvement.

A common tendency that undermines effective conversations is leaders relying too heavily on their own ideas. You might have worked with someone like this yourself. Not much fun! Of the frontline leaders we assessed, 25 percent were less than effective at inviting ideas from others.[7] And even if they do encourage others to participate in discussions and decisions, they might miss the next opportunity to get other people truly on board with the ideas discussed. We call that gaining buy-in. Getting the commitment of the people you work with is an essential part of your job as a new leader.

The ability to have effective conversations is critical at every level of leadership. So, we all can be forgiven for assuming that senior leaders have mastered these skills while they moved up the career ladder. After all, they've been at it for a longer time, right? Nothing is further from the truth. Our assessment data found that executives are actually worse at asking questions and facilitating others' involvement (36 percent are less than effective).[8] The stakes are real. The more senior the leader, the more damage poor quality interactions will have on the entire organization—and the less likely he'll find someone to help him improve.

The Involvement Key Principle goes beyond breaking our natural habit as leaders to solve versus ask others for input. It's about reframing how to get things done. Asking for help is a sign of strength, not weakness. It clears space for you and frees your time and energy. Asking for help is about tapping valuable resources to get the best outcome most quickly with the fewest resources expended. Let people know that you're asking for help because you value their time and talent, not because you are in over your head.

Think about what you'll gain from asking—a chance to connect, value a colleague, get something done faster or better, optimize your own time and talents.

There are pitfalls to avoid, however. Asking for help and encouraging involvement doesn't mean seeking input from everyone on everything. Some people aren't in a position to contribute, and we know that asking everyone slows the process. Not to mention that you won't be able to use every idea you ask for. Instead, your job is to involve the right person (or people) for the particular job, without over-relying on the same people. The more you know about your team, the more effectively you can tap the collective wisdom, and the stronger it will be.

While it also can be tempting to share your burden, be aware of how you frame what you ask. Make your request part of a shared win. For example, *Jim, given your extensive experience working on the same kind of equipment, what technical problems should we address in the procedures manual?*

Or, *This change will affect your group's process, so we want your ideas. Sandy, how do you think plan A will work for you?* Or, *Mark, I was impressed with your leadership of the team through the last changeover. Would you consider chairing this committee?*

One last thought on this Key Principle, and it can be difficult for a new leader: People sometimes suggest ideas and solutions that, for some reason, aren't viable. You can maintain their self-esteem by explaining why an idea isn't workable.

Better yet, explore the pros and cons together to help them understand the risks or downsides. Wherever possible, build on the usable parts of ideas.

KEY TIPS:

Ask for Help and Encourage Involvement

- Make involvement your first choice.

- Unleash everyone's ideas with questions.

- Encourage responsibility through involvement.

For new frontline leaders, the Esteem, Empathy, and Involvement Key Principles are among the most powerful skills you can master. If you take them on as a serious goal, you will be a good leader forever.

 Identify the Key Principle

So far we've introduced three Key Principles and shown how they pave the way to effective interactions. In this next quiz you'll see all three in action. Read the following situation and circle the Key Principle that is reflected in this leader's statement.

I'm sorry you had to miss the meeting. I know you were looking forward to it and excited to share the data you collected [**Q1.** Esteem/Empathy/Involvement]. *Your charts were helpful. Everyone said so. You highlighted a lot of complex information, and made the meeting move quickly* [**Q2.** Esteem/Empathy/Involvement]. *In fact, some people asked if they could have similar analysis for their departments. I wanted to check with you how we can best honor their requests* [**Q3.** Esteem/Empathy/ Involvement] *I know you're feeling swamped right now with other projects* [**Q4.** Esteem/Empathy/ Involvement] *so I wonder what ideas you have to help make this happen* [**Q5.** Esteem/Empathy/ Involvement]

ANSWER KEY: Q1. Empathy; Q2. Esteem; Q3. Involvement; Q4. Empathy; Q5. Involvement

In the next chapter we'll introduce the last two Key Principles and explore how you can use them in your conversations to build trust and ownership within your team.

> Your job is to make sure that
> all your people are productive,
> engaged, and working up to
> their fullest capacity.

7 LEADERSHIP IS A CONVERSATION, PART 2
How to Build Trust and Ownership

In the previous chapter you learned that using the first three Key Principles in your conversations will make your team members feel valued, heard, and involved. The two Key Principles explored in this chapter will enable you to cultivate employees' trust and help them take responsibility for their own success.

Share Thoughts, Feelings, and Rationale *(to build trust)*

This one is all about trust.

Rhea learned the hard way that trust takes work. When she took over as a director of sales for an engineering firm, she expected to lose a few people right away. *It happens*, she thought. But a few months into her new job, Aaron, one of her superstar sales guys, decided to join another team within the company. This was a potentially thorny problem, and Rhea knew she would have to plan carefully for his departure. The deals Aaron was working on were complex and had reached a crucial stage. To make matters even more dicey, he had the department's biggest customers. *I asked him* not *to share with his customers that he was leaving*, Rhea said. *I needed time to find a replacement, and it could take about two months.*

One month later, Rhea got an urgent email from Aaron's biggest customer—one she was most worried about alienating—asking what was going to happen with their account now that Aaron was leaving. Rhea was very upset. To her credit, she attempted to understand his actions after the fact. *Aaron is very much a relationship seller; he's good friends with a lot of his customers,* Rhea told us. *In hind-sight, I should have known that it was an impossible task to ask Aaron not to share his impending role change with his customers.* But she confronted him angrily, and he got very defensive. *He was like, "These people are my friends. You just don't understand. You haven't been in sales before, so you don't know what kind of relationship you can develop with these folks,"* Rhea said. She chose to give Aaron a negative performance review because he put his own relationships before the needs of the company. *I hope he would think twice about doing something like that again,* she said. But she doubted it. *He just felt like he was keeping something important from them.*

In the workplace, sharing thoughts, feelings, and the rationale behind decisions builds a more trusting environment. When leaders and team members open up, they encourage others (direct reports, colleagues, even customers) to do the same. In addition to making everyone more productive, it helps a manager avoid sticky situations like the one in which Rhea found herself. She assumed that Aaron would do what he agreed to do. But by failing to walk him through the more complicated reasons why she needed his cooperation, she missed an opportunity to gain his understanding, and without that, he took her request to remain silent for a period as a recommendation versus an expectation.

Perhaps even more crucially, by failing to get Aaron to talk about his relationship with his customers—specifically, how he builds trust with them—she enabled a nasty surprise that could have cost the company money and people their jobs. By sharing rationale for her decisions, she might have been able to jointly forge a solution with Aaron that would have met everyone's needs.

Sharing your thoughts, feelings, and the reasons for your decisions lets people know that you trust them enough to see what's inside you. You can show your trust in and respect for people by having enough confidence in them to discuss these issues. This helps them understand you and encourages them to be open with you. And, as trust and understanding grow, people communicate more openly and effectively.

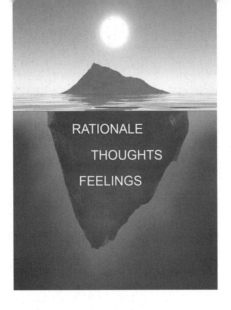

RATIONALE

THOUGHTS

FEELINGS

To understand how this Key Principle works, imagine you're an iceberg—part of you is above the surface where people can see it. This is the part you're most comfortable letting people see and know. But, like an iceberg, much more of you—your motives, beliefs, emotions, thoughts, and reasons—lies beneath the surface. This is the deeper you. Letting people get to know this part of you is what the Share Key Principle is all about.

Share Rationale

Sharing rationale helps people understand and accept new ideas or decisions. When people know why something was done, they work better because they're not guessing—they know what's going on. That context helps everyone work better. It's that simple.

Andrew worked for a technology company as a designer. By the third time he'd shown up at work in a one-month period to find that his team's projects had been summarily reassigned to other teams, he got angry. Was the work no good? Was this just standard procedure? *Not only was nobody telling us what was going on, or when or why it was happening, my supervisor told me to just do the new work we were being given and stop being so "dramatic,"* he said. But it felt like everyone was lying to them. *We'd see [our supervisor] in these meetings before it happened, and he obviously didn't like what was going on.*

What if Andrew's supervisor had said, *Hey, I get that you're frustrated with the way we're reassigning projects. And maybe it feels random or that we don't have faith in you. That's not what's going on here. Let me tell you what we're doing and why.* Would this rationale have made a difference? We feel confident that it would have.

Share Thoughts

Your group benefits when you share your approaches to tasks, problems, or situations, or simply your knowledge and opinions about a situation or issue. But, as you recall from our discussion of the Involvement Key Principle, you should seek more than tell—so share only the thoughts, opinions, and experiences that others can build on. Be judicious, and be careful not to override others' thoughts or monopolize conversations.

Embrace chances to share your own experience, particularly when it includes mistakes you've made as well as what you've learned from them. If experience has taught you a lesson that will help others, by all means bring it up. Disclosure of this type is a powerful way to build trust. Leaders will continue to struggle getting things done through others if team members don't trust them.

Here are some examples of sharing thoughts:

- **Share an experience:** *The first time I led a team meeting, I spent a lot of time preparing. But I didn't think to ask anyone for agenda ideas, so I missed some important topics.*

- **Share an idea:** *Overall, this is a solid plan. One thing you might consider, though, is scheduling time between the two tests to make adjustments, then retest the improved product.*

Share Feelings Appropriately

How you feel about a team member or issue is often well beneath the waterline, at the bottom of the iceberg. And sometimes it's very difficult to let these deep feelings rise to the surface.

> *Trust is like the air we breathe. When it's present, nobody really notices. But when it's absent, everybody notices.*
>
> —**Warren Buffett,** chairman and CEO, Berkshire Hathaway Inc.

But, sharing feelings is an excellent technique for communicating and building trust. When people see that you trust them enough to share your feelings, they're likely to be more open with you. This mutual trust supports understanding and good working relationships and can sound something like this: *Frankly, I'm concerned about not using the feedback we got from our partners. If we don't make some of the changes they suggested, they might not support us in the future.*

Because this can be challenging for a new leader, we offer two additional tips: First, when you share feelings, consider starting from a truly personal place, such as the emotions you are feeling, poor decisions you've made in the past and the corresponding unintended consequences, or your vulnerabilities and imperfections. Personal admissions such as these help team members and others understand you better. They also deepen your relationship with them while teaching an important lesson. But, as with anything, be aware of appropriate disclosure. Share only true feelings that *directly* relate to the situation and that will benefit people to hear in some way. For example, if everyone else on the team is complaining about the new companywide process for audits, disclosing your frustrations via a half-hour grandstand in a company meeting is neither helpful nor leader-like. Instead, acknowledge the situation and empathize with your team as you help them put it behind them.

Want to Build Trust? Disclose

Again, we have Neil Rackham[1] to thank for his pivotal research study on sales effectiveness in major multinational companies. Rackham's research focused on the impact of interaction skills training and the importance of motivation and emotions during work conversations. He demonstrated that to build trust, leaders must disclose their own thoughts and feelings. According to his research, trust in leadership is a critical requirement for employees to have, and their degree of trust affects overall organizational and work-group effectiveness, employee satisfaction with leadership, and the overall level of innovation. But do be careful. You can't disclose to people who will use the information against you or take it out of context, or when it would be unethical to do so. When in doubt, double-check your thinking with your own supervisor or human resources rep.

Make sharing a very active, ongoing part of your life and leadership brand. Disclosure shouldn't happen only in response to a onetime incident. And although you might disclose to a group, it's more effective when done one to one. As you interact with your team over time, you'll find more and more opportunities to share your feelings and insights in ways that feel natural and authentic.

Reflection Point

Think back to a time when you were surprised by a major development at work. What happened? How did it make you feel? What could your boss have shared with you in advance that would have helped? How did it affect your relationship with your boss going forward? Your colleagues?

KEY TIPS:

Share Thoughts, Feelings, and Rationale *(to build trust)*

- Disclose feelings and insights appropriately.

- Offer the *whys* behind a decision, idea, or change.

- Make sure your ideas, opinions, and experiences supplement—not replace—those of others.

- Be honest—disclosing true feelings builds trusting relationships and can help others see issues in a new light.

 Avoiding the Pitfalls of Sharing

Read the following statements and select the best answer.

Q1. You cannot disclose too much about yourself because sharing your feelings is very beneficial in building trust with someone.

A. True   **B.** False

Q2. If you fail to discuss the rationale behind a decision, or even how you feel about it, you *(select the one best answer)*:

A. Risk escalating people's concerns, especially if the decision is an unpopular one.

B. Fail to give people the knowledge they need to implement the decision successfully.

C. Limit your effectiveness as a leader.

D. All of the above

ANSWER KEY: **Q1.** The correct answer is B. It is possible to share too much. So, take care to disclose appropriately. **Q2.** The correct answer is D. By disclosing inappropriate information or too much information about yourself, you can make people uncomfortable or dominate the conversation, thereby causing them to close up and distrust you and your judgment.

Provide Support without Removing Responsibility *(to build ownership)*

This is the most straightforward Key Principle of the bunch. As a leader, you need to give assignments to different people. You need to make sure that people are fulfilling what you've asked them to do. And you need to provide the support they need to be successful. Your job is to make sure that all of your people are productive, engaged, and working up to their fullest capacity. You don't want to take an assignment away from somebody and reassign it somewhere else—or take it on yourself. Not only will that diminish self-esteem and erode trust, but it also will wear you out.

This Key Principle is all about ownership—helping your team accomplish meaningful work while maintaining their accountability. As you recall from Chapter 2, catalyst leaders spark action in others. This Key Principle is a critical leadership tactic to deploy on your journey to becoming a catalyst who helps others grow and succeed.

A classic *Harvard Business Review* article titled "Who's Got the Monkey?"[2] illustrates this topic quite well. The article tells the engaging story of an overburdened manager who has unwittingly taken on all of his direct reports' problems. If, for example, an employee has a problem and the manager says, *Let me think about that and get back to you*, the monkey has just leaped from the employee's back to the manager's. The net effect is a tribe of monkeys on the manager's back. He didn't support employees in their development but instead reclaimed all their responsibility. Why? Because he was probably thinking:

- *It's probably quicker if I just do it myself.*
- *They're probably too busy to do it anyway.*
- *I hate giving this up. I enjoy doing it so much. Maybe just this one time.*

When a *group owns* a task, they are responsible not only for doing it, but also for the thinking behind it. To cultivate this sense of ownership, a statement like this would work wonders, *You've been working with this customer for three months and are most qualified to handle this problem. I know you're concerned about phone coverage while you work with him. What can I do to help there? Let's talk about who else can cover the phone while you work on the customer issue.*

You can avoid the temptation to take over if you:

- Encourage the person or group to identify the type and extent of support they'll need. Don't guess or take for granted that they know where to go for help.

- Don't assume *you* know the best way to approach an issue. The way you handled it in the past might not be appropriate now.

- Don't automatically say yes when someone asks you to take responsibility. While it might be possible—and even make you feel needed—to take it on, that might not be the best route. Explore other ways for providing support that enable people to be more self-sufficient.

You'll learn much more about the nuts and bolts of this principle in the Mastery chapters, where we provide more specific advice about delegating, coaching others, and leading meetings.

KEY TIPS:

Provide Support without Removing Responsibility
(to build ownership)

- Help others think and do.

- Be realistic about what you can do and keep your commitments.

- Resist the temptation to take over—keep responsibility where it belongs.

 QUIZ YOURSELF   Good or Excellent?

Read the following pairs of statements. Choose the statement in each pair that is a *more effective* use of the Support Key Principle.

Q1. **A.** How can I help you resolve your problems with John? Your idea about early testing seems like a good one.

  B. It sounds like you're having trouble with John. I could try talking with him if you think that would help.

Q2. **A.** Do you know how we handled a similar problem at the TACAR Corporation? You might check that out.

  B. I'll check around and see if I can come up with any ideas.

ANSWER KEY: Q1. Statement A is correct. Q2. Statement A is correct.

Over the past two chapters, we've introduced the five Key Principles. We hope you're starting to see how they can be an effective tool for meeting people's personal needs during the important conversations you'll be having. Your goal, of course, is to ultimately be remembered as the best boss ever. When we asked associates what the best leaders are doing, they told us (see Figure 7.1). Not surprisingly, those who are most skilled at using the Key Principles rated highest.[3]

FIG **7.1** What are the best leaders doing?

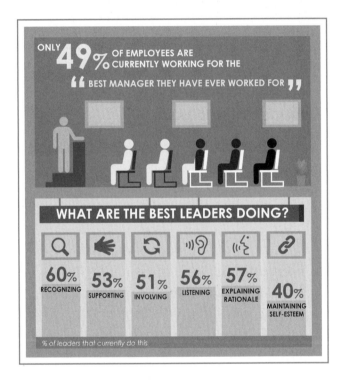

Remember earlier when we introduced you to the skills you'll need to be a catalyst and spark action in others? In the next chapter we dive into the Interaction Guidelines, which offer greater detail on addressing the practical side of working with people to develop effective action plans, which is crucial for any leader.

What we're saying might seem a bit counterintuitive—but to have quicker, more productive conversations, you need to slow down.

8 YOUR FIVE-STEP CONVERSATION ROAD MAP
Taking a Practical Approach to Get Results

It wasn't for lack of trying. We were always at least a week behind, no matter what the task.

John worked for a software development company that made apps for mobile phones and other devices. It was a small company—fewer than 50 people. And John had just inherited a design team that was incredibly talented, but its members couldn't meet a deadline to save their lives. If all-nighters and dirty coffee cups are effective lag measures, then the effort was clearly there. *I knew part of my job was to turn that around,* he told us. *I was going to be judged on that. But besides giving lots of pep talks and making people stay late, I really didn't have a clue where to start.*

In the two previous chapters, we introduced you to five Key Principles designed to help you better understand and speak to people's *personal needs.* Make no mistake—these are key relationship skills that build trust and enthusiasm so people want to support you and your ideas. But this personal connection isn't enough; there's the practical matter of getting the work done. To do that, you'll need to make sure everyone understands exactly what's expected of him or her, which is more difficult than it sounds. To accomplish this consistently, you'll need a clear road map for the conversations you have with your team about the work it does—one that minimizes miscommunication and unmet expectations, and gets everyone moving toward the common goal. In other words, meet the team's *practical needs.* We call this road map the *Interaction Guidelines.*

The Interaction Guidelines provide a vehicle to frame conversations in a quick, logical, and thorough way—from start to finish—to cover all the specific information people need to do their jobs. The guidelines also help you confirm that people understand what's expected of them. Using these techniques doesn't have to be a big deal; you don't need to follow a script or sound like someone other than yourself. They are simple enough to be incorporated easily into most discussions. And because conversations that employ them tend to stay on track, everyone involved comes away with a clear action plan. This makes for a happier, more successful, and more collaborative team. With time and dedication, using the Interaction Guidelines will become second nature to you.

To Meet Practical Needs, Take Five

Imagine you're in John's shoes. You need to have a series of conversations with your new team members about what they're working on and what they need to be successful, but also why they're always late. To ensure that this conversation runs smoothly, we encourage you to plan for it by focusing on five steps: *Open, Clarify, Develop, Agree,* and *Close.* To be consistently successful, you'll need to cover every step.

But wait, you say. You're so busy trying to get a handle on everything that, like John, you haven't even thought about your meeting ahead of time. This is not uncommon. Instead of using all five Interaction Guidelines, many leaders tend to minimize, shortchange, or even skip steps. Let's see how doing that can play out via three possible scenarios.

Scenario 1 (Jumping Straight to a Solution): John might say, *I need to talk to you about the XYZ project. We're behind by a week. What are we going to do to get back on track?* We bet you noticed that he skipped Clarify and went right to Develop. Or, John could say, *We're behind on the XYZ project by about a week, and I want to talk to you about it.* And, in turn, a team member might reply, *Let me tell you what I'm going to do. I have it figured out.* In this case, John's team member jumped right to Develop, skipping Clarify.

Again, this behavior is not uncommon. In our day-in-the-life assessments,[1] we found that frontline leaders skipped this step 50 percent of the time. When leaders jump straight to solutions, they fail to understand the context of a situation and miss opportunities to involve others. Also, their solutions are more likely to miss the root cause of the problem.

Scenario 2 (Overlooking Good Ideas from Others): John might say, *To help us meet our deadlines for the XYZ project, I think we need to think of some process efficiencies. One idea I have is. . . .* In other words, John's actions overlooked (or otherwise failed to capitalize on) good ideas from his team, because he didn't bother to identify problems and potential causes. He just forged ahead with his own solutions. Again, he's not alone; frontline leaders in the assessments relied on their own ideas and skipped Develop 54 percent of the time. By doing so, leaders deprive their teams of ownership, buy-in, and commitment toward finding a solution. And without buy-in, a team's energy and enthusiasm are sapped. But, more importantly, there is a chain reaction when leaders rely too heavily on their own ideas. It can stifle critical business activities like innovation and continuous improvement. It also can inhibit safety initiatives. In short, only limited improvement can be achieved when there's just one person (in this case, John, the leader) offering improvement ideas.

Scenario 3 (Too Quick to Close): Once leaders develop ideas with others, they often skip Agree and move to Close. And once again, things go wrong. For example, two days removed from the meeting, John asks a team member, *So where's the data?* and she counters with, *What data?* John pauses and slowly says, *The data you told me you were going to get for me.* Looking confused, the team member responds, *No, John, I told you I'd get the data to you after you talked to Sergio.* As we can see, action-oriented John attempted to take a shortcut, and his conversation was a less-than-effective, three-step process. For the record, frontline leaders in the assessment skipped Agree 43 percent of the time.

So, what we're saying might seem a bit counterintuitive—but to have quicker, more productive conversations, you need to *slow down*. Invest a bit of time planning your conversations, so you can really be active in the moment with your team when you speak. You'll also be less tempted to shortchange the process, which will enable you to reach a full understanding of your situation. Only then will you be able to move on to a real action plan that sticks.

Figure 8.1 shows the Conversation Road Map, which depicts the Interaction Guidelines in a circle. *Why?* you ask. Because for discussions with many topics, after Open you'd work through the Clarify–Develop–Agree sequence for each issue to be addressed until you covered them all. Then you would Close. For discussions with a single topic, you'd cycle through them in sequence—covering each guideline only once.

FIG 8.1 The Conversation Road Map

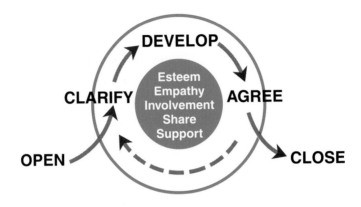

Now, let's imagine how John might incorporate all the Interaction Guidelines into a conversation with his team.

Open: John's first step is to declare the meeting topic and why it's important: *Good morning. I want to talk about the XYZ project, which is a week behind schedule. We need to get back on track for two reasons: It's for one of our biggest clients, and if we're late again, our other projects will be thrown off schedule. I want to talk to you about that and why we always seem to be running late.*

Clarify: John's next step is to understand what's happening. For this, he needs to be both partner and detective: *Why do you think we're behind by a week? What are some of the things keeping you from meeting your goals?* John asks these questions without strong emotion or placing blame. And then he does something that many other managers fail to do: He listens. Based on what he hears, he may ask additional questions about how the work is being done and what concerns people have that aren't being addressed. He might share some information from his own experience. And then he'll listen some more. If he discovers barriers that have been preventing his team from succeeding—like lack of support from other parts of the organization—he notes it. This critical Clarify step helps John gain a deeper insight into what work is like for his team in a very practical way.

Develop: *OK, I hear you—the delays are due to handoffs among our team as well as a bit of version control. What can we do about that? How do we get back up to speed?* Again, listening is key. Once John is certain he understands what's happened and why, it's time to create a plan to move forward. John's job is to encourage the team to share ideas and map out next steps as a group, based on the situation that was clarified. This should be conversational. He should also be listening for action items to note on the calendar.

Agree: This is where everyone commits. *So, here's the plan: Jane will handle formatting, and Jason will generate the reports. And we agreed that my job is to find someone from Marketing to give us feedback in writing—that's been a big problem in the past. And all this needs to be done by Friday. Is that right?* This step is essential to executing the new action plan; agreements must be clear, linked to a date, and in writing. If not, expect a lot of head-scratching and blank looks when your team fails to deliver at the next meeting.

Close: John needs to end the conversation with a quick summary. A smart move is to ask another team member to do it: *Alison, you're the project lead. Can you summarize next steps and double-check that we're all ready to go?* Finally, John needs to take the team's temperature: *So, how is everyone feeling? Did we forget anything? Can we get this thing back on track?*

Personal and Practical Needs—Putting It All Together

You'll find the Key Principles at the heart of our Conversations Road Map (Figure 8.1), because they belong at the center of every practical business conversation. And there is no way to predict when they'll be needed. So, while you move a conversation through its practical stages, remain ready to address people's personal needs when appropriate. It will be up to you to figure out how to tailor your conversations to fit the person. For some folks, just the facts will do. For others, you might need to employ more empathy to be sure that they feel valued and understood. The ongoing conversations you have with your team will prepare you to make increasingly better judgments about what each individual needs from you to do his or her best work.

Together, the Key Principles and Interaction Guidelines equip you with the skills to conduct effective discussions. And they make the difference! See Figure 8.2 for the impact we see from leaders who consistently demonstrate the core interaction skills of managing people's personal needs, asking powerful questions, and listening carefully to others.

FIG 8.2 Interaction Skills Make the Difference

Common Leadership Interaction Styles

DDI has observed tens of thousands of leaders in common interaction situations. Based on our observations and assessment of key interaction behaviors, we have identified a number of common leadership interaction styles. While these styles may be situational, many leaders display a preference toward one or two styles.

For each of the common interaction styles there will be inherent strengths and weaknesses. With a better understanding of *your* style, *you will be* better equipped to leverage your strengths and manage the potential risks.

Which Ones Are You?

THE PROBLEM SOLVER feels the need to solve problems on behalf of the other party. She may either jump straight to presenting the solution or clarify the situation simply to help her identify a solution.

> *Tip: Focus on using the Clarify and Develop stages of the Interaction Guidelines to better understand the perspective and ideas of the other party. Be sure to include these in your assessment of the situation and development of the ideas. Focus on involvement and provide support while being mindful not to remove responsibility.*

THE INTERROGATOR asks lots of questions (often with an overreliance on closed questions). He typically focuses on drawing out the facts of a situation and less on feelings. The other party can often feel under the spotlight and may be reluctant to share perspectives or ideas.

> *Tip: Need to place greater emphasis on the personal needs of the discussion through Key Principles such as enhancing and maintaining self-esteem, sharing thoughts and feelings to build trust, and involvement. Focus on the use of more open questions to enhance involvement. Be sure to seek feedback and input on your own ideas.*

THE RELATIONSHIP BUILDER tends to focus more on the relationship and less on the outcomes of a discussion. She will be very sensitive to the feelings of others and may not address the practical needs of the conversation. She may also be less likely to tackle the tough issues. She can often confuse empathy and sympathy. People can leave a conversation feeling "good" but with little resolution or direction.

> *Tip: Need to place greater emphasis on the practical needs of the discussion through the use of the Interaction Guidelines. In the Open stage, be sure to clearly state the purpose and importance of the discussion. In the Agree stage, ensure there are clear actions and check for understanding.*

THE STRAIGHT TALKER believes that everyone wants things out on the table and handled directly. He is less interested in the personal needs and will quickly dismiss any emotional responses or references. He believes an open and "brutally" honest approach is the best. He relies on presenting facts and business rationale to gain support for a view or idea.

> *Tip: Need to put greater emphasis on the use of Key Principles, in particular empathy and self-esteem. Need to recognize that others may not respond to a direct approach and therefore may need to Clarify both the facts and feelings associated with an issue. Consider using these essential skills with one-on-one conversations for potentially sensitive issues before jumping into an open group discussion.*

THE SKEPTIC, whether consciously or subconsciously, appears to question the intentions of the other party. She tends to favor the tried and tested and will be less open to exploring creative or alternative approaches. The skeptic tends to use a lot of *why* questions. To the other party she can often appear challenging, overly pessimistic, and lacking receptivity to new ideas.

> **Tip:** *Need to involve the other person more through the use of open questions. Focus on maintaining the other party's self-esteem in response to ideas and opinions offered and be open to developing ideas collaboratively. Can use the Share Thoughts and Feelings Key Principle to build trust.*

THE MOTIVATOR emphasizes the positive and opportunities. While recipients may feel motivated and engaged, they often leave discussions lacking clarity on actions and next steps. Furthermore, perspectives and ideas are not openly questioned or challenged. The positive nature of the conversation may mask inherent skill and confidence gaps.

> **Tip:** *Need to focus on the Clarify and Agree stages of the Interaction Guidelines. The Clarify stage will help to draw out all perspectives (both positive and negative). The Agree stage will ensure clarity and accountability for next steps. Involve the other party, provide support as needed, and check for understanding throughout.*

THE DETACHED avoids getting emotionally involved in discussions. While he remains very neutral, he can often appear distracted or even disengaged. Furthermore, he can be very difficult to read. As a result, others may misinterpret his intentions or actions and come to the conclusion that he doesn't seem to care.

> **Tip:** *Listen for, acknowledge, and respond to the emotions of the other person through the use of Empathy. Use Self-Esteem statements to show you value the other person's perspective and ideas. Share to help the other person understand your own perspective. Collaboratively Develop solutions and check for agreement on actions and next steps in the Agree stage.*

THE ASSENTER often relies on the other party to take the lead in conversations. While she can be seen as agreeable and open to other perspectives, she often lacks self-confidence and may not be willing to share her own perspective or ideas. In the end she may simply embrace the other person's point of view. As a result, she will often miss the opportunity to express her own point of view, avoid the tough issues, and leave issues unresolved.

> **Tip:** *Be clear on the purpose and importance of the meeting during the Open stage. During the Clarify and Develop stages, share your own perspective and use the Share Key Principle to help others understand your perspective. Try not to overuse Involvement and be sure to close the discussion with clear actions and outcomes.*

Planning Your Conversations

Remember the leader who needed to have a difficult conversation with his 15-year-old son? To prepare, he used a form, the Discussion Planner, to help him think through that crucial conversation. We've provided a copy of this essential tool at the end of this chapter. Tool 8.1 represents one of the single-greatest tools you can use on your path to better conversations. Just as great public speakers write out their speeches in advance (full sentences or bullet points, whichever they prefer), great leaders also plan their discussions. The Discussion Planner takes only a few minutes to complete, but the results for you will be amazing (we promise!). It helps you plan what you'll say at each Interaction Guideline (to meet practical needs) as well as when you'll use the Key Principles. A copy of the Discussion Planner can be found on the microsite. We hope it becomes part of your regular practice when planning conversations.

Together, the Key Principles, Interaction Guidelines, and Discussion Planner demystify what those great leaders do and help you make it part of your day-to-day practice. We're not saying you'll need to plan out everything you say for the rest of your life! Eventually, you'll build conversational muscle memory and naturally use the skills without even focusing on them. But even executives tell us that they pull out their Discussion Planners when they need to think through a tough conversation, like having a difficult discussion with a poor performer. Planning helps ensure that they confront the issue, deliver the difficult messages, seek input, respond appropriately, and resolve key issues. That's a win-win for both personal and practical needs in conversations!

It Takes Practice

As Malcolm Gladwell suggested in his book, *Outliers*, it takes 10,000 hours to master a skill.[2] It won't take you that long to master these conversation skills, but you'll get there with practice. It has been said that the soft skills are the hard skills. (They're also the essential ones for work, family, and life.) And mastering these soft skills, sometimes called emotional intelligence, is ultimately *the* most important thing you can do to achieve success as a leader. Yes, it's true! While smarts are important, they aren't *the* thing that makes for success. According to Daniel Goleman,[3] the father of emotional intelligence, success is 33 percent IQ and 66 percent EQ (emotional intelligence) for all jobs and all levels. But if you consider just leaders, that number soars. Success for leaders is 15 percent IQ and 85 percent EQ.

As you move through your leadership career, you'll have many chances to practice conversations leveraging the Interaction Guidelines and Key Principles.

Some will flow better than others. But take a moment to imagine the impact of those many conversations over time and how they'll color what people will say about your leadership ability. What would you like them to say about you? Perhaps you'd like it to go something like this:

I, LEADER

A One-Minute Play about You

Scene: Your company's break room.
A researcher comes in and talks to one of your direct reports.

Researcher: *So, what can you tell me about your boss? Is he one of those micromanagers? Does he even know your name?*

Direct Report: *You know what? My boss never dumps a job on me and then just walks away—even if it's a stretch project. He always checks to see what support I need and asks what I think will make things work better. He really understands me, how I work, what I care about. Even though he doesn't act on all my ideas, he asks for my opinion. And he tells me the truth—in a good way. When he makes decisions that affect me, he explains them. I might not always agree with them, but at least I understand why he made them. But most of all, he makes me feel valued and like I have a real chance to grow.*

Researcher: *He sounds like a great boss!*

Direct Report: *You said it!*

END

Discussion Planner

Discussion with _____ Date _____

Topic/Issue to discuss _____

Key Principles *(to meet personal needs)*

❑ **Esteem**
   - Be specific and sincere

❑ **Empathy**
   - Describe facts and feelings

❑ **Involvement**
   - Unleash ideas with questions

❑ **Share**
   - Disclose feelings and insights
     to build trust

❑ **Support**
   - Specify the level of support
     you'll provide

MY APPROACH

What are my objectives for this discussion?

How will I know I've accomplished these
objectives?

What personal needs of the person/team
do I need to consider?

Interaction Guidelines *(to meet practical needs)*

Time

❑ **1. OPEN**
   - Describe purpose of discussion
   - Identify importance

❑ Make procedural suggestions
❑ Check for understanding

❑ **2. CLARIFY**
   - Seek and share information about the situation
   - Seek issues and concerns

❑ Make procedural suggestions
❑ Check for understanding

Discussion Planner *(cont'd)*

Interaction Guidelines *(to meet practical needs)*

Time

☐ **3. DEVELOP**
- Seek and discuss ideas
- Explore needed resources/support

☐ Make procedural suggestions
☐ Check for understanding

☐ **4. AGREE**
- Specify actions, including contingency plans
- Confirm how to track progress and measure results

☐ Make procedural suggestions
☐ Check for understanding

☐ **5. CLOSE**
- Highlight important features of plans
- Confirm confidence and commitment

☐ Make procedural suggestions
☐ Check for understanding

Post-Discussion Notes

- What did I say or do to use the skills effectively?

- What could I say or do to use the skills more effectively next time?

But the first step to executing well is to start thinking differently about how you define success.

9 NOTHING ELSE MATTERS UNLESS YOU GET RESULTS
How to Execute with Focus, Measurement, and Accountability

To Kelly, it seemed like the fifteenth time that day that her boss was in crisis.

Her name is Joan, but we called her The Stresscalator, Kelly told us. *She was always changing things at the last minute, totally disorganized, and had no plan for anything. And everything was equally important and always a priority.* Success? *"I'll know it when I see it." That's what she told us!*

Joan had terrific ideas but little ability to apply them effectively at work. In her defense, the problem partly came from above. Her boss, a sink-or-swim sort of manager, gave Joan no direction or training. So, Joan committed a common mistake made by the anxious and unprepared leader: She avoided leaning on her boss and peers for support and micromanaged her team instead. And if this wasn't bad enough, Joan's worst habits magnified exponentially when she was under pressure.

This particular crisis flared over preparation for an internal presentation Joan would be giving to her manager and his peers regarding potential new lines of business. It was clearly a big deal. But Joan waited until a few days before the presentation to ask her team to assemble the slide show. Then, the day before the big meeting, The Stresscalator swooped in and took over. *She started changing the slides, putting words and concepts together that didn't make sense,* Kelly recalled. *The team didn't want their names associated with it. She was going to crash and burn.*

After Kelly and her colleagues spent a brutal all-nighter fighting with their panicked boss and fixing the slides, Joan made a last-minute decision to scrap the visuals altogether. She presented with her exhausted team seething on the other side of the closed-door meeting. Kelly transferred out of the group the first chance she got. *It was never going to get any better.*

The funny thing about leadership is that it seems so much easier when you talk about it in a job interview, review it in a training class, or even when you read about it in a book. But Joan's constant crashing—and the subsequent burning of her team—is a fairly common occurrence among new leaders. The pressures of having to get the work out—on deadline and under budget—can quickly launch a new leader into panic mode. When faced with the first test of execution—you know, getting actual stuff done—you, too, will be tempted to become very task focused, tossing aside much of the training and good advice you received. But the first step to executing well—on behalf of yourself, your team, your manager and company—is to start thinking differently about how you define success.

Reflection Point

Are You a Stresscalator?

We work in an always-on, global world. It's easy to equate "frantic busy-ness" with working hard. But they're actually not the same. Think about what gets you the most stressed at work. How can you address it before it becomes a problem for others?

There's No "I" in "Results": Team Comes First

When you were responsible for only your own work, what you were doing flowed smoothly and was under control. You had your own deadlines to meet, your own agreements to make, and you sought feedback on yourself alone. When someone complimented your work, it was clearly a cause for celebration. Then you became a leader, and the rules changed. Now, you're responsible for seeing your company's needs through a new lens. You'll need to know how to get things done through a larger network—upper managers, your new peer group, and of course, your team. (Yes, you probably have to do some work yourself, as well.) In the most practical terms, you now need to understand what constitutes success for your team. Instead of focusing only on your achievements, now you'll celebrate your team members hitting their goals or when someone compliments them.

Instead of focusing only on your achievements, now you'll celebrate your team members hitting their goals or when someone compliments them.

There's no magic formula for how to be good at both, but there are actions you can take to dramatically increase your odds of success. In the earlier example, Kelly and her colleagues were able to deliver what Joan needed, but under unnecessarily stressful circumstances and without any confidence that their hard work actually mattered in the big picture. Joan had little ability to do her work in a way that made sense to everyone she worked with—especially to her team. It's something that a seasoned leader—one who understands the best way to keep an eye on *how* direct reports are doing their jobs—should know. This is the roll-up-your-sleeves part of being a leader. In business terms, this is called *execution*. But really, it's all about getting results.

The Essential Elements of Execution

In Chapter 4 we talked about your leadership brand and how the authentic conversations you have with people are key to a truly engaged team. The Key Principles and Interaction Guidelines we introduced in Chapters 6, 7, and 8 help you address the personal and practical needs of the people you work with. They are going to be an important part of mastering execution.

In this chapter, we're going further. This is bigger than one conversation at a time. There's a larger business ecosystem in play here, and you'll need to work across your network, interacting with your boss, peers, customers, vendors, and of course, your direct reports. All of these groups have their own needs and priorities that will play a role in how well you execute.

You'll need to create a working environment where focusing on and getting results becomes second nature to you and your team. This is known as an *execution culture*. To do that, you must learn to apply and live by the three essential elements of what we call *strategy execution* (Figure 9.1).

FIG **9.1** Three Essential Elements

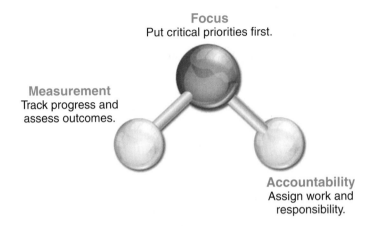

Focus
Put critical priorities first.

Measurement
Track progress and
assess outcomes.

Accountability
Assign work and
responsibility.

There's a reason that we call Focus, Measurement, and Accountability essential elements. Think back to your middle school science class. Essential elements are the building blocks for every living system. We all know the formula for water contains two elements, hydrogen and oxygen. Both must be present in the right amounts for water—H_2O—to exist. This is also true of strategy. If a single element is missing or insufficient, execution won't happen, and any strategy you thought you had will fail.

Notice we said "will" fail, not "could" fail.

Even if your team manages to achieve some goals, as in the Joan example, it won't be because of the strategy you put in place. Instead, it will be because individuals rose to the occasion in spite of all the barriers. Executing a strategy means that you can keep a close eye on the work your team is doing, but also repeat your successes.

So, let's start with figuring out where you are now. Complete the following self-assessment (Tool 9.1) to help you take an honest look at what you need to know about execution strategy.

How Well Do I Execute?

Read the set of statements for each essential element. For each statement, circle the number that best represents the frequency with which you currently take that action. Use the rating scale below. Answer frankly so you can target your strengths and areas for improvement. Add your ratings for each element, writing your total on the line provided.

Rating Scale:
1=Seldom or Never   2=Sometimes   3=Often   4=Always or Almost Always

FOCUS				
1. I invest my time and energy in the few most critical priorities that my team is responsible for achieving.	1	2	3	4
2. I inform my team members of our most critical priorities and how they support the organization's goals.	1	2	3	4
3. When distracted by urgent matters, I quickly refocus myself and my team on what's important.	1	2	3	4
4. I anticipate potential barriers and concerns.	1	2	3	4

TOTAL: _____

MEASUREMENT				
5. I measure the right things, so I know when my team has achieved our priorities.	1	2	3	4
6. I consistently use milestones to help my team determine what might need to be adjusted.	1	2	3	4
7. I establish deadlines and clear definitions of success for high-priority work.	1	2	3	4
8. I make our priorities and our progress toward them visible for my team members.	1	2	3	4

TOTAL: _____

Rating Scale:
1=Seldom or Never   2=Sometimes   3=Often   4=Always or Almost Always

ACCOUNTABILITY				
9. I make sure that each action needed to achieve our priorities is carried out by the appropriate team member.	1	2	3	4
10. I establish monitoring and follow-up procedures with the accountable team members.	1	2	3	4
11. I provide the coaching and feedback that team members need in order to achieve our priorities.	1	2	3	4
12. To each accountable team member, I communicate up front the consequences (both personal and higher level) of accomplishing his or her work successfully and unsuccessfully.	1	2	3	4

TOTAL: _____

Which element had the *highest* total?   _____

Which element had the *lowest* total?   _____

How did you do? Are you surprised by the results? If you're like most first-time leaders, you'll have scored lower than you hoped on all three elements. Or, if you're a bit more seasoned, you're saying, "Ah, I never knew how much attention I needed to give to measurement." This chapter is rich with content, tools, tips, and exercises that will help you develop the skills and tactics you'll need to execute a strategy consistently and with confidence. You'll find it helpful to use some of them, like the radar chart (Tool 9.4), throughout your career.

Put Critical Priorities First

Being a leader can get overwhelming (we should tell you something you don't already know, right?). The whole world is conspiring against your focus. Everyone needs your immediate attention: family, boss, your matrix boss, your peers, your team. And from the moment you wake up to the moment you log off for the day (which for some of us may be around midnight), you are barraged by requests from other people who hope that they can convince you to put their emergency before your own. Only one example: On average, just 10 percent of emails relate to the most critical things a leader must do.[1] Everyone who works in the modern world experiences this tyranny of the urgent. It's up to you to separate the urgent from what is truly important for you to do. Surprise: Now you need to do this for your team as well.

But here's the worst case scenario. Your boss hands you goals for the year. You agree that these are the priorities for you and your team. Then, fast-forward 12 months, and you're in your performance review. You have to sheepishly say, *Oh no, where did the time go? We just didn't get to that*. And now you feel like a giant "L" (for "Loser") is etched on your forehead.

The Three Possible Paths

So, what can you do? You have three choices:

1. Turn into a crazy zombie, staggering unproductively through your life while good ideas, meeting requests, and emails swell to epic proportions around you. This has the added benefit of scale: Your lunatic behavior spills over to others' work, passing along the zombie curse.

2. You actually take on more and more work yourself and plod forward alone, martyred and exhausted. This has a depressing effect over time, which adds dramatic flair.

3. Figure out what is important and *focus* your time on clear priorities.

In this section we're going to help you choose the right path. But first, stop and look at the adorable cat videos on YouTube!

(If you fell for that, please start this chapter over.)

Distractions

What causes people to lose focus at work? The leaders we've trained confirm what we've long known—it's the sheer volume of work to be done, limited resources, and an always-on world, where customers, vendors, partners, and colleagues can reach us at any time of the day. Things like these:

- Changes due to external requirements.
- Urgent issues that distract us from the priorities.
- Competing priorities—others want part of our resources.
- Customers who need quick responses regardless of our other work.
- Sheer volume of work to be done; limited resources.

So, to remedy the pull of these constant distractions, you need to create focus. Of course, this is easier said than done. When you and your team are focused, you consistently take actions and invest time and energy on what's most important to accomplishing your organization's goals, all while balancing your daily operational needs, customer demands, and financial requirements.

Focus means:

- Prioritizing a few important goals, communicating this concentration to the team, and reminding members of it periodically.
- Giving these goals more attention, review, and discussion because they're the most critical for your team's and the organization's success.

Here's an opportunity to identify the highest-priority work you are expected to deliver through your team this business cycle. We're looking for the big things—like reducing processing time for client orders or filling staffing needs more efficiently—that require your strategic focus. Then, use Tool 9.2 to identify your top three priorities. Why three? Execution experts suggest that you can't have more focus areas than three sides of a triangle. (It's a pretty cool metaphor—the triangle is the strongest shape for withstanding collapses due to fatigue or distortion.) Then, note how they align with the broader organization's business goals. If you don't know your organization, department, or business goals, a conversation with your manager can help you confirm or adjust.

Identifying Your Top Priorities

Instructions:

1. List your team's top three priorities on the left.

2. Then, link those priorities with the team's, department's, or organization's broader business goals by writing them in on the right.

3. Refer to the following two examples for guidance.

Important note: This is the most important exercise in this chapter. Don't skip it! This is your opportunity to document your team's top priorities, which is the critical first step in clarifying and driving focus.

My Team's Most Critical Priorities	Organization, Department, or Business Unit Goals
(Example) Integrate our technology databases (financial, client records, order-entry systems) across the enterprise.	Increase operational efficiencies in accounting systems.
(Example) Increase overall customer service rating at front desk to 95 percent Satisfied or Very Satisfied.	Improve customers' first impressions under the Customer-First service initiative.
1.	
2.	
3.	

Now, let's take a closer look at the role focus plays in the success of you and your team. For example, we always hear leaders say things like *I'm crazy busy.* But, being busy doesn't mean you're focused. In fact, crazy-busy types of activities can dilute your focus and distract you from your execution targets. In essence, these activities (planning, doing admin work, scheduling, and so on) help us manage our job and are significantly different than interacting with others to get things done. In fact, interacting is far more critical to successful leadership than managing and results in fewer damaging effects. A heavier focus on managing leads to less job satisfaction, higher turnover, and lower engagement among leaders. Figure 9.2 from the *Global Leadership Forecast* (2014) shows how the leaders surveyed balance their time. You can see that they currently spend twice as much time managing as they do interacting.

FIG 9.2 Interacting versus Managing

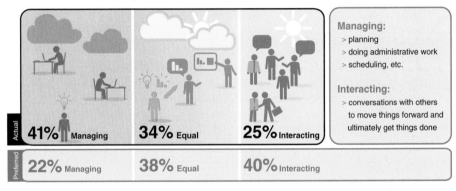

| Actual | 41% Managing | 34% Equal | 25% Interacting |
| Preferred | 22% Managing | 38% Equal | 40% Interacting |

Managing:
> planning
> doing administrative work
> scheduling, etc.

Interacting:
> conversations with others to move things forward and ultimately get things done

What does your balance look like? We all spend time in meetings and on emails; these tasks can be monumental time drains. Let's look beyond them and think about the type of work that they support. For example, you might spend 25 percent of your time in meetings, but if these meetings enable progress on the focus areas you listed earlier, this is a good thing. On the other hand, if you spend hours on emails that don't move your priorities forward, then that's a different matter . . . and something you'll need to address. Tool 9.3 will help you determine the activities that typically consume most of your time.

Where Does My Time Go?

1. On the following table check the activities (first column) on which you regularly spend at least 10 percent of your time in a typical week. If needed, add more relevant activities at the end of the list.
   Note: "Attending meetings" and "processing email" were intentionally left off this list. Account for your meeting and email times by considering what work they support.

2. For the items you checked, estimate the percentage of total time you spend (second column) during a typical week. Your percentages do not need to total 100 percent.

3. For each of your most time-consuming activities, mark the continuum (below each activity) to indicate the degree to which your work supports the priorities you noted earlier.

My Typical Week

Activity	% of Time

❏ Providing my expert opinion to others.
[_____]   _____
Not Priority   Priority

❏ Producing work product using my technical expertise.
[_____]   _____
Not Priority   Priority

❏ Working on a team as an individual contributor.
[_____]   _____
Not Priority   Priority

❏ Solving technical problems.
[_____]   _____
Not Priority   Priority

❏ Intervening to solve customer issues.
[_____]   _____
Not Priority   Priority

❏ Developing project plans.
[_____]   _____
Not Priority   Priority

❏ Tracking projects against schedules and deadlines.
[_____]   _____
Not Priority   Priority

Activity	% of Time

❑ Monitoring my team members' performance and providing timely feedback.

[_____]

Not Priority   Priority

_____

❑ Using appropriate quantitative measures (for example, to monitor production, quality, sales).

[_____]

Not Priority   Priority

_____

❑ Following up on delegated work.

[_____]

Not Priority   Priority

_____

❑ Intervening to resolve interpersonal conflicts.

[_____]

Not Priority   Priority

_____

❑ Communicating progress to my team and key stakeholders.

[_____]

Not Priority   Priority

_____

❑ Removing barriers to facilitate my team's progress.

[_____]

Not Priority   Priority

_____

❑ Keeping my team informed about organizational and departmental issues.

[_____]

Not Priority   Priority

_____

❑ Establishing decision-making and problem-solving processes.

[_____]

Not Priority   Priority

_____

❑ Managing a budget.

[_____]

Not Priority   Priority

_____

❑ Intervening to solve process issues.

[_____]

Not Priority   Priority

_____

❑ _____

[_____]

Not Priority   Priority

_____

❑ _____

[_____]

Not Priority   Priority

_____

What Did You Discover?

- What insights have you gained about how you regularly spend your time?

- How does that time allocation affect your ability to focus on your priorities?

- Did you check more items at the beginning of the list versus the end? You might have noticed that we listed the tasks in order from *individual contributions* to more *leader-like* activities. Spending much of your time toward the beginning of the list might be an indication as to where you are on your transition into leadership.

Join the conversation! Head to our microsite for our take on how to manage the energy magnets in your life that distract you at work.

Measurement

Here's a saying we live by at DDI: *You can't manage what you don't measure.* There's real wisdom here. Like a compass pointing you in the right direction, clear measures are indicators that show progress. They help you answer these two questions: *How will we know we are on track?* and *Have we been successful?* Sometimes the answers are not fun to hear. But measures allow

You can't manage what you don't measure.

you to see your team's goals more clearly and figure out how far in the weeds you may actually be before it's too late. You can't manage work after the fact—you need to measure it as it's happening. And, execution depends on knowing—not *guessing*—where you've been, where you are, and where you need to be.

But if you're like the majority of the leaders we work with, measurement is a gap in your quest to become an awesome executor of your team's strategies and goals. Areas like manufacturing and health care are highly regulated and measurement tools are easy to come by. But for many, many others, measurement can be a challenge. But because it's one of the three essential elements to your execution success, it's not a "should do" but a "must do."

Here's another saying to tuck away: *Not everything you can measure matters.* We live in a world fueled by new technologies that let you track all sorts of things. But measuring the right aspects of your organization enables you to track and improve the performance of its products, services, processes, and operations. This section will help you determine which measures you need to pay attention to and what to do with the data you collect.

Progress and Outcome Measures

To be successful, you and your team need to be able to establish measures in two distinct areas. These are called *progress* and *outcome* measures:

- **Progress measures predict future success.** They help you assess your ability to reach a goal or an objective.

- **Outcome measures are end results.** They describe what success will look like.

Progress measures (sometimes called *lead indicators*) operate like a real-time diagnosis. They give you the kind of feedback and information that can let you confirm you're on track, change course, or take preventive steps to avoid potential problems. Good examples are the marine radar that ships use to detect other vessels and obstacles, and a daily caloric intake count for someone trying to hit a specific goal with his weight. Lead indicators' power comes primarily from one thing: They tell you if you are on course.

An outcome measure (sometimes called a *lag indicator*) confirms your success (or not!) after something has happened—sometimes long after. Sometimes, if the results aren't what you hoped, this measure can help you separate what worked from what didn't, so you can work toward a different outcome next time. But it's all in the past—you can't do anything about it now. Most people are familiar with the concept of outcome measures. In fact, the final exams you took in secondary school are good examples. They measured whether (and how well) you absorbed the semester's material. A wonderfully morbid example is an autopsy—the ultimate outcome measure of how someone lived and died. But unless you work in a morgue, you probably use things like quarterly reports as lag measures in your work.

Part of your new job as a leader is to keep an eye on the progress and outcome measures that will help your team be successful. In some cases, it may be pretty clear what those are. In other cases, it might be necessary for you to determine some for yourself.

Safety First

Here's a good example: Troy is an engineer with a Canadian mining organization and leads the company's safety initiatives. He's a self-confessed numbers-and-measurement guy. (Our kind of guy.) Because he took his role so seriously, he developed a three-pronged approach to actively manage mine safety performance. Each prong had a name and a distinct set of progress indicators associated with it: Leadership and Training, Safety Management System, and an active Internal Responsibility System.

Troy knew that if his organization and all departments actively completed the activities under each indicator, they would be well on their way to achieving their safety goals.

Figure 9.3 shows the milestones and actions for the Safety Team in the form of a Safety Calendar. These were the items that were of the utmost importance to the company when it came to mine safety accidents: frequency rates, severity rates, and vehicle incident rates. They serve as Troy's progress measures.

FIG 9.3 Example Progress Measures

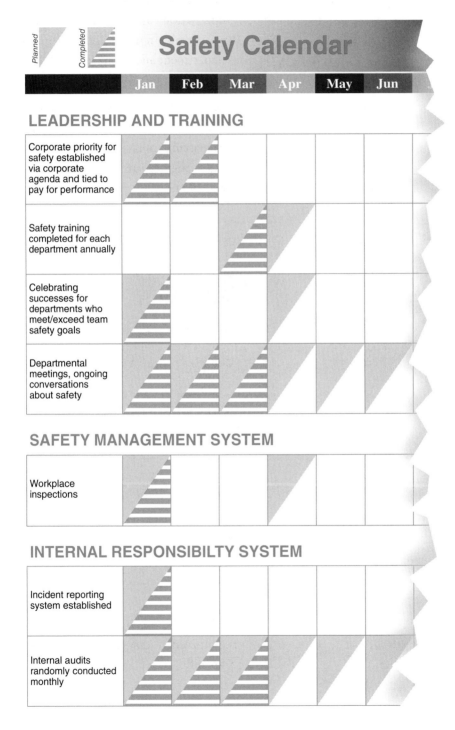

Safety Calendar

Planned / Completed

	Jan	Feb	Mar	Apr	May	Jun

LEADERSHIP AND TRAINING

Corporate priority for safety established via corporate agenda and tied to pay for performance	◨	◨				
Safety training completed for each department annually			◨			
Celebrating successes for departments who meet/exceed team safety goals	◨					
Departmental meetings, ongoing conversations about safety	◨	◨	◨		◨	

SAFETY MANAGEMENT SYSTEM

| Workplace inspections | ◨ | | | ◨ | | |

INTERNAL RESPONSIBILTY SYSTEM

| Incident reporting system established | ◨ | | | | | |
| Internal audits randomly conducted monthly | ◨ | ◨ | ◨ | ◨ | | |

The company already collected plenty of information about how safe they were acting as an organization, and this information could easily be tied to safety outcomes—things like lost time, worker's compensation (medical) claims, motor vehicle incidents, and property damage. But the problem was that this data was held by the Finance Team and the facilities department and wasn't being shared with key teams, like Troy's, that could take action on them.

But that didn't stop Troy. He then created two visuals that regularly rotated on a computer screen in the lunch rooms to help the company make improvements to sustain its focus on results. He found that the visual results—which he updated regularly—motivated the team. They served as a tangible reminder of where the team stood relative to their goals. See Figures 9.4 and 9.5.

FIG 9.4 Example Outcome Measures

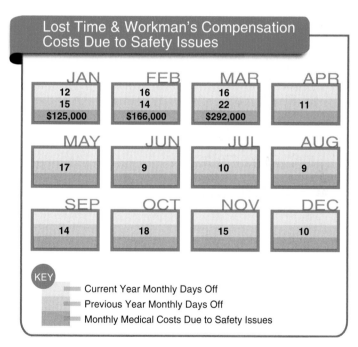

Troy told us that he never would have succeeded in this execution journey without setting key milestones to ensure that the outcome measures were achieved. His progression highlights were realistic, specific, observable, relevant, and, above all, measurable.

FIG 9.5 Another Example Outcome Measures

As a result, all safety outcomes over a five-year period showed substantial improvement. As Troy told us, *It was a lot of work, but it was the focus on the measures that helped us reach our goals and execute. Because of the team's measurement discipline, we could look at their execution road map and plan appropriately for contingencies. And, more importantly, our discipline on measurement helped me appropriately respond to requests from my boss. Oftentimes the big boss would go to a conference and hear a new idea. He'd come back and expect us to implement it ASAP. But, for the most part, these ideas would draw our attention and could pull us off track. I mean, I don't really like to say "no" because that's an ugly word to say to your boss. But, if I showed him our measures . . . instead of "no" I was saying, "if something needs to slip . . . what would it be?" or "We're 50 percent of the way there; if we pull resources it will involve risk that we'll slip on the progress we've already made." I had a lot more understanding given the data I had to back us up. Incidentally, my team won the president's award for our efforts in both saving lives and making our workplace (almost) injury free.*

We encourage you to draft measures for your team and confirm together. Don't worry, you don't need to be a measurement junkie to accomplish this. Just work through them together. The following sample metrics may help.

Sample Metrics

If you're having difficulty defining progress measures, you might first choose an outcome measure, and then think about what markers, milestones, or contributing factors would be needed to achieve it. Following are examples of related measures. (Although the table shows only one progress measure per outcome measure, additional progress measures might well be appropriate.)

Progress measures ....help you achieve........Outcome measures.
• Number of team handoff statistics ....New product cycle time
• Error rates...Quality scores
• Identification of variances.....................................Process improvements
• Employee development plans ....Retention of key personnel
• Coaching interventions ....Employee skill development
• Pilot projects...New products
• On-time delivery...Customer satisfaction

Measurement Prompts

The following prompts will help you craft relevant, quantifiable, and actionable measures for your team.

- How much/How many?
- By when?
- How much cheaper?
- How much better?
- How much faster?
- Related to what?
- Implemented how?
- To what standard?
- To what level of detail?

- With what impact?
- Using what units?
- From what baseline?
- With what form/method?
- With what data?
- What source of data?
- Tracked how?
- Tracked by whom?
- How often to update?

Accountability

Assigning Work and Reinforcing Responsibility

Leaders often struggle with setting expectations and holding people accountable for meeting them. As a new leader, you're responsible for holding people accountable in appropriate ways and ensuring that the right people do the right things at the right times.

Although some people think of accountability as negative, when it is applied well, people who want to get things done accept—and even welcome—it.

- Accountability reinforces the importance of responsibility and role clarity.

- Holding others accountable requires systems that support responsibility and ownership for results.

Reflection Point

Who is accountable for each important piece of work in a project? Even when your team works together on something, it's essential that each piece has one person who is on task and accountable for getting that work done on time and to clear quality standards.

Holding people accountable could always be difficult; today, it's even more so. Our modern approach to work can be much more complicated. For example, many matrix organizations have joint accountabilities, and confusion reigns in determining who is ultimately responsible for completing the work.

Here's a typical example. Let's say a large chemical company identifies product gross margin (roughly, the difference between the money coming in and the costs of doing business) as a joint responsibility of the marketing and sales departments. Focusing on money is an important job, right? But here's where it gets tricky: Marketing personnel set the prices, but salespeople change them when they need wiggle room to make a sale. While both departments are held accountable, neither has the authority to fully control the outcome—in this case, profit. Only clear-cut roles and accountabilities increase the probability of objectives being accomplished.

Best Practices for Ensuring Accountability

Even if there are conflicts like this baked into the organization you work for, there are some things you can do. Following are four best practices for holding people accountable.

1. **Hold *one* person accountable for each progress measure.** Avoid joint accountability; it leads to inaction or confusion. (However, in some cases it's appropriate for multiple team members to have an identical individual measure, such as a quota or rate.) If a task is complex (like a major product launch), you are wise to assign different accountabilities to each person (e.g., one person for marketing, one for pricing, the third for sales force training). Each element should have a single person for accountability, and progress should be measured separately.

2. **Communicate accountability, including consequences.** Discuss your expectations with each person, including the consequences (positive and negative) if the work exceeds or falls short of the measures you've outlined.

3. **Set monitoring and/or follow-up methods.** Discuss with each person the ways in which the work will be monitored. Confirm that you'll be following up regularly, and encourage people to speak up when obstacles arise.

4. **Offer feedback and coaching.** Indicate to each person that you will provide feedback and coaching to ensure that they are successful.

Don't worry, the Mastery section will guide you through accountability via the chapters on performance management, delegation, coaching, and feedback.

As a leader, you must demonstrate accountability yourself and expect it of your team members and others in your organization. This takes consistency and focus. In particular, you must be transparent in setting and tracking measures, and vocal about accomplishing priorities

Radar Chart

We'd like to introduce a tool that will help you with strategy execution. In fact, it puts all three elements of execution in one place—the priorities you need to *focus* on, the progress and outcome *measures* associated with these priorities, and *accountability* for accomplishing the work.

Your *Strategy Execution Tool* provides you with a comprehensive inventory of how you spend your time within a given time frame. It's a more advanced tool, so feel free to play with it a bit. But if you stick with it, the results you get will help you to see how your daily tasks relate to:

- Your organization's business priorities.

- Your role as leader.

- Your personal goals and motivations.

Consider sharing this tool with your manager when you meet to discuss your progress. It also will give real insight into how you spend your time. It's a good vehicle for discussing ways to make improvements, as well as identify trends, concerns, or any potential corrective actions, if necessary.

A sample of the Strategy Execution Tool is included next, and a copy of this highly useful resource can be found on the book's microsite. Next, we'll show you how to use the radar chart as an ongoing tool for managing your work. With your manager, you might agree on a schedule for repeating this analysis.

TOOL 9.4

Strategy Execution Tool (Sample)

Instructions:

1. In the space below, write in the priorities you identified in Tool 9.2.
2. Note one outcome measure under each priority.
3. List the progress measures for each outcome measure.
4. Check the appropriate circle between On Track and At Risk to show that measure's status.
5. Note who is accountable for each progress measure. If that person is external to your team, circle "Ex."

Priority 1: *Increase customer loyalty.*

Outcome Measure:	*Increase customer satisfaction by 5%.*	On Track	At Risk	
Progress Measures:	• *Process client transaction requests within 24 hours of receipt.*	○ ○ ☑ ○		Who: *John* Ex
	• *Maintain 97% or better individual transaction accuracy.*	○ ☑ ○ ○		Who: *John* Ex
	• *Follow up on customer complaints within 24 hours.*	☑ ○ ○ ○		Who: *Christy* Ex

Priority 2: *Increase number of new clients.*

Outcome Measure:	*Increase conversion of marketing leads to sales opportunities by 5%.*	On Track	At Risk	
Progress Measures:	• *Qualify a minimum of 30 leads each month.*	☑ ○ ○ ○		Who: *Rita* Ex
	• *Send new customer information packets within two business days of request.*	○ ○ ☑ ○		Who: *Anne* Ex
	• *Conduct two feedback surveys per month to identify opportunities for improvement.*	○ ○ ○ ☑		Who: *George* (Ex)

Priority 3: *Reduce overall business unit costs.*

Outcome Measure:	*Reduce supplier costs by 10%.*	On Track	At Risk	
Progress Measures:	• *Evaluate 15 new contracts per month.*	○ ☑ ○ ○		Who: *Sarah* Ex
	• *Reduce number of vendors by 25%.*	○ ☑ ○ ○		Who: *Charles* (Ex)
	• *Renegotiate 10 of the highest-volume contracts.*	☑ ○ ○ ○		Who: *Sarah* Ex

Ex = External to team

Transfer abbreviated priorities, measures, and names (with "Ex" if relevant) to the following chart to create a concise visual representation.

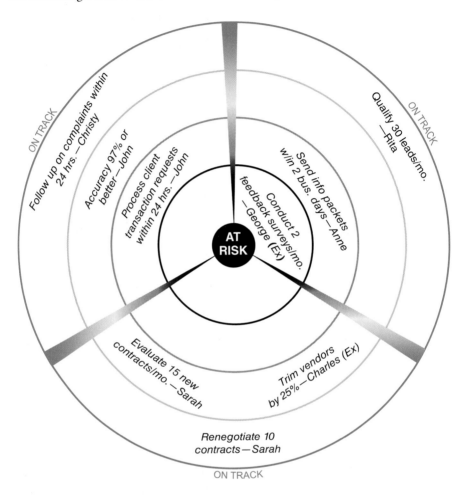

Excellent! You are now well on your way to Focus, Measurement, and Accountability. In other words, if you keep this up you'll be an Execution God/Goddess!

The next step is to keep your radar chart active; it will help you prioritize what's important versus what's not. You should even share this with your manager, who can be your biggest distractor of focus or your greatest ally. The radar chart can help you collaborate and prioritize with your manager. Here are some tips for meeting with your manager.

How to Use Your Radar Chart in a Meeting with Your Manager

1. Together, examine where you spend your time and determine if it's appropriate. *Tip:* Make sure you truly get down to the activity level.

2. Given your team and the organization's strategic priorities, determine whether you're spending the right amount of time on driving business priorities or are focusing on tasks that either are energy magnets or can be delegated. Discuss why you continue to hold on to this task and how you can let it go.

3. Determine whether the priorities need to change or if you need to adjust your focus on the activities within each wedge.

4. Discuss how your current radar chart aligns with each of the following:

   - How have you appropriately cascaded accountabilities to the team?

   - Is your radar chart leveraging your personal strengths?

   - Is your radar chart aligned with your personal development plan?

   - How does it reflect your personal motivations?

5. Periodically reflect on your radar chart and discuss challenges for eliminating existing gaps.

6. Repeat this process with your manager every three to six months.

Today's leaders are now called upon to lead increasingly geographically dispersed teams, operate within a matrix with blurred accountabilities and dotted-line reporting relationships, and take on a greater share of the work required to execute strategy and meet customer needs. That means that their organizations are counting on them as never before. But also, that the challenges of focus are amplified.

If you're in a matrix reporting to two managers, the radar chart can be your savior. In matrix-type structures, role clarity is often at the heart of focus problems. To address this issue, the radar chart and your discussions will ensure that everyone understands what's expected of them.

And that work gets done, and you don't pull out your hair.

Leveraging the Radar Chart with Your Team

The Strategic Execution Tool is also an excellent tool to share with your team. (We know of one manager who has taught her team members to use it themselves with great results. In update meetings they talk through progress and what's taking them off target.)

We suggest the following steps to leverage using radar charts with your team:

- Model using a radar chart by sharing one of your own with your team. This will provide members with instructional guidance as well as build trust within the team because you've allowed them to see your personal focus areas.

- Instruct each team member to complete his or her own radar chart. Then, with each person, follow the same development process you did with your manager (see earlier discussion).

- Create an opportunity for your team members to share their radar charts with one another in a team meeting. During this time, optimize the team's workload balance, leverage logical collaboration opportunities, eliminate unnecessary redundancies, and fill gaps in coverage. This can be especially important after adding a new team member or adjusting to the loss of one.

- Make a six-month target plan to review their strategy execution tool as a team.

The Calm in the Eye of Your Storm

Execution can be very different in a crisis. In fact, it's often effortless. A hospital administrator told us that hers was the only children's hospital open after a hurricane in Texas. As a team, the hospital went directly into crisis mode. You can picture it from all of those hospital-based TV shows. People shouting, gurneys flying, and patients waiting to be seen. In this crisis mode, communications were clear, everyone reported in on the hour, casuality charts were actively posted and used to monitor the flow of patient care, and most importantly, everyone knew exactly who was accountable for what. It's a type of flow that is rare in the day-to-day work world, but one worth aspiring to. Practice will get you there.

Part 2: Mastery and Leadership Skills

Early on, we made a statement that now bears repeating: Great leadership takes place every day, in the smallest of ways. Pieced together, these moments might not seem notable. But put them together, and over time they will make for a successful career and a happy life. By taking your leadership journey seriously, you will grow not only your own capabilities, but also those of the people around you. This is where the real work—and the satisfaction—will happen for you.

But it will take practice.

Think of this Mastery section as a practical guide to the situations you'll face every day. As you lead meetings, when a nervous colleague knocks on your door, or as you wonder whether to click "Send" and launch that hasty email, you'll find yourself making (or not!) a series of decisions about how to best meet your goals and keep your team feeling confident and engaged.

The next chapters are all about your behavior—what you'll need to do, when, and why, to be a successful leader. You're on a journey to become the best leader you can be and fulfill your leadership legacy. But, there is no magic button that will instantly transform you into a perfect leader. You'll encounter unexpected diversions, tough challenges, and brand-new experiences.

In the following Mastery and Leadership Skills chapters, you'll learn how to handle an array of typical leadership tasks such as coaching for success, influencing others, selecting new employees, and giving feedback. There are 12 Mastery chapters, each full of practical tips to help you bridge what you learn from these pages to immediate application to your job. Additionally, we've created even more resources for you online. Part 3, available on the microsite, includes bonus chapters and tools, along with a checklist that can serve as a "travel map" for your first six months as a leader.

This Mastery section is also chock-full of tools that can be used repeatedly to plan the challenging conversations you'll need to have. We've also included tips for using technology to help you become a more effective leader. Technology is not just about doing more work in a fast-moving world. It's about keeping your leadership voice alive for your team, colleagues, customers, and the people you care about—even when you're not in the room.

There are thousands of books on leadership—twice as many as cookbooks! Many are very good, but most sit on the shelf. Very little is actually applied. We're counting on you to change that. If there are four or five things you can apply right away, we'll have accomplished our goal. If you do so, you'll be well on your way to becoming a leadership master!

Mastery and Leadership Skills
10 HIRING AND SELECTING THE BEST
Behavior Predicts Behavior

Pre:Think
Remember back to when you were hired for a job or picked for a team, committee, or board. What was the process like? Were you a good fit every time? What was missing? What clicked?

Surround Yourself with the Best

The late management guru Peter Drucker said, *Of all the decisions a leader makes, none are as important as the decision about people.*[1] He wasn't wrong. When the right people are in the right jobs, performance soars. The conversations you have with your team become rich and meaningful, and your company—and everyone who works there—benefits. As one leader put it, *The key to my success is hiring people far better than I am.* The intent is spot on. But the truth is, most people don't know how to identify and hire the better people they need.

There are lots of reasons why this matters. Conservatively, a wrong hiring decision can cost a company three times the person's salary. Other sources have calculated the cost of a bad hire at 24 times the position's base salary.[2]

But for you, a new leader, a hiring mistake can be immediately expensive, and not just monetarily:

- Your credibility and judgment may be called into question by your team, peers, managers, partners, and customers.

- The new hire is likely to be unproductive, inefficient, and unengaged. If the person does show up for work, he may be unable to meet his goals. This is a leadership emergency.

- You'll burn time, energy, and money involved in hiring and on-boarding a replacement.

- And if you can't find a replacement, leaving a position vacant for months can be a nightmare to manage. Who will do the person's work?

- You face potential damage to customer relationships and brand image, especially if your bad hire worked directly with clients.

- Your team struggles to fill the gaps left by the poor performer and do damage control with internal and external customers.

- Firing someone is always a legal issue. Labor laws are complex around the world. You'll need to spend a lot of time understanding how the laws in your land come into play every step of the way.

It doesn't have to be that way. You're in a unique position to influence smart selection decisions. This chapter contains some of the challenges and best practices to help you identify the talent you need to meet your company's business goals.

Selection Traps

Over the last four decades, we've trained thousands of managers to make better hiring decisions. As we worked with our clients, we began to document some of their most common mistakes. Some of the major ones are listed here.

1. **Failing to seek complete and consistent information from applicants on the specific competencies needed for success in the job.**

In fact, if you were to ask a group of managers hiring for the same position to identify the key requirements for success, they're often likely to come up with different lists.

2. **Misinterpreting applicant information.**

Some managers play amateur psychiatrist. Trying to determine an applicant's underlying personality trait or innate talents is likely to lead a hiring manager astray. So too is asking applicants to describe themselves in a sentence, or to name three strengths or weaknesses. And asking a theoretical question (e.g., "What would you do . . . ?") in a certain situation, rather than what she actually did, can easily mislead a hiring manager. Explaining how she might handle a situation is far different than having done it.

3. Disregarding job motivation.

Many hiring leaders tend to focus only on an applicant's skills, asking whether that person can do the job. It's just as important to find out if the candidate is motivated to do the job.

4. Allowing biases and stereotypes to affect judgment.

The hiring manager's biases can reflect negatively or positively on decisions for reasons that have no relationship to the job responsibilities. For example, a manager might be biased against an applicant who has an unusual hairstyle, has belonged to certain college groups, or shares common interests with the manager.

5. Making wrong decisions based on first impressions.

Reaching quick decisions based on information in the person's application or resume, attire, or even a handshake is the wrong way to go. Accuracy is diminished because objectivity is lost. When interviewing, first impressions definitely should not become lasting impressions.

6. Allowing pressure to fill the position to affect judgment.

The pressure to fill an open position can come from a variety of sources: How long the position has been open, the degree to which business or resources are affected by it, or the level of attention paid to the vacancy by senior management. Within reason, a selection decision is not one to make without gathering all the right information.

7. Failing to sell applicants on the advantages of the job, organization, or job location.

Remember, top candidates are likely in high demand. A key part of any hiring process is conveying a positive impression of you and your organization. A story from an IT candidate: He was in demand and had three offers. He decided not to accept one from his top choice, based on the callous way he was treated during the interview process.

The Interview: Making the Grade

The interview remains the key decision-making tool for virtually every job in the world—including the ones you'll be hiring for. The interview is so common, so expected, that many leaders take it for granted. They consider themselves to be good judges of character and believe they don't need formal training. The stark reality? Nothing could be further from the truth. In a study of hundreds of hiring managers, we found that almost half of managers spend less than 30 minutes deliberating each hiring decision—less time than it takes to deliver a pizza or watch a favorite television show. Amazingly, 44 percent rely on gut instinct to make a decision. This sense of overconfidence leads to boast such as these: *Ten minutes is all I need with a candidate, then I know*, or *I can pursue good interview questions on the fly*. Finally, over 50 percent have never had any formal interview training. That's too bad. Those leaders who receive formal training are far more likely to have confidence in making the right choices.[3]

Interviewing is a skill. Building a skill takes training and practice. You can't build these skills by reading a book—no one can. We advise you to seek out formal interviewing training through your HR department, or from online, publically available options. Following are some quick tips for making your interview and ultimate hiring decision more effective.

TIP 1: Keep your focus on job-related competencies, knowledge, and experience.

Simple, right? Sadly, not. Many hiring managers and their HR teams fail to identify what's required for successful performance in a given job. To make matters worse, the requirements exist, but aren't used as the foundation of the interview process.

Like any decision you have made, know what you're looking for, make sure it's job relevant, and interview around those requirements. A funny story: One of Rich's associates drew up a list of criteria for a potential spouse and used them in making her final decision. They've been happily married for over a decade! In Chapter 2 we provided a success profile that will help you frame questions for your prospective new hire, spouse, or any other role you're selecting for.

TIP 2: **Use behavior to predict behavior.**

The best predictor of behavior is behavior. The more evidence you can gather about a person's behaviors (and experiences), the more likely you will make an effective hiring decision. In an interview, most of your evidence will come from a candidate's past behavior. However, HR often will supplement the hiring processes with simulations and tests to augment interview data. As we mentioned earlier, leaders often ask theoretical questions, thinking they are testing an applicant's intelligence. Unfortunately, these types of questions are poor predictors of performance. For example, asking a candidate to define good teamwork is a far cry from hearing about his or her actual experience as a team player. Research has proven that behavior-based interviewing is 16 times more valid than loosely structured, "What would you do if?" types of questions.[4] Keeping your questions focused on behavior related to the open job avoids another problem: Both theoretical questions and those unrelated to a specific job often violate multiple employment laws.

Following is a list of some potentially legally dangerous and just plain stupid questions candidates told us they were asked during an interview:

- What would you do if I gave you an elephant?
- Is that your natural hair color?
- Would you be available at times to watch my children?
- Are you single? Why not?

Tool 10.1 provides a better feel of what we mean by behavioral questions.

TOOL 10.1

Asking Behavioral Questions

It's important to ask only questions that prompt a rich answer on what a candidate has done in the past. Following are some sample questions to do that for three key areas: customer focus, building partnerships, and driving for results.

Customer Focus

1. Tell me about a time when you had to gather information to better understand a customer's needs/concerns? Did the information make a difference?

2. Describe a time when you may have overpromised something to a client? What happened?

Building Partnerships

1. Tell me about a time when you participated with someone outside of your own team that turned out to benefit you and the other person? What were the details?

2. Think of someone from your department with whom you've worked who would say you're a good partner. What did that person say?

Driving for Results

1. Achieving required work goals is not always easy. Describe a difficult goal that you were able to achieve. Why was it difficult?

2. Tell me about a time when you were very satisfied with your team's or business unit's level of performance. How were the results achieved?

TIP 3: Search for the STARs.

The best way to keep your interview focused on behavioral information is to use a simple concept we call STAR.

"ST" stands for the *situation or task* the candidate faced. The "A" stands for the *action* the candidate took. The "R" references the *results* of the action. Let's take a closer look at a STAR question an interviewer might ask to uncover a candidate's behavior for teamwork.

Interviewer Question:

Describe a time when you needed to work closely with others to complete a project. How did you go about including them? What was the outcome?

Candidate Answer:

I was working on a new product launch that involved a team of people from R&D and sales [S/T]. To meet our timelines, I put together an informal team with a representative from sales and product development. We met once every two weeks to plan actions and deal with issues [A]. It really was a team effort. We launched on time and ended with some very creative ideas, thanks to everyone's participation [R].

Don't expect a candidate to give you complete STARs every time. And you don't want to ask questions in the same format every time! This will require you to probe further, asking for more information about the situation/task the person faced, actions she took, or results she achieved.

Tool 10.2 presents a few examples of complete or incomplete STARs. As you go through the exercise, identify which STAR component(s) is missing.

Seeking STARs

Instructions: Identify the missing **STAR** component in the candidate responses below. Use the Answer Key below to check your responses.

S/T = Situation/Task   **A** = Action Taken   **R** = Result

Leader Question 1: *Tell me about a time when you worked on a project with a tight deadline. How did you go about meeting the due dates?* (Hiring manager is seeking a STAR for Planning/Organizing.)

Candidate Response: *I was working with an IT team to install new customer analyses software. My boss was under a lot of pressure to meet a late August date, leaving us 30 days. We actually finished the project three days early.*

What **STAR** component is missing?

Leader Question 2: *Can you tell me about one of the toughest decisions you had to make within the past two years? What did you do to feel comfortable with your decision?* (Hiring manager is seeking a STAR for Decision Making.)

Candidate Response: *I was asked to recommend a marketing theme for a new product we were about to launch. I took a close look at the competition and personally spoke to a group of clients. In addition, I did some online research on market trends. I came up with two possible themes and then did a pro/con analysis of each.*

What **STAR** component is missing?

Leader Question 3: *Occasionally, we all need to work with people who seem to have their own agenda, making it difficult to accomplish our goals. Can you give me an example of working with someone you really didn't get along with, but whose help and support you needed? How did you handle it?* (Leader is seeking a STAR for Influencing.)

Candidate Response: *I took Mary to lunch to discuss the project and how we could best work together. I listened carefully to her side of the story. She ended up being a big supporter.*

What **STAR** component is missing?

Answer Key: **Q1.** The missing component is the action. There's no mention of what the candidate actually did to meet the deadline. **Q2.** We know what the applicant faced and what she did to make a decision. What's missing is the outcome, or result of her decision. **Q3.** In this response, we have both an action and a result. What's missing is any background information on the situation/task.

TIP 4: Interview for "will do" as well as "can do."

Yes, a candidate's skills and past behaviors are powerful predictors of performance. Ultimate job satisfaction, retention, and performance also can depend on a host of motivational issues, which, by the way, includes the person's relationship with you! Let's take an example: Suppose you're hiring an associate to help manage a complex and high-visibility project. The candidate might have excellent planning skills, yet dislike any sort of collaboration or management control. As a highly independent individual, this candidate might not be the best match to the job.

Examples of motivational facets include external customer focus, job complexity, detail orientation, need for rapid promotion, and so on. As part of your selection process, it's your responsibility to evaluate job motivation. This means identifying facets inherent in the job and matching them to an applicant's motivations. Now, you don't do this by asking, *Do you like a diverse work environment or a job that requires attention to details?* Nine times out of 10, the person knows why you're asking this question and will answer yes. You want to use the same behavioral questions we described above. For example, *Tell me about an assignment that required high attention to detail. What was it you were working on? What sort of results did you achieve? How satisfied or dissatisfied were you with the assignment?*

Tool 10.3 helps you identify some key motivational facets, which you can then use as a basis for determining the questions you will want to ask.

Motivation Matters

DDI's research has identified 30 common sources of employee satisfaction or dissatisfaction. We call these motivational facets. In the following exercise, use the scale to determine which might be most prevalent for the job you are hiring. Some facets are likely to be prevalent for a single role, while others may cross multiple roles. Your job is to then be sure you gather interview or background data from candidates to determine the fit between a candidate's motivations, and those offered in the position you are hiring for.

Scale:
- **LO** Few opportunities available in job/organization.
- **SO** Some opportunities available in job/organization.
- **MO** Multiple opportunities available in job/organization.

Rating	Motivational Facets
	Achievement—meeting increasing work challenges.
	Compensation—receiving a high salary or generous monetary compensation for work.
	Complexity—performing complex tasks or working on complex projects.
	Continuous Learning—increasing knowledge and skill when circumstances call for additional learning.
	Detail Orientation—working on tasks requiring great attention to detail.
	Formal Recognition—receiving formal recognition (inside and outside the organization) for accomplishments.
	Bias for Action—orientation toward aggressive, proactive responses to problems and opportunities.
	Challenging the Status Quo—emphasis on asking questions and challenging the norms and standard procedures to achieve breakthrough advances.
	Social Responsibility—support of and involvement in community activities.
	Continuous Improvement—emphasis on constantly improving processes, products, and services and exploring innovative ways to do the job.
	Customer Focus—emphasis on understanding, meeting, and exceeding customer needs and maximizing customer satisfaction.
	Interdepartmental Cooperation—cultivation of an atmosphere of interdependence, collaboration, and reciprocal communication among divisions within the company.

TIP 5: Don't go it alone.

At the end of the day, it's your decision whom to bring on board. However, like any key decision, the quality improves when others are involved. While HR might be screening candidates, it's common to find selection decisions are made on the basis of one interview—yours. We recommend involving one or two additional associates in the interview process. The person you choose may be a peer leader, your boss, a partner from HR, or even a team member. We also recommend dividing up the areas you cover and the questions you ask. We've heard too many bewildered candidates ask, *Why did three people ask exactly the same question?* The goal is to get multiple inputs on a candidate's abilities and then share the STARs that were gathered in a systematic fashion to gain consensus on the applicant's abilities.

TIP 6: Check references.

Before making any hiring decisions, it's highly worthwhile to check several references. Sources for references can be provided by people who have worked with the applicant—former bosses, team members, clients, college professors, vendors, and so on. Candidates are usually asked to provide references. Review the candidate's resume for possible reference sources. We recall a situation where an applicant worked at a company for two years, but listed no references there. We were able follow up with the applicant's previous supervisor and got an earful—none of it very good!

There are two general categories of information you can gather from references. The first is to verify facts that candidates have provided. Examples include dates of actual employment, salary, job history, educational level, and types of job experiences. While not typical, some applicants do bend the truth—or flat-out lie. We've seen some high-profile examples. Kenneth Conchar resigned from Veritas Software after it was found that he never got the Stanford MBA he claimed. Yahoo!'s past CEO, Scott Thompson, listed a computer science degree he never earned. If your HR people get involved in the hiring process, they're often responsible for verification reference checks.

The second type of reference check, which should be conducted by you, is to probe further for behavioral information. For example, if after several interviews you remain concerned about a candidate's ability to handle difficult customer interactions, you can ask a reference for additional STAR examples that might alleviate or confirm your concern.

TIP 7: Sell the job and your company.

It doesn't matter whether you're in an abundant or tight labor market—the candidate you really want to hire will be in top demand. How you treat this person before, during, and after the interview will likely impact his final decision. Unfortunately, many candidates give low marks to their experience with company selection processes. In one study, 42 percent felt the interviewer did not show interest in their career goals; that number was the same for conveying excitement about the job. And candidates felt that only about one in three interviewers came across as professional![5]

How can you make sure the candidates you interview walk away with a favorable impression of you and your company?

- Use the tips provided throughout this chapter.

- Take time to ask questions about their career goals and what is motivating them to work for your company. Allow them time to ask questions as well.

- Be prepared to sell the benefits of the job and your company. Let your actions show that you want the candidate.

- Pay attention to details, such as being on time, greeting the candidate, and promptly following up. All of these will make a difference.

- Keep the following simple rule in mind. The candidate you really want likely will get several offers. And even those you don't want might very well become future customers—treat them all that way!

TIP 8: Keep it legal.

Multiple companies find themselves in legal hot water because of the way a hiring manager handled the selection process. There are laws and guidelines that should be followed by both you and your organization. Almost all have to do with discrimination, and they differ from country to country. Some good news: You don't need to be a lawyer to avoid many common discriminatory practices. Many of the tips in this chapter not only will help you make the right decision, but also will help you make the more fair decision. Some considerations:

- Keep your questions related to job competencies/requirements.

- Follow our suggestions for gathering STARs.

- Handle all applicants in a consistent fashion. The steps and processes used for selecting candidates within a particular job category should be the same for all candidates.

- Avoid your own tendency toward stereotyping and bias.

- Seek professional training and advice from your HR team.

Mastery and Leadership Skills
11 WHAT YOUR BOSS REALLY WANTS FROM YOU
Become an Adviser

Pre:Think

Take a moment to think about all the bosses you've ever worked for. Or, if you're still pretty new to work, any "boss" type characters you've seen in movies, in books, or on television. What made them bad? Good? What made them tick?

At a recent conference attended by more than 5,000 people, we had participants stop by our booth to post some attributes of what they thought constituted a good boss and a bad boss. You'll find some of those posts on the next page. And, they confirm our earlier discussion of a catalyst leader (see Chapter 2). Based on their responses, we created a scale for you to assess your own boss. If you circle a 1, 2, or 3, he's bad news; an 8, 9, or 10, and consider yourself fortunate.

Bad Boss   Good Boss

1   2   3   4   5   6   7   8   9   10

Attributes of a Good Boss	Attributes of a Bad Boss
• Makes a difference in business and people's lives.	• Is inconsistent.
• Empowers others.	• Focuses on tasks, not on people.
• Develops people.	• Is a poor listener.
• Provides coaching.	• Micromanages.
• Holds self and others accountable.	• Withholds information.
• Gives constructive feedback.	• Gives vague, nonconstructive, or no feedback.
• Creates more leaders.	• Doesn't develop people.
• Is a good and compassionate listener.	• Ignores performance issues.
	• Is not team oriented.
• Builds trust.	
• Is a good role model.	

You, of course, are either now a boss or about to become one. The very fact that you're reading this book means that you aspire to be a good one. Yes, there are terrible bosses and excellent ones. But, if you are like most people, you likely placed your leader somewhere in the middle.

Key Relationship

Make no mistake: Your relationship with your boss is paramount—it can make or break your career. If you're on your boss's bad side, don't count on pay increases, promotions, or other perks—perhaps, regardless of how well you are performing. Our research shows that those working for poor leaders are less likely to be productive and engaged in their work.[1] But, the state of your relationship goes far beyond career success. Gallup has shown a direct relationship between good leadership and employee well-being. According to their researchers, "when leaders opt to ignore employee well-being, they erode the confidence of those that follow them and limit their organizations' ability to grow."[2] Not to mention a study from Sweden that showed a positive relationship between poor leadership and the risk of serious heart disease.[3] Let's face it—working for a bad boss will follow you home!

Here are some tips for making your relationship with your boss a better one.

Select Your Boss

Peggy was thinking about leaving her job for a team leader position in another department with a hefty salary increase. The job promised new challenges, an opportunity to learn, and most of all, the chance to lead. After two months of deliberation, she withdrew her application. The reason? It had nothing to do with the job; it had everything to do with the (poor) reputation of her boss-to-be. The point of this short story is pretty straightforward: If you have significant concerns about who you're going to work for, think twice. By the way, the reverse is also true. A boss with a good reputation should enter into your equation for accepting a new role.

Cut Your Boss a Break

You don't deserve to be belittled, bullied, or mistreated—period. That said, your boss is a human being, too. We've heard employees hold their bosses in contempt for the smallest offenses because they expect absolute perfection. Take Arun. He told us that one day everything seemed to be going wrong. During his last meeting of the day, he lost his temper. *I didn't yell, I just got angry,* he said later. Arun's anger surge had a definite effect on his team members; they seemed to avoid him for weeks. You'll make mistakes as a new leader, and so will your boss. You might want to provide feedback, but a few missteps might not justify putting your boss in the dog house forever. And, on the other side of the equation, it doesn't hurt to maintain or enhance your boss's self-esteem by paying a sincere compliment every now and then!

Get to Know Your Boss

If you have a good boss, she is doing her best to learn what makes you tick. It helps her to help you perform, continue to grow, and increase your level of engagement. The reverse is also true. Steve Arneson, author of a great book—*What Your Boss Really Wants From You: 15 Insights to Improve Your Relationship*—calls it studying your boss. He feels that if employees want better relationships with their bosses, they need to better understand where they are coming from.[4] And, if the following list of questions looks familiar, you're right; this is a parallel exercise to "What Do I Need to Know?" in Chapter 3 to help you get to know your team. Arneson suggests a number of questions, the answers to which will enable you to learn more about your boss:

- When and how is he most approachable?
- What is her preferred management style?
- What behaviors does he tend to reward?

- What is she most worried about?
- What is his primary motivation?

Just look at the advantage knowing your boss brings you. Christina avoided her boss first thing in the morning. She knew he needed time to get his day in order. She also soon understood his hands-off management style. She never bogged him down with the details. And Ricardo, a supervisor in an automobile production facility, knew his manager was asked to take charge of a plant-wide lean initiative. Ricardo, who respected his boss, knew the project was critical and went out of his way to help him succeed.

Getting Off—and Staying—on the Right Foot

No matter how you dice it, you and your boss will have a two-way relationship— a good one, bad one, or one in between. And, like any relationship, a good one not only takes an investment of time and effort, but it's also one that you own! All relationships begin with a strong start. On the microsite you'll find a checklist for your first six months as a leader, with a set of actions you should specifically engage in with your boss. Following are a few questions you should consider before your first one-on-one meetings.

- What are the expectations/goals for your relationship?
- What are the potential barriers in working together, and how will you resolve them?
- What sort of support will you require from one another?
- In what ways, and how often, do you want to communicate/keep each other informed?
- How will you informally assess how the relationship is going?
  (Note: We don't mean an appraisal of your work, but rather a meaningful discussion on how things are going between the two of you.)

And, while it's important to ask these questions in the very beginning of your relationship, come back to them every so often.

Watch Surprises

While some bosses are micromanagers and want to know every little detail of whatever you're doing, most merely want to know what's going on. It's not an unreasonable request. Steve told us about an incident that temporarily derailed his relationship with his boss, Janice, who was working on a complex project involving several teams. During a project coordination meeting with senior management, Janice learned that the project would miss its deadline by three months because of some technical difficulties within Steve's team. *She was pretty upset*, Steve told us, *I should have let her know in advance.*

Ask for Help in Solving the Problem

Remember this Key Principle from Chapter 6? We hope you'll be using it with your team. You want team members to come up with their own ideas as they tackle problems and opportunities. A good boss rarely should be telling you *how* to solve a problem. On the other hand, she often may have suggestions on how you can tackle a new challenge or implement a new idea based on her experience. It makes sense to seek out your boss's support. And, there's an added benefit: Nothing makes a leader feel better than being asked for help! The key point here is to view your boss as a valuable resource, as someone who can help you get your job done.

Become an Adviser, Not a Whiner

Our boss, who happens to be a good one, recently kicked off one of our more challenging business planning meetings. He had, as always, an interesting, but relatively common-sense, piece of advice: *I like to surround myself with positive people. I'd rather spend my time with people who have ideas and advice to tackle our challenges than to whine about them.* Your boss's respect for you increases exponentially when you help solve problems, not cause them. Don't mistake this for buttering up your boss (or other phrases we choose not to use). It's about becoming a respected adviser. How will you know if you're doing this well? Easy—your boss will begin to seek out your thoughts and advice.

Take a Step Back

One hectic work pace means you're likely to focus on tasks—getting things done. And that undoubtedly will filter up in the types of discussions you'll have with your boss in performance appraisals, project updates, coaching, and planning. This means it's important every now and then to take a short breather to work on your relationship with your boss (and others). Your own reflections and conversations occasionally need to focus on the quality of your relationship—not the quality of your work. There's likely no other simple factor that will make the difference between hating every morning and enjoying your job as a leader.

Mastery and Leadership Skills
12 ENGAGEMENT AND RETENTION
Creating the Environment to Energize
People

Pre:Think
Think about a time when you considered leaving your job. What was missing
for you? Did you think things would be different? Did you have needs that
weren't being addressed? Think back to the moment when you just knew:
This isn't working for me. I have to find something else.

Perhaps you've heard senior leaders use the term *engagement* or *employee engagement*
as a way to describe how people are feeling about their jobs.

The quest for engaged employees is a mantra at many organizations these days,
possibly yours. It evokes questions such as these: *Are people showing up energized and
ready to work? Feeling hopeful about the future? Bringing their best effort to the table?* And
there's another term permeating today's organizations: *Retention*. Are employees
happy enough to stick around? Or are you always looking for new people?

Employee engagement and retention are more than just buzzwords—they're
real vehicles for measuring the health and potential of any company.
There are hundreds of studies showing that groups with highly engaged teams
are more profitable, more productive (based on their stated business goals),
have more satisfied customers, and suffer fewer accidents.[1] And as you learned
in Chapter 10 ("Hiring and Selecting the Best"), losing, replacing, and then
training new employees costs businesses and the global economy billions of
dollars every year. But the cost to the economy is not the hot issue here.

No organization can afford a culture where unhappiness thrives. Nor, as a new leader, can you.

Engage Early and Often

Let's talk about engagement first. It's tempting to think that as a first-time leader you don't have much power to keep other employees from jumping ship for other jobs or companies. And to a certain extent, that's true. Some overarching features that attract talent—like the company mission and strategy, benefits, and other perks—are out of your hands. But our research has found that the most influential factor in a person's decision to bring her total effort or energy to her job is her immediate leader—you.[2] When people show up for work feeling strong and full of enthusiasm, they develop a loyalty that makes them want to push through obstacles, bring new ideas to the table, and do their part to help the company meet its goals. And they stick around. Does this feel like a lot of pressure on you? It shouldn't. This puts you in the driver's seat in a very meaningful way. By authentically speaking to the hearts and minds of your team and colleagues, you're more likely to drive higher levels of commitment, energy, and loyalty in the people around you.

Few people leave a **job**; they leave a **leader**.

> It wasn't until my third week on the job that I realized that my manager didn't remember my name. Worse, he thought I was someone else. Sure, we were both women and had blonde hair, but that was where the similarity ended. By the end of the second month—and eight excruciating staff meetings later—it was clear that he didn't really know who any of us really were or what we were doing. And he didn't care beyond the reports we filed. I was gone before the ninth staff meeting.
>
> —Tara, former data analyst

Some of what you'll learn in this chapter will build on the important foundational work from Chapters 6 and 7. You'll see how applying the Key Principles to everyday interactions with your team will help them feel engaged and want to stick around.

Engaged employees find meaning in their work and know that they are growing and developing. Your job is to *create the best environment* for that to happen. You'll need all the skills you've developed to make sure you're continually identifying how to keep your people engaged before they lose their drive. You've heard us say in many different ways that leadership is getting work done through others. Engagement is the way you'll do that.

Here are three examples of how leadership and engagement are intertwined:

- When you delegate tasks with an eye to helping people develop, your people have a real chance to gain experience and grow their skills.

- Focus on the *why* whenever you can. When you share the connection between the tasks people do and the company's goals, they see where they fit into the big picture. Explaining the reasons behind something employees consider routine—such as a monthly report—helps people understand why their role is valuable to the greater whole.

  The single highest driver of employee engagement is whether or not workers feel their managers are genuinely interested in their well-being. Only about 40 percent of workers actually believe that to be true.[3]

- When you get good at coaching people along the way—*before* there's a problem—they feel valued, protected, and ready to take on the next challenge.

Engagement Is Energy

The **ENGAGED Employee** is positively charged, passionate, optimistic, and brimming with ideas.

The **STUCK Employee** operates in neutral, is checked out, has low energy, and does the bare minimum, but isn't leaving. She slows everyone else down.

The **DISENGAGED Employee** is negatively charged, complains, spreads discontent, and causes conflict. He typically leaves, often with a bang.

Driving Engagement

When people are empowered and passionate about their work, their productivity, morale, and, ultimately, business performance increase significantly. As a leader, you can increase employee engagement by addressing three factors that get to the heart of what really matters to people and their job satisfaction. And they're universal; we've found these categories to be largely true for most humans, regardless of generation, gender, job type, race, nationality or geography. We call them *engagement and retention drivers*, and they are fairly straightforward. They are:

- **Individual Value**—*I'm appreciated and encouraged to grow.*

- **Meaningful Work**—*What I do matters.*

- **Positive Environment**—*This is a great place to work.*

Part of your new role as leader is to help your people identify their source of job and career satisfaction. Through an ongoing series of engagement conversations, you can help your people make the connection between what fulfills them and the work they do. Then, it's up to you to create an environment where they can thrive and grow by overcoming any obstacles that they might be experiencing. Each person on your team might need something different from you in order to be successful. Understanding these engagement drivers will help you do that.

Figure 12.1 lists the drivers, work values they represent, and a list of questions you might ask your team members during individual engagement conversations.

Reflection Point

Do you regularly meet with your team members to ask about their level of engagement? If so, do you cover all three engagement and retention drivers? If not, how would they react to the questions posed in Figure 12.1?

FIG 12.1 Practice an Engagement Conversation

Meaningful Work	Positive Environment	Individual Value
Purpose, Information, Empowerment	Respect, Collaboration, Trust	Development, Recognition
❏ *What would make you extremely satisfied with your job?*	❏ *How do you work best?*	❏ *What skill, areas of expertise, or interests do you have that we are currently overlooking?*
❏ *Are you aware of how much you contribute to the organization's success?*	❏ *How would you describe your ideal working environment relative to working with others?*	❏ *In what areas would you like to grow and develop?*
❏ *What would make you feel more empowered in your job?*	❏ *What change would make the biggest difference in your work or work environment right now?*	❏ *How do you prefer to be recognized? What do you think should be recognized?*

You're probably starting to see why you're so important to employee engagement. As a frontline leader, you have a direct influence on every one of the drivers just mentioned. Not only that, but you're also *personally* influential. (See Chapter 20 for more on influencing others.) Your people naturally look to you to provide direction and support for their day-to-day work. But they also need you to recognize their unique needs, capabilities, and potential. And your voice will set the tone for the entire group. Sound familiar? It should. This is one of many, many direct real-world applications of the interaction skills—Key Principles and Interaction Guidelines. Your ability to address people's practical and personal needs will go a long way toward fostering an environment where people feel they're doing meaningful work. (You'll also be a happier, more productive leader.) We encourage you to use the *interaction skills* to help you plan your engagement conversations to address both sides of these very human needs.

Just a reminder:

Interaction skills have two parts:

Key Principles—to help address people's personal needs.

Interaction Guidelines—to help address people's practical needs.

Everyday Engagers

If you're having conversations with people about how they're feeling, how much they matter, or what they'll need to grow their skills, then you must prepare. Your first step is to make a real, human connection. This can be easier said than done, as starting a conversation about engagement can feel awkward. Figure 12.2 offers some pointers on how you can do this more comfortably.

FIG **12.2** Simple Tips for Getting People Engaged

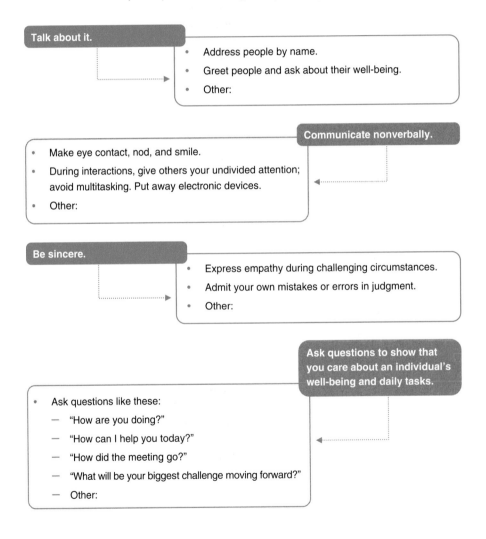

Talk about it.
- Address people by name.
- Greet people and ask about their well-being.
- Other:

Communicate nonverbally.
- Make eye contact, nod, and smile.
- During interactions, give others your undivided attention; avoid multitasking. Put away electronic devices.
- Other:

Be sincere.
- Express empathy during challenging circumstances.
- Admit your own mistakes or errors in judgment.
- Other:

Ask questions to show that you care about an individual's well-being and daily tasks.
- Ask questions like these:
  - "How are you doing?"
  - "How can I help you today?"
  - "How did the meeting go?"
  - "What will be your biggest challenge moving forward?"
  - Other:

Simple Tips for Getting People Engaged *cont'd*

Respect others' time and efforts.

- Say "please" and "thank you" to genuinely express your request for an individual's help or your appreciation for her work.
- Ask, "Do you have a few minutes to talk?" or "Is this a good time?"
- Respond in a timely manner to communications, even if only to say you need more time to respond or to express appreciation for people's efforts.
- Be on time for meetings and teleconferences. If you're running late, send a brief email or text to let people know.
- Other:

Listen first, then offer guidance.

- Quickly note your comments, ideas, and questions beforehand so that you can offer them after you've listened fully.
- Ask questions like these:
  - "Let's hear your ideas first. What do you think?"
  - "Can you help me to better understand your perspective?"
  - "What concerns do you have?"
  - Other:

Compliment and recognize results, constructive efforts, and positive attributes.

- Write a personal note of appreciation showing that you cared enough to acknowledge the person.
- Congratulate the person face-to-face.
- Know and be able to share the specifics of people's actions, efforts, and accomplishments.
- Other:

Simple Tips for Getting People Engaged *cont'd*

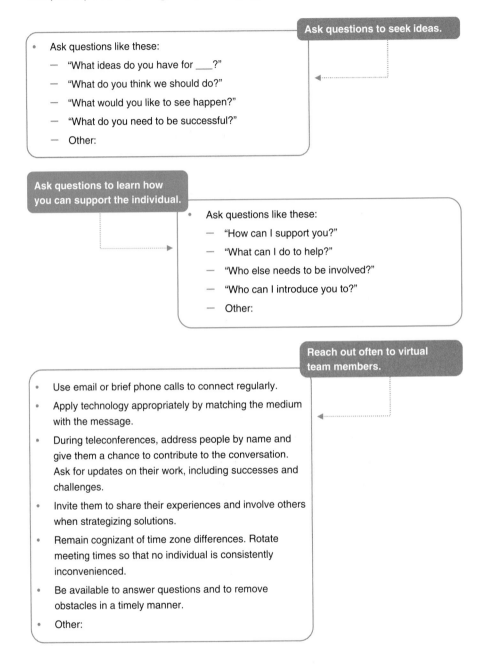

- Ask questions like these:
  - "What ideas do you have for ___?"
  - "What do you think we should do?"
  - "What would you like to see happen?"
  - "What do you need to be successful?"
  - Other:

- Ask questions like these:
  - "How can I support you?"
  - "What can I do to help?"
  - "Who else needs to be involved?"
  - "Who can I introduce you to?"
  - Other:

- Use email or brief phone calls to connect regularly.
- Apply technology appropriately by matching the medium with the message.
- During teleconferences, address people by name and give them a chance to contribute to the conversation. Ask for updates on their work, including successes and challenges.
- Invite them to share their experiences and involve others when strategizing solutions.
- Remain cognizant of time zone differences. Rotate meeting times so that no individual is consistently inconvenienced.
- Be available to answer questions and to remove obstacles in a timely manner.
- Other:

Engagement Conversations: More Than Just Eye Contact

Every conversation you have with a team member is an opportunity to understand what he or she is thinking and why—and to show that the person's work is important. But a formal engagement conversation at least once a year keeps focus on the drivers that are most likely to keep team members working with maximum energy. If that seems like a lot of emotional heavy lifting, it's not. It simply means you recognize that each person is unique and that each has value to share. These small conversations need not be long or complicated, but they do have to be personal—to the people involved. You're more likely to keep people happy and fulfilled at work—and solve problems more quickly—if you know them. And if you're really good, you'll ask questions that get them thinking about their own potential in new and exciting ways.

 **KEY TIPS:**

- Prepare for an engagement conversation by thinking about which of the three drivers might be most important to the person, and why.

- Ask the person to talk about what means the most to him about his job *lately*. Notice if this changes over time.

- Ask what she's been learning that excites her. Does it track with her job duties?

- Keep the conversation brief, informal, and friendly. If a work problem pops up unrelated to the conversation, get the information you need to address it and schedule a follow-up meeting.

- Think about actions you might want to take to raise the person's level of engagement.

Praise: Recognizing Individual Achievement and Effort

The research is clear: Praise is good for the bottom line. People who receive regular recognition and praise for their good work increase individual productivity, receive higher loyalty and satisfaction scores from customers, have better safety records and fewer accidents, and are more likely to stay with their company.[4]

New leaders tend to get tripped up on praise because they worry that it will seem unprofessional or that people will get overconfident and complacent. It isn't and they won't. So, we encourage you to overcome your resistance. Praise doesn't have to be a big production, but it is a big deal to the receiver. And it can and should take place in the regular interactions you have with people.

We often think to offer praise when a team member has gone that extra mile—he completed a project ahead of time, volunteered to be part of the interview process for a new hire, or suggested a process improvement for the group. But it's just as important to offer praise appropriately even when someone has delivered mixed or disappointing results on an assignment. Of course, this is also an opportunity to coach the individual for improvement. But chances are the person tried hard. *Very* hard. Her effort represents an opportunity for you to deliver authentic praise in a difficult coaching situation. Be sure to explore the effort she put into her assignment in detail and deliver specific, sincere compliments around it.

WE ASKED, YOU ANSWERED via Facebook

Q. What praise did you get from your boss that meant the most?

Chris Allieri—*We need to have a strong presence at events, on stage and off. This feedback came after a particularly difficult presentation, one that we'd spent ages prepping for. Afterward, my boss said, "You are fearless in a room full of strangers. That's good." I was thrilled, and it gave me a sense of myself that I didn't already have.*

- Find out how individuals prefer to be recognized. Some don't like being the center of attention in meetings; some people prefer individual to group emails.

- There are three things to think about when you recognize others: their *efforts*, their *contributions*, and their *results*. If you praise just the results, you'll miss mentioning the valuable work that was done to achieve them.

- Get to know how people approach their work and why others like working with them. Mention how their personal style affects others.

- Regularly inform senior management about individual accomplishments. (First, check with your manager to find out how she prefers to be informed.)

- Don't forget about virtual team members! Even though they're out of sight, you can foster their engagement with the team when you let them know they are valuable contributors, too.

- Send handwritten thank-you notes. On paper. Yes! They work! Now more than ever.

DDI PRO TIP: Don't think that it always has to be you giving the high fives and good feedback. Consider ways for peers to recognize each other's work. Think about informal approaches like employee achievement awards tailored to the kind of recognition that is meaningful to your team. Or, simply ask for peer recognition in your regular group meetings: *We had a busy week. Who has a shout-out for someone on the team that went above and beyond?*

But don't stop there. You might want to lobby for something more formal at your company, like software that can give your employees a chance to publicly acknowledge each other and earn meaningful rewards. (DDI uses Yammer, but there are tons of good options.) Head to our microsite for a list of ways to recognize individuals. We can help you make the case that an acknowledgment culture is good business.

Retention Conversations

No matter how expert you've become at keeping your team engaged, sometimes people will think about leaving. Smart leaders understand that retention conversations—where they identify people who have become disenchanted or distracted by other job possibilities—can help them stop a valuable contributor from heading for the door. They might even learn something that can make the organization work better.

But with all you've got on your plate, it would be impossible for you to check in with everyone all the time. Although you do need to keep scanning the horizon for potential retention issues, you can't take care of everyone all at once. Your *first* efforts should focus on people who (1) provide *significant value* to you and the organization and (2) are *most likely to leave*.

It's important to prioritize your retention efforts by thinking about whom to focus on first and what you can do to make a difference in retaining that person. Use Tool 12.1 to help you think this through.

Identify Talent to Retain

1. Choose the person from your team whom you want to have a retention conversation with first. You can use the following parameters as a guide; check those that apply to this person. Then, use the space below "Other:" to note why you want to speak with this person first.

   ❑ Has expertise, knowledge, and experience that are significant assets.

   ❑ Has specialized skills that would be difficult to replace.

   ❑ Would be difficult for someone to assume this person's duties quickly and competently.

   ❑ Consistently gets positive feedback from customers, team members, and internal partners.

   ❑ Generally earns high performance ratings.

   ❑ Is highly employable and marketable.

   ❑ Remains open to change and is unafraid to take risks.

   ❑ Would be a valuable asset to the competition.

   ❑ Other:

2. Think about the risk or likelihood of this person leaving the organization.

Now that you've identified whom you should talk to first, it's time to have the conversation! Typically, these talks take place one-on-one. These are important conversations, so be sure to find a quiet time for your chat. After you've identified, in her own words, the person's primary motivators, your job as leader is to take concrete steps to keep her on board. Although most people think that money is the primary motivator for anyone to leave his or her job, people most commonly cite lack of career advancement—with related promotions, of course—as the reasons why they are thinking about leaving.

At least 75 percent of the reasons for voluntary turnover can be influenced by managers. Find out what matters most to individuals on your team, and then take proactive steps to provide it as much as possible.[5]

KEY TIPS:

- Think back to earlier conversations with this person. What mattered most to him about his jobs?

- Let the person know this is a conversation about keeping her at the company.

- Ask him direct, relevant questions:

  - *How are you feeling about where you are and where you're going in your career?*

  - *Given your valuable experience and expertise, I'm concerned that you could be approached by another organization. What can we do to keep you?*

  - *What would make you feel successful in your job or career?*

- Ask for specific ideas about what she wants or needs. Share your thoughts.

- Summarize what was discussed and plan next steps.

- If you discover that a top performer wants to move on to another team or project within the organization, do what you can to make it happen. The key here is that keeping the person in the organization is still a win.

Reflection Point

What about you? How engaged are you? Engagement is all about energy. Engaged leaders create an engaged team. Take a moment to reflect on your personal level of engagement:

- On a scale of 1 to 4, with 1 being "not at all engaged" and 4 being "highly engaged," how would you rate yourself? And, what impact does your level of engagement have on your direct reports?

- What will you say to share with your supervisor what matters most to you at work? What ideas will you suggest to your leader to increase your own interest and job satisfaction?

Mastery and Leadership Skills
13 MEETINGS
Make Them Count!

Pre:Think

Jot down a list of five things you've observed someone do or say in meetings that really got your attention in a bad way. Something truly awful, unproductive, or just plain bizarre. What happened? How did others respond? How did you wish they had responded? If you could have done something without getting into trouble, what would you have said or done?

If I wasn't tied up in meetings all day, I really could get something done here.

Most of you, leader yet or not, have felt like this at some point, and likely for the right reasons. A recent study of more than 1,000 UK workers revealed that their country lost more than £26 billion (about $43 billion) through wasted meetings. On average, the study reported that individuals are wasting two hours and 39 minutes in meetings each week![1] The United Kingdom, of course, is not alone. Extrapolate the £26 billion around the world, and you easily assume that hundreds of billions are lost in inefficient meetings each year. Trying to estimate the real cost of meetings yourself? Thanks to the magic of technology, there are over a dozen apps that allow you to easily calculate meeting costs. Some are like a stop watch. Insert your average per-person hourly rate and the number of people attending the meeting, start the clock, and watch the money add up.

In spite of the challenges inherent in meetings, they are not going away! While you may need to work on reducing the number of meetings, and/or time spent in meetings, they still serve an important purpose. There are a number of reasons why well-run meetings are well worth the time spent. They make sense if you need to:

- Identify problems and opportunities and how to best address them. There is an abundance of research showing that groups of people are better at solving problems than a single person.[2]

- Make a decision or seek input on a decision, and the commitment of those attending the meeting is crucial.

- Communicate a change that affects everyone at the meeting and provides an opportunity to address their issues and concerns.

- Accomplish projects or everyday tasks that require coordination and communication among team members.

What Makes Meetings More Difficult Than Ever?

We've identified three things that make meetings more difficult than ever before.

You Are on Stage

If you have a positive or negative interaction with a single person, the consequences are usually limited. However, in a single one-hour meeting, you can damage or enhance your leadership credibility with every single person attending. If you are chronically disorganized, combative with others, or unable to moderate people's bad behavior in a group setting, people will begin to dread meeting with you. Further, expect your reputation to take a hit as people talk to colleagues about your (in)ability to lead a meeting, and even a team. The consequences to your leadership career could be amplified exponentially.

Tina recalled the first time her colleagues convened to meet their new leader. The team of 12 created a monthly financial newsletter for accountants, planners, and other professionals. The new leader had previously run a larger publication and had been brought in to help team members refresh their basic product and develop new digital ones. There were lots of details to address. *We were pretty excited to take our work to a new level*, said Tina. *But it was clear from the beginning that there were going to be problems.* The new boss began by having the attendees brainstorm a group of words to describe the newsletter they currently produced. *We said things like "informative, accurate, timely"—stuff like that*, Tina recalled.

Then he wrote "BORING" above the list. Really big! Then other words like "pedantic" and "talks down to people" and "REALLY BORING." We were shocked and hurt. Things fell apart from there. *People got very upset. He was unable to answer even the most basic question—like how we were going to fix our work flow or how we were going to address production changes that were coming. A plan for the upcoming website redesign? Please? Nothing.*

To make matters worse, every meeting was similarly tense and unproductive. The team reacted predictably. It was rebellion. For the rest of the year, the team privately mocked every memo the boss sent—labeling it "BORING" and circulating it among the group for feedback. *We spent more time than we should have making fun of him behind his back,* Tina admitted. Members also did their best to solve the production issues on their own. *It got to the point where we just gave up trying to work it through with him.* Later that year, when it came time to provide manager feedback for the firm's annual employee survey, team members coordinated their answers so that everyone's was exactly the same. *We all told the same story about that first awful meeting, and documented what we thought was his unwillingness to do his job,* she said. *Every single answer was exactly the same. We thought it would send a message.*

Competing for Attention

About a decade ago, one of the biggest consequences of ineffective meetings was that attendees tuned out. They were bored, unengaged, and might even doze off. Not today! With laptop screens open and smart phones on, you're not competing with boredom, but rather with the other tasks team members will be working on during your meeting. While this might be a bit ego-deflating, it's not entirely bad. When people use technology to multitask, they are often keeping an eye on urgent needs from customers, peers, and clients that would cause bigger problems if they didn't respond quickly. You don't want your meetings to be the reason other projects fall apart. Technology that connects to the outside world also helps solve questions that arise in meetings—like finding a key data point, or getting a quick email from an outside expert on a pressing issue.

But, imagine the reaction of one leader we spoke with who was told by one of his closer peers that meeting members were actually spending time text messaging each other on how poorly the meeting was being run! When the technology becomes a way for people to escape the meeting, then you've got a problem on your hands.

Virtual Technology

Many meetings today use virtual technology, some with voice and some with video (in varying degrees of quality). It's much harder to stay in tune with attendees' feelings and reactions when everyone may be in different locations, sometimes in different countries. What could go wrong?

WE ASKED, YOU ANSWERED via QUORA

Q: What's the worst meeting you ever attended?

Neel Kumar:

I used to work for a LARGE software company. I was told to attend a conference call at 10:00 p.m. that was "critical" to the product that I was working on and was close to shipping.

1st bad sign—*No agenda. But normal for my company.*

2nd bad sign—*There were no pre-meeting emails. Again, normal for the company.*

3rd bad sign—*There will be people on it from West Coast, East Coast, Europe, China, and India.*

So, I log in at 10:00 p.m. I was the first one to connect. 5 minutes later, another guy logs in from Germany. At 10:15 p.m., my boss (the organizer) logs in. Asks if Mr X has logged in. I say "No." Boss: "Oh, it is critical for Mr X to be here." Logs off.

At 10:30 p.m., there are 30+ people on the conference call, when my boss logs back in. He cannot find Mr X, but the meeting should continue. Meeting starts. Questions start flying. But there is no one actually answering anything. Most of the questions are not for my area of expertise. The few that are get hijacked by my boss and deferred till another time. At 11:30 p.m., Mr X logs in. My boss starts recapping everything for him. Meanwhile, someone is snoring and we can all hear him. My boss shouts over the noise to finish his recap. All of a sudden we hear a woman screaming at her husband in Hindi (my mother tongue) that he is still puttering around the house. It is now midnight and the meeting is still going on. I don't know whether I should simply hang up or start making random noises. :-)

Finally, at 1:00 a.m., the meeting ends. None of the questions posed have been answered satisfactorily (at least in my opinion). The only conclusion is that this meeting should be repeated at the same time the next day.

I managed to conveniently forget to attend the following 4 meetings. The first meeting had eaten up 100+ man-hours. I did not want to feed the monster.

TECH TIP!! Conducting Virtual Meetings

Choose the tips that best apply to your situation or that you think will help you lead a productive, worthwhile virtual meeting.

- Call the roll at the beginning of the meeting and after breaks.

- Create a virtual seating chart to give you a visual of your team.

- Help participants get to know one another by asking them to share some personal information before beginning the meeting.

- Designate a note taker so participants can concentrate on the discussion.

- Set ground rules about multitasking during the virtual meeting.

- Use appropriate technology tools to enhance collaboration, display information and visuals, summarize key points, and gain consensus. Tools such as white boarding, desktop sharing, and polling are common.

- Check for understanding, and prompt people to participate more often than they would in a face-to-face meeting.

- Pay close attention to each person during the meeting and jot down your observations. This can be valuable in revealing patterns of behavior you might otherwise not recognize. In future meetings you can head off problems by knowing in advance who has been quiet or domineering, and then using the Key Principles to ensure everyone is involved.

- Talk to disruptive participants privately during a break, or send them an instant message or email. Share the importance of completing the meeting's agenda with as few distractions as possible.

Questions You Don't Want Meeting Participants to Ask

In the earlier unfortunate, yet funny, real-world example, we heard from just one participant (Neel). But imagine the conversations that go on between peers when meetings go poorly. Consider the example of Thomas, who just led a key two-hour meeting with seven associates to work on next year's operational plan. The meeting did not go quite as well as he expected. After the meeting, participants began a side conversation with one another—but not with Thomas! Why? Because they'd lost faith in his ability to run a meeting. And the attendees naturally begin the process of checking in with each other, to diagnose what they think went wrong.

The questions people ask after poorly run meetings run the gamut from its purpose to the behavior of others. For example:

- *Did we really need a meeting to cover this topic? Seems to me soliciting some input from each of us separately might have been more efficient.*

- *What was the purpose of the meeting, anyway? We went back and forth with no clear goals.*

- *Why did I get invited? It really didn't seem like I belonged. I had very little to add to the discussion.*

- *Why did no one control Judy? She talked half the time. No one else could get a word in edgewise.*

- *What happened to Amit? He called in late at night to accommodate time zone differences. I only heard him offer a comment once.*

- *What was going on between Janice and Ricardo? Toward the end, they were both constantly arguing. It was embarrassing for the rest of us.*

- *Why did we run over by 30 minutes? One hour was plenty. I had to rearrange my day. Perhaps if we had started on time? Does anyone have any idea of next steps? Lots of issues. Not sure what will happen with them.*

Once these types of questions start popping up after meetings, it's very hard to regain momentum. There are plenty of good, practical tips to consider when planning and running meetings, but there are also some philosophical ones for you to think about—like how to treat people, particularly in a public setting. And they are useful whether a meeting is in person, or virtual.

Know When Not to Hold a Meeting!

Decide whether a meeting is the best vehicle for addressing the topic(s). Earlier in this chapter, we provided examples of when a meeting might make sense. There are many times when it doesn't. Such as when:

- You're not entirely certain about why you're calling a meeting and/or the objectives you want to achieve.

- Your only purpose is to communicate information. With technology today, there are many more dynamic ways to do this.

- A key attendee can't make it. You're better off to cancel. If you don't, you can rest assured that you'll need to start all over again.

- Only a few people are really crucial to accomplishing your goal, but a dozen people are in the meeting. This is not only inefficient, but it makes others wonder why they were invited.

- A decision has already been made or needs to be made quickly. Some first-time leaders err in over-involving everyone.

Occasionally there are times when a small meeting is necessary, but you don't need to be there. The more you can trust others who work for you to meet themselves, the better off you'll be.

The Right Start: Clear Purpose and Importance

Meeting horror stories often can be avoided by having a clear purpose or goal and spelling out why it's critical to you, the meeting participants, and your organization. Often, this can be communicated in advance, but should still be the first step in beginning a meeting.

Set the Agenda in Advance

Creating and sticking to an agenda is an important part of any meeting. In fact, it becomes your road map to navigate through the topics you want to discuss. Agendas include meeting purpose and importance, names/roles of people attending, time and place, the set of topics you plan to cover (with time allocations), and expected outcomes. Don't wait to hand out the agenda at the meeting; instead, send it two or three days in advance. Also, any meeting prework or expectations should be sent along with the agenda. We've attended meetings where half the time is consumed by reading documents that should have been read in advance.

No Minutes Equals Lost Minutes

This sounds like a no-brainer, but we can't tell you the number of times we've been in a meeting when midway through someone asks, "Who's taking notes?" Always designate a note taker, preferably not yourself. If you do a little homework, you'll find there are very inexpensive app tools (e.g., Evernote) that can simplify the task of taking, storing, and distributing meeting notes.

Meeting Leaders Make Poor Participants

It's pretty hard to conduct an orchestra and play an instrument at the same time! Rajev, in his leadership role for just six months, realized he was doing most of the talking during his meetings. As a meeting leader, you need a laser focus on each attendee, bringing each into the fold. (You'll find more facilitation tips later in this chapter.) You may need to mediate conflict between participants, and you'll need to keep things moving. As meeting leader, you'll need to use your facilitation skills to follow the agenda and encourage the people in the room to share their ideas and concerns. If you want to be a meeting contributor, you might think about asking someone else to fill in as a facilitator.

Keep the Time

Nothing is more disruptive to an effective meeting than starting late and running long. This tip is pretty simple: Make it a habit to start and end on time. You, of course, need to set the example. If you find some meeting participants frequently arriving late or leaving early, some coaching may be helpful.

Command and Control Multitasking

Dealing with multitasking attendees is a significant challenge for many first-time leaders. A meeting attendee who is emailing, texting, or doing other work is decidedly not focused on the task at hand. If you want to make sure you have their undivided attention, be sure to *set your expectations early in the meeting*. Ask that people stay off of laptops, tablets, and smartphones unless they are absolutely necessary to their jobs, are being used to take notes, or are needed to contribute external information to the discussion.

The Next Step

Most of the power of a well-run meeting is realized *after* it ends. Almost every meeting should close with a clear set of next steps, who is accountable, and by when. Make sure you build in time to do this, as it often gets shortchanged. One leader we interviewed also takes a few minutes to get feedback on the effectiveness of the meeting itself. Was it efficient? Did everyone get to participate? Are the outcomes clear? A great idea!

The Foundation of Meeting Success: Interaction Skills

One of the most difficult leadership roles is *facilitating* a meeting. In Part 1, we introduced a set of critical interaction skills that help you meet people's personal and practical needs. Tool 13.1 describes some of the typical meeting challenges you'll face and how to use these skills to overcome them.

Anticipate and Prevent Problems

An ounce of prevention is worth a pound of cure. If you can anticipate roadblocks, you can plan a way around problems in the meeting itself. Here are some questions you can ask yourself before the meeting:

- Do any attendees have an ongoing conflict?
- Could someone with strong opinions dominate the discussion?
- Will any topics you plan to discuss surprise people or cause them to react negatively?

Tool 13.1 will help you apply the preceding tips to special meeting situations. It will put you on the right path to becoming a master meeting leader.

TOOL 13.1

Using Interaction Skills to Solve Meeting Problems

PROBLEM	SYMPTOMS	SUGGEST THAT YOU ...
Arguing	• Teamwork decreasing. • Someone will not compromise. • Emotions rise. • People criticize each other personally. • Listening not to understand, but to refute.	• **Encourage others to take turns talking.** • **Summarize ideas/actions.** Ask the arguers to summarize each other's views to promote better understanding. • **Take a break.** Let people cool off. Talk privately with the arguers, using the appropriate *Key Principles.*
Dominating	• The discussion becomes a monologue; other participants tune out. • Someone takes too long to make a point. • Someone insists on his own ideas and won't listen to others.	• **Focus on agenda/desired outcomes.** • **Summarize ideas/actions.** Interrupt the dominator, summarize your understanding of what's been said, and redirect the discussion to someone else. • **Take a break.** Then, talk privately with the person dominating the meeting. • **Esteem.** This can keep the person from going to the other extreme and withdrawing. • **Share.** Describe how you believe the person's behavior is affecting other people. • **Involvement.** Ask for the person's ideas about participating differently.

Using Interaction Skills to Solve Meeting Problems

PROBLEM	SYMPTOMS	SUGGEST THAT YOU . . .
Floundering	• Progress slows or stops altogether. • People are not participating. • The group lets you (the leader) do most of the talking. • Decisions are postponed.	• **Focus on agenda/desired outcomes.** Restate the meeting's desired outcomes and why they're important. • **Listen and respond with empathy.** Jump-start the discussion by asking people for an idea or suggestion. • **Take a break.** Allow everyone, yourself included, to get refreshed. • **Resolve an issue later.** If people have trouble working out an issue, ask a subgroup to work on it later.
Getting Off Track	• People discuss topics that aren't on the agenda or don't support the desired outcomes. • People jump ahead in the agenda. • People spend more time on a topic than is allotted.	• **Focus on agenda/desired outcomes.** Ask how some-one's comments are relevant. • **Share thoughts, feelings, and rationale.** Explain the consequences you think will occur if the agenda is not completed. • **Maintain self-esteem and summarize ideas/actions.** Carefully interrupt the person, summarize what she said, and redirect the discussion to someone else. • **Resolve an issue later.** When people raise relevant issues that aren't on the agenda, list them on a flip chart titled "Issues." Agree to discuss them at the end of the meeting or some later time.

Using Interaction Skills to Solve Meeting Problems

PROBLEM	SYMPTOMS	SUGGEST THAT YOU . . .
Interrupting	• Someone cuts off people while they're talking. • People have side conversations. • Someone asks you to repeat information after arriving late or leaving to do other business.	• **Encourage others to take turns talking.** Politely stop the discussion and ask the person who interrupted to wait to speak. • **Take a break.** If someone continues disrupting, talk privately to him at the break. • **Focus on agenda/desired outcomes.** Reinforce the importance of completing the agenda to encourage people to withhold any unnecessary comments.
Venting Emotions	• People complain loudly or get upset. • The group blames a problem on others. • One participant implies things would be better if another participant had done her job better.	• **Listen and respond with empathy.** Help people move on; show that you understand how they are feeling and why. • **Focus on agenda/desired outcomes.** Emphasize that the best way to improve the situation is by focusing on factors the group can control. • **Resolve an issue later.** Schedule a time to follow up on the concerns people have.
Withdrawing	• Someone seems unwilling to contribute at all. • A person does other work during meeting.	**Use appropriate Key Principles:** **Encourage involvement.** Draw out the person by asking for his or her ideas. **Appropriately enhance self-esteem.** Show how much you value the person's contributions.

Mastery and Leadership Skills
14 COACHING
Learning from Success

Pre:Think
Think back to anything you've worked hard to get good at. It could be school, sports, dancing, making videos, public speaking, mastering spreadsheets—anything. Do you prefer to learn from your successes or your failures?

Put Me In, Coach!

If you ask most people to explain what they mean by "leadership," you'll probably get a vague description of "coaching" accompanied by a flurry of sports metaphors. It's easy to see why. The sports version of a coach offers a romantic and dramatic example of leadership in which one person brings out the best in others while bringing home the title. It's heroic! The tear-jerking halftime pep talks, the towel-chewing sideline anxiety, and the victory lap on the shoulders of a grateful team all make for emotionally satisfying, inspiring imagery. There's a reason why winning coaches end up populating "great leaders" lists in magazines every year: They seem like a perfect model for winning at business and at life. Who doesn't crave the roar of the crowd to commemorate our success?

But that's not the kind of coaching we mean. In fact, the sports coach may be a counterproductive metaphor for the kind of coaching you'll need to do in almost every way but one. Why? Because game-day inspiration is a poor substitute for the regular, timely guidance your team needs from you to help members gain the skills, knowledge, and behaviors they must have to accomplish their work and grow the business. That type of true coaching occurs in small, but powerful, ways every day. Gatorade baths are optional.

Most people would prefer to learn from their successes. In the Pre:Think exercise, we asked if you preferred to learn from success or failure. If you're like most of the people who have taken our course, "Coaching for Peak Performance," you said success. Easy, right? Learning from your mistakes can be effective, but also exhausting, time-consuming, and embarrassing. And workplace failures can trip up an entire team, delay or derail projects, and lose money. Learning from a success experience builds enthusiasm, reinforces good habits, and fosters good will. The members of your team, like most people, would prefer to *learn from their successes, while confidently taking on the risks associated with new responsibilities*. And now it's your job to provide the kind of coaching that will help them do that. Unlike running fast, jumping high, or kicking a ball accurately, it's a skill that anyone can learn. (We'll end the sports metaphors here.)

If you know nothing else, know this: As a leader, you'll need to recognize, apply, and master two types of coaching: *proactive* and *reactive*. Proactive coaching, as the name suggests, helps you get in front of opportunities and situations before they happen. It's part of helping people learn from success. Reactive coaching inserts you in the mix after something has happened or is in progress. It's part of helping people change course after a problem or setback. To succeed as a frontline leader, you'll need to master both. But even more important is understanding what they are and why they are distinct.

Define and Conquer

Proactive coaching happens *before* something has occurred and guides people toward success in new or challenging situations, such as:

- Taking on a new responsibility or an unfamiliar task or assignment.
- Learning a different skill or job function.
- Working with new partners or suppliers.
- Planning to conduct a first meeting or a difficult conversation.
- Preparing to resolve a conflict.

Reactive coaching happens *after* something has occurred and guides people toward improving or enhancing their work performance, such as:

- Making good results even better.

- Improving low or weak performance ratings.

- Reaching goals or deadlines that aren't being met.

- Reviewing completed assignments or tasks for ways to improve.

- Addressing poor work habits like punctuality, meeting prep, and so on.

Here's an unfortunate truth: Most leaders are lousy coaches, even if they don't mean to be. Even if they're great people. There are many reasons for this. Sometimes, it's because they want to avoid conflict. Often, they believe it would be better if their direct reports were entrepreneurial or independent and figured things out on their own. And sometimes they're swayed by the heroic allure of coaching. You may have worked with someone who liked to swoop in and tell you what you should have done differently after the fact, then help you duct-tape things back together. You may even be that person. We call it the firefighter syndrome. Rescuing people feels good, looks great—and is sometimes necessary—but it's reactive coaching.

But once we explain the distinction, most of the leaders we survey will admit to relying on reactive coaching for one reason: They don't believe they have enough time to do their jobs *and* do a good job proactively coaching their people. Our data reveals a surprising paradox: The more time you spend coaching people proactively, the more time you'll free up in your schedule. Bottom line, reactive coaching burns through time, energy, and other valuable resources.

The scorecard in Figure 14.1 suggests that leaders have a long way to go to develop the skills necessary to be a proactive coach.[1]

FIG 14.1 Coaching Behavior Scorecard

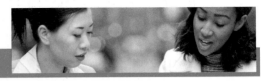

SCORECARD

Does your manager ask for ideas about how to solve problems?

51%

49%

Does your manager help you solve problems without solving them for you?

53%

47%

Does your manager give you sufficient feedback on your performance?

55%

45%

In conversations, does your manager ask questions to ensure he or she understands what you are saying?

59%

41%

Does your manager adequately recognize your efforts/contributions?

60%

40%

Does your manager handle work conversations efficiently?

64%

36%

Most of the Time or Always
Only Sometimes or Never

You might remember John, the urban planner, from Chapter 1. He discovered the hard way that his failure to coach his most-senior direct report delayed projects and undermined her confidence. *I only gave her direction when there was a problem*, he said. *And it looked like I was micromanaging her. I just thought everyone does better when they figure things out on their own.* After six months on the job, office productivity dropped precipitously. The irony of John's situation was that his new supervisor did the same thing to him. *Looking back, I needed help figuring out how to get in front of some big things—like the first time I gave a presentation to the staff*, John said. There were new partner relationships to manage, human resource functions, and, of course, monthly meetings, all of which would have been much easier if he had felt better prepared. Let's take another leader, Marta, who knew that her go-to high performer, William, was a prickly sort, yet utterly failed to proactively coach anyone when she plopped him into the midst of an already established team. *At some point, the personality stuff just feels like noise to me*, she admitted. *I just want them to work things out.* Instead, Marta lost valuable time in soothing ruffled feathers, fixing problems, and trying to jump-start morale.

 TECH TIP!! Things move fast today. Don't wait for an ideal moment or the weekly staff meeting to find out how people are doing. You can use technology to help you take advantage of coaching opportunities when they arise. Short messages with insightful questions or comments can keep people on track and motivated. Use email and text (based on the preferences of your team) to ask quick questions or provide brief feedback to make sure people are making progress. One "how did it go, and how can I help?" text after a crucial presentation can boost a team member and keep his momentum up.

Assessing Impact

A person's work performance, exceptional or poor, can greatly affect the entire work ecosystem. When a team member is scattered and unsure about a project or task, she needs proactive coaching from you. Without it, the entire work department's focus may be cannibalized by the last-minute prep. Or, if a desk clerk doesn't return colleagues' emails in a timely fashion, this can cause confusion and loss of productivity for the entire team.

Use the following questions to gauge the impact of an individual's performance in each area. This information will help you prep for either a proactive or reactive coaching session.

People

- Who is currently (or could, in the future) being affected by your team member's performance (e.g., customers, team members, and so on)? How?

- What personal or practical needs does this person have? Are they being met?

- What positive or negative impact might your team member's behavior have on other individuals? The rest of the team? The organization?

Productivity

- How is your team member's performance affecting processes, deadlines, or others' work?

- What positive or negative impact might your team member's performance have on others' productivity? Overall productivity?

Profitability

- What positive or negative impact might your team member's performance have on profitability?

- If the team member is not performing successfully, how much money could be lost?

DDI PRO TIP: If you want a quick way to think about the distinction between proactive and reactive coaching, remember **seeking** and **telling** from Chapter 6. Proactive coaching emphasizes *seeking* a person's commitment by asking powerful questions or sharing insights to build empathy. Reactive coaching emphasizes *telling* someone what to do to solve a problem or address an issue. Seeking and telling live on a spectrum of coaching techniques. It's your job to balance them in every coaching interaction.

And, as much as you can, *seek more than you tell*. Use Tool 14.1 to plan whether you'll need to seek or tell more at specific points during your coaching conversation.

My Approach

SEEKING		TELLING
❏	Benefits to person, team, organization	❏
❏	Background information	❏
❏	Issues, concerns, barriers	❏
❏	Ideas for achieving success	❏
❏	Needed resources/support	❏
❏	Specific actions to be taken	❏
❏	Ways to observe performance and measure results	❏
❏	Summary of next steps	❏

The Perfect Coach

Some say that the Perfect Coach is a myth. But, Tacy and Rich both know one. Both have benefited from a career full of candid moments with this person. He is too humble to be named here, but here's what he does that makes him a perfect coach:

- Always has an open door, making himself available for advice.

- Can be trusted with confidential information.

- **Never** opens a coaching conversation by putting you on the defensive.

- Is always asking you questions. He has a knack for getting you to come up with what to do!

So, at the end of the day, he is a person others want to go to for coaching and advice . . . again and again. An enviable reputation for any leader!

Oh, the Humanity

Coaching is a deeply human endeavor. When you talk openly and authentically with your direct reports, you'll quickly discover that they have personal needs that they bring to work every day, such as the need to be involved, listened to, and understood. They also have practical needs, like insufficient resources, problems to solve, and a plan of action that they can apply immediately. And you might discover them having real trouble feeling good about their jobs, and are at risk for leaving. (Head to Chapter 12 for more on retention and engagement.) We encourage you to use the interaction skills we introduced in Part 1 to help you design your coaching conversations to address both sides of these very human needs. As you recall, the interaction skills have two parts:

- Key Principles—to address personal needs.
- Interaction Guidelines—to address practical needs.

Coaching with Interaction Guidelines

A coaching conversation to meet practical needs has five distinct parts that we mentioned earlier: *Open, Clarify, Develop, Agree,* and *Close.* To be successful, you must work through all five. By the way, it won't ultimately matter whether this conversation takes place face-to-face or over a series of meetings, email, or IM. But for now, try to have as many of these conversations as you can in person or voice-to-voice. Twenty minutes, face-to-face, is the gold standard; make as much time for them in your first 90 days as you can.

Figure 14.2 will help you think about the Interaction Guidelines in the *context* of proactive and reactive coaching discussions, where they can have great impact. The callout boxes in the graphic cite specific tips for using each Interaction Guideline.

FIG 14.2 Interaction Guidelines in Coaching Conversations

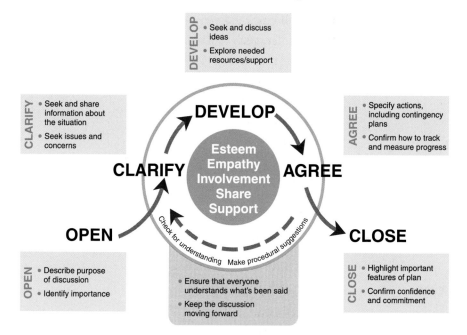

DEVELOP
- Seek and discuss ideas
- Explore needed resources/support

CLARIFY
- Seek and share information about the situation
- Seek issues and concerns

AGREE
- Specify actions, including contingency plans
- Confirm how to track and measure progress

Esteem
Empathy
Involvement
Share
Support

OPEN
- Describe purpose of discussion
- Identify importance

Check for understanding   Make procedural suggestions
- Ensure that everyone understands what's been said
- Keep the discussion moving forward

CLOSE
- Highlight important features of plan
- Confirm confidence and commitment

DDI PRO TIP: In our experience, most people skip Clarify when they coach. It feels faster and more leader-like to jump straight from Open to Develop—a big mistake. Why? The Clarify step helps the person you're coaching understand the situation in a deeper way. You foster this understanding by asking powerful questions to get the person considering the situation from other perspectives and encouraging him to think out loud with you. Only then do you move to the Develop stage, to start floating ideas. At that point, most of the ideas that are generated should be his.

Coaching with the Key Principles

The personal side of coaching can feel more challenging because the outcome isn't based on external benchmarks—like an agreed-upon plan—but on the sense that people understand each other. This is where many frontline leaders get nervous or impatient. *Is this really necessary?* But by asking probing, high-gain questions—or judiciously sharing a part of your inner self—you can better understand and respond to the personal motivations of the people who work for you. It's during these moments that people develop or reaffirm their trust in you based on your ability to incorporate their needs and values into your leadership vision.

Following is a brief Q&A around the Key Principles and both proactive and reactive coaching conversations:

1. What *personal needs* might people have during a *reactive coaching* discussion? Which Key Principles would you use to meet those personal needs?

   - **To feel valued and respected.** People might be feeling vulnerable about their performance, so you'll want to acknowledge and reinforce their skills and abilities. To meet this personal need, you could use the *Esteem Key Principle.*

   - **To be heard and understood.** People might express strong emotions when discussing their work performance. The *Empathy Key Principle* helps defuse those emotions so people can think more rationally.

   - **To be involved.** People want to be part of any plan for how they will improve; you'll want to build their commitment to making a change. To meet this personal need, you could use the *Involvement Key Principle.*

2. Why is it important to *ask for help and encourage involvement* in both proactive and reactive coaching discussions?

   - During proactive coaching discussions, using the Involvement Key Principle helps you better understand people's needs and engages them in planning their approach.

   - During reactive coaching discussions, using involvement can build commitment to making a change or improvement.

   - In both discussions it's important for people to take ownership of their actions.

3. Why might using the *Esteem Key Principle* be important in a reactive coaching discussion?

   - To maintain esteem. Reinforcing people's skills and abilities helps them understand that there are aspects of their work that are going well.

4. If you had to maintain a person's self-esteem in a reactive coaching discussion, what might that sound like? Give a specific dialogue example.

   - *We've identified areas you need to work on. Now I'd like to share with you the areas in which you're doing very well. . . .*

- *While the results aren't where they should be right now, you have the experience and the motivation to make it happen.*

5. Why might it be important in a reactive coaching discussion to *listen and respond with empathy*?

- Empathizing enables you to defuse strong emotions and gives people a way to move past those emotions.

So, it's simply a few provocative questions balanced with authentic listening and empathy and you're on your way to becoming a perfect coach. As such, you focus your energy on your team, the members' challenges, and their coaching needs. How you *share your thoughts, feelings, and rationale* in both proactive and reactive coaching discussions is just as important. People want to know what you're thinking and feeling as a leader; for example, *I'm worried that if this isn't resolved, we'll miss the deadline.* By sharing your feelings, you help others connect with you; at the same time, you build trust, which is a precious commodity for any leader.

 TECH TIP!! What should you do when you need to coach but don't have time for a full-blown coaching discussion? For starters, don't wait! You can break up the discussion into smaller conversations around each of the five Interaction Guidelines and use technology to move from one step to the next. For example, you can use an email exchange to Open a coaching discussion (proactive or reactive) and Clarify information and details. The Develop step usually requires an exchange of ideas, so conducting it in real time via phone, web conference, or instant messaging is usually best. The Agree and Close steps can be done by email, instant messaging, or even text message.

Is it harder to coach piecemeal using technology? Yes, and it will take some practice. However, the only thing worse is to delay the conversation, which too often results in skipping it. For leaders who manage remote associates, tech-based coaching may be the norm and in-person discussions a rare luxury. Either way, get good at it so that you give people the support they need regardless of time, schedule, or location.

Try Out Your Coaching Skills

We invite you to try DDI's Interaction Skills Experience to practice the skills you've just learned about in this chapter. This online, video-based simulation on the microsite will provide insights about your strengths and development areas as a coach.

When you log in, you'll find yourself in a discussion with one of your team members—a person whose bad behavior is alienating other team members and starting to affect the whole team's performance. The discussion is representative of the types of interactions leaders typically face every day. You'll be given a number of opportunities to respond to the team member by using Key Principles, with the goal of coaching the person to improve work performance.

You'll get a scorecard on your mastery of each Key Principle—where you are best and where you need to improve. Give it a try.

You Believe They Can Fly, Right?

At the start of this chapter we said that sports offer an imperfect metaphor for business coaching in many ways except for one: The coach, by definition, can't do the job for each player. As we explored in Chapter 3, your transition from individual contributor to leader marks a shift from doing the work yourself to becoming a catalyst who can ignite the efforts of others. Coaching is an excellent way to help people prepare, learn, and ultimately grow into their jobs. But you have to let them do it. As absurd as it would be to watch, say, a World Cup coach dash onto the pitch and run for a goal himself, it's equally ludicrous for you to attempt to do your team's work, whether in desperation or because you miss the thrill of victory. You'll have to take a risk and let the team members do their jobs. It's one sports analogy we hope you keep in mind.

If you find yourself having difficulty letting go, spend more time referring to and thinking about the *Support Key Principle*. This is where you establish a plan to provide support for your direct reports' goals, with realistic monitoring in place to help you all feel more secure. As you master the difference between proactive and reactive coaching, and practice using the Interaction Guidelines, the elements of coaching will start to feel more natural to you.

Mastery and Leadership Skills
15 FEEDBACK FUNDAMENTALS
Specific, Timely, and Balanced

Pre:Think

We've all had that bit of feedback in our career where we said, *That was insightful.* And days or weeks later, we even stopped to thank the feedback provider. Think about it: Do people in your organization get enough feedback? How confident do you feel about giving both positive and constructive feedback? And, most importantly, does your team's performance suffer because people don't get the feedback they need to perform to their potential?

Sometimes, it's just as good to receive as it is to give.

That was the situation facing the Apollo 11 crew on their legendary lunar mission in 1969. Midway through their flight, the crew was way off course, and their fuel was almost gone. In this situation astronauts could have ignored the data (feedback) they got from the flight controllers and computers. Neil Armstrong controlled the command module, and he could have steered it anywhere he wished. But he accepted the data and made the course corrections that enabled him to hit a moving target a quarter of a million miles away from Earth.

While exchanging feedback in space can be a life-or-death proposition, the principles of effective feedback apply just as well here on Earth as they do up in space. (Though for most of us, these conversations won't have such dramatic consequences.) Feedback answers the question, "How am I doing?" and is a common

That is one small step for man, one giant step for mankind.

—**Neil Armstrong** (1969)

element in a number of conversations you'll have as a leader. People typically enjoy receiving *positive feedback*, as it meets the common personal need to feel valued and appreciated. More than that, when someone does well and receives positive feedback, it helps that person know what behavior to repeat in the future. *Developmental feedback* is just as critical for helping people build good or better working relationships and improve performance to achieve results. When delivered effectively, it lets people know what they can do to correct mistakes and helps them develop and grow professionally. However, many leaders are often hesitant to give it, and employees to accept it.

Effective feedback is more than merely saying, "Thanks" or "Nice job." While people appreciate being noticed for their hard work, vaguely worded positive feedback has little impact. The same applies to developmental feedback. To have real value and lasting effect, feedback needs to be *specific, timely,* and *balanced.* Effective feedback is also focused on the performance or behavior, and not on the person or the person's motives. Keep these principles in mind when you're asking for feedback on how you are doing.

Leaders Give Feedback All the Time—Myth or Fact?

Noted speaker Jack Welch, the former chairman and CEO of General Electric, has made many presentations in front of thousands of people. He typically asks his audience, *How many of you work for an organization that values integrity?* The majority of hands in the audience usually go up. Then he asks, *How many of you get straight-between-the-eyes, honest feedback on your performance?* Without fail, very few people raise their hands. Welch then points out that an organization can't have integrity if it fails to provide straightforward, honest feedback to its employees.[1]

And, that's our role as leaders—to support our team's job performance, growth, and development. And feedback is the key. But, as noted, it's a myth that people generally receive regular, useful feedback about their job performance. In fact, our own research shows that 42 percent of individual contributors (your team members) said that "more feedback and guidance from my new manager" would have significantly eased their transitions in their role.[2]

But, is feedback a tool to be used only with your team? No, it's an effective business tool that reaches across all levels. The most sought-after leaders coach their peers when situations arise. They also become exceptional mentors to the next generation of leaders. So, feedback can, and should, be used to help your broader team, function, and organization grow. As such, feedback not only should be regularly accepted by you, but regularly provided to your peers, customers (if appropriate), and even your boss. An organization that is populated by individuals who are skilled at sharing both positive and developmental feedback is one that has a distinct competitive edge.

Reflection Point

Let's say Jack Welch was giving a private speech to just your team. Would the members' hands have been raised in response to his second question? Why or why not?

Feedback Deflectors

It's important to take into account your team and the personalities of the people who will be on the receiving end of your feedback. We're sure you can picture thoughts like these coming out of the heads of team members when they're sitting across from you receiving feedback:

"It's not my fault. Too many elements are beyond my control. Would you like to hear who and what are to blame?"

Sydney Side-Stepper

"Are you out there to get me or to cover your own actions? I might need to improve something, but you are 10 times worse. How are you deficient—shall I count the ways?"

Augustus Aggressor

"I've been a winner my whole life. I know more about this work than most people. I'm a top expert in my job. Doesn't that count for something?"

Stephanie Star

"You have the facts wrong. I need to set you straight. Otherwise, why should I listen to you?"

Rodney Refuter

"You've always given me positive feedback before. Now you suddenly think I should improve. Why have you turned against me? How can you not remember what a good person I am?"

Belinda Betrayed

"I don't want to get along with people. The important thing is to just listen, nod, and smile. You don't really expect me to take action, do you?"

Fredrick Faker

No wonder leaders dread feedback! But as catalyst leaders, our challenge is to give feedback that is delivered in a way that is constructive and not punitive. So, don't worry; there are two sets of skills that will ensure that the feedback you give not only is delivered in an actionable fashion, but also is accepted by the receiver. We've already discussed the first skill set, which is using the Key Principles to meet the personal needs of the feedback receiver. For example, when you give developmental feedback, the best Key Principle to use is *maintain or enhance self-esteem* (particularly "maintain"), as this will help you overcome defensiveness and move toward a productive outcome. The other four Key Principles also will play a strong role, depending on the situation. Using the Empathy Key Principle will help you respond to the receiver's emotions and challenges and using involvement will help you and the receiver determine alternative approaches. To build trust, you might share a similar situation that you faced. And, you can offer support (without taking responsibility) to help move forward.

Keep the STARs Shining

The second skill set you'll need consists of a simple process—we call it the STAR approach—to deliver complete, specific feedback. If you've already reviewed the Mastery chapter on selection, you'll recognize the STAR mnemonic. In this case, STAR extends its versatility as it applies to both positive and developmental feedback.

STAR is a handy way to remember how to structure your feedback for maximum positive impact.

Giving Positive Feedback

STAR reminds you to describe:

- The Situation or Task (ST) the person or group handled, such as a problem, business opportunity, special challenge, or routine task.

- The Action (A) the person or group took, or what they actually said or did that was effective.

- The positive Result (R) or what changed for the better or how it impacted the situation.

DDI PRO TIP: Make sure your comments are:

- **Specific**—Feedback must reflect what was accomplished in terms that are precise and can be measured. For example:

- *You submitted the proposal a day ahead of your due date.*

- *As of last Friday, your sales were 101 percent of your target for the quarter.*

- *Last week's printout shows that you averaged 55 calls a day.*

- **Timely**—Praise the person's action (and any positive results) as soon as possible after it happens. The details will be fresh in your mind, and your comments will be most relevant to the work the person is currently doing. Also, timely feedback seems the most sincere, as if you were so impressed that you had to tell the person right away.

- **Balanced**—Over time, you should balance your positive feedback with developmental feedback. If all your feedback is positive, you'll miss opportunities to help people strive for higher goals. Also, people might question your sincerity if your feedback is nothing more than an endless stream of positive comments.

Giving Developmental Feedback

To give effective developmental feedback, you'll need to adapt STAR slightly and add an AR. The result, called STAR/AR reminds you to share the Situation/Task (ST), Action (A), and Result (R). Effective developmental feedback also must include:

- An *alternative* Action—what the person might have said or done instead.

- The expected *enhanced* Result—why the alternative action might have been more effective.

DDI PRO TIP: Make sure your comments are:

- **Specific**—When you specifically compare current performance to goals, people can see clearly what adjustments they need to make to ensure success in the future.

- **Timely**—You need to give feedback for improvement as soon as possible because:

  - When the details of performance are fresh, you'll be able to explain exactly what the person did that was less than effective.

  - The person receiving the feedback probably will remember what he or she did and why these actions were less than effective.

  - You'll help people make adjustments before they face similar situations.

- **Balanced**—It's important to balance developmental feedback with positive feedback in order to maintain a person's self-esteem and openness to feedback. Even when someone performed very poorly or made a major mistake, it's still possible to balance feedback—to find something the person did well and provide developmental feedback at the same time.

- **More seeking/Less telling**—Sometimes seeking the person's ideas for alternative approaches can be more effective than simply telling him or her what should or could have been said or done differently.

Here are some examples:

INCOMPLETE FEEDBACK	COMPLETE STAR OR STAR/AR
• *You did a great job in getting that hot order out yesterday.* This feedback isn't specific; the person receiving it won't know what actions to repeat. • *Jane, when you were teaching Mark to operate the system, you told him he just wasn't "getting it." He got angry and stopped asking questions. You need to go easier on him.* This feedback doesn't describe an alternative Action or the enhanced Result it would achieve.	• *You showed a lot of initiative when you discovered a problem with the shipping procedure in the order processing system* [Situation/Task]. *Instead of waiting for the supervisor to take care of it, you contacted MIS and showed them the problem* [Action]. *The system was fixed, and the materials were shipped on time* [Result]. • *Jane, when you were teaching Mark to operate the system* [Situation/Task], *you told him he just wasn't "getting it"* [Action]. *He got angry and stopped asking questions* [Result]. *A better approach would have been to acknowledge that it's difficult to operate the system and that his questions are appropriate* [Alternative action]. *That would have maintained his self-esteem and encouraged him to keep trying* [enhanced Result].

You now have the power to wisely choose the opportunities to give feedback to others. We know these skills will help you create authentic, trusting relationships with colleagues that show you have their best interest in mind. But, practice in giving and receiving feedback will be the key.

How Can Feedback, the Key Principles, and Interaction Guidelines Drive Lean Organizations?[3]

Looking for lean? Despite good faith initiatives to identify and eliminate waste, you may have overlooked an in-plain-sight source: workplace interactions.

All interactions between managers and team members are potential sources of waste. These include formal interactions (team meetings, coaching, feedback and performance discussions, and so on) and informal (e.g., phone calls, emails, instant messages, and hallway/elevator conversations)—each critical to the day-to-day operations of manufacturing groups.

And, when these interactions don't go well or aren't effective, they can add to the negative impact of the eight recognized forms of waste: defects, overproduction, downtime, underutilized skills, transportation, inventory, motion (e.g., bending, lifting, reaching), and overprocessing. The end result? Organizations fail to meet essential lean objectives: continuous improvement and improved performance.

Therefore, if we are serious about eliminating waste, we must give equal consideration to the softer side of production, or those skills that allow leaders to manage their interactions and their teams effectively. Trend research shows that the manufacturing industry is hit the hardest by the gap in these soft skills.[4] Additionally, the Accenture 2013 Global Manufacturing Study reveals that 35 percent of supervisors and 20 percent of operational leaders report having "significant" skill gaps.[5]

Mastery and Leadership Skills
16 HANDLING DIFFICULT EMPLOYEE SITUATIONS
Focus on the Behavior, Not the Person

Pre:Think
When was the last time you became angry (or hurt, or confused) by something someone did or said? What went wrong? How did it resolve? To whom did you turn for advice? What do you wish you had done differently?

Evan had recently taken on the leadership role of a 12-person call center after working as a team member for three years.

One of his newer direct reports, Judy, worked on scheduling appointments for the sales force. While she had started her job with abundant enthusiasm, she soon fell into a pattern of poor work habits, either coming in late or claiming sick days that she had already used up.

Evan was hesitant to confront Judy. All of his other team members were above-average performers, and he had yet to have a discussion with anyone regarding performance issues. After a month or so, he began getting complaints from his other team members about Judy. Not only was she not carrying her weight, they said, but she was bringing down the entire team's performance levels. Evan wisely sought advice from his manager, who encouraged him to take action and helped him plan the discussion. While not easy, Evan's task was relatively straightforward: He had to make Judy see that she needed to start turning around her performance or leave.

Jing, a leader for two years, was in a more difficult situation with Sam, a one-year super IT programmer. Sam was well liked outside his team, got most of his projects done on time, and had high work standards. Just one minor problem! Everyone else on Jing's team detested him. Sam was uncooperative, would talk about his peers behind their backs, and was constantly complaining to Jing about others. (He made the mistake of bad-mouthing Jing, as well.) Unfortunately for Sam, he needed other team members' support to do his work. So, when two of Sam's team members asked for a transfer, Jing knew she had to act. It was going to be a difficult conversation.

These real stories hint at some of the messy interpersonal situations you'll likely encounter as a new leader. They can be annoying and upsetting for a number of reasons. No matter the size of your team, the nature of your business, or how good you become at selecting team members, you cannot completely avoid all the possible failures, conflicts, and squabbles that can happen whenever people work together. And now it's your job to deal with them.

First, the good news: 85 percent of your employees are likely to be just fine. The other 15 percent? Some of the time you'll have to confront very serious issues. But, most likely, the employees in that 15 percent bracket are not bad people—there are often good reasons behind their behavior.

But to turn these situations around, you must focus on the behavior that needs to change, and our number one rule is to not attack the character or personality of the individuals involved. We like to say, *Be hard on the issues and soft on the people*. Not only is it the right thing to do, but by focusing your feedback and coaching on the situation, not the person, you are far less likely to evoke strong negative emotion and far more likely to achieve a positive resolution.

To turn disruptive situations around, you'll need to focus on the behavior that needs to change, not the person. We like to say, *Be hard on the issues and soft on the people.*

Doing Nothing Is Not an Option

This is the part of the job that leaders fear most. These conversations can be fraught with strong emotions and stronger words, which came out loud and clear during our interviews. And even those leaders who can muster the courage to address such situations directly often lack the skills to do so. But, at the end of the day, you can't ignore a difficult employee's behavior for a number of important reasons:

You Owe It to the Employee

Employees have the right to know where they stand. More often than not, open and constructive coaching can put a person back on the right path, avoiding what could lead to more severe consequences for her future and yours.

You Owe It to Yourself

When things get messy, every leader we've ever interviewed suffers. Stress, sleepless nights, self-doubt. That's no fun. And even one of these issues can become a drain on your time that will keep you from hitting your own goals. One new leader we coached confessed that he was spending more than 20 percent of his time on a single employee issue. What was he not getting done? How was the rest of the team being affected?

You Owe It to Your Team

An employee like Judy or Sam can play havoc on team collaboration, morale, and engagement. The other members don't deserve it! And, they'll point fingers at you for not holding the person accountable for the team's poor performance and/or lack of collaboration.

You Owe It to Your Organization

Even a single interpersonal mess can hurt your organization's performance. In a world where the quality of talent is the number one factor in a company's ability to perform, you cannot afford to have these unhelpful behaviors define the culture. In some cases, severe violations of company policies, substance abuse, sexual harassment, safety violations, and the like can lead to serious and costly legal consequences you don't want on your shoulders. In these cases, probation or termination may be in order. If you confront those types of situations, we strongly suggest you seek counsel from your HR team, which will likely help you with the discussion and avoid risky legal issues.

Eight Tips to Get Results

We absolutely believe that as a leader you are a powerful, creative, and indispensible force for good in society. But you're not a mind reader, nor are you a psychiatrist (most likely). You may discover that the employees you'll be coaching have personal issues beyond your scope that make it necessary to enlist your HR contact for help. But by approaching the entire situation with empathy and planning—and considering the personal and practical needs of all involved—you'll be better able to help your team consistently work well together. The following tips can help.

Start with a Comprehensive Hiring Process

In Chapter 10 ("Hiring and Selecting the Best") we showed you how to choose team members in ways that lead to top employee performance and engagement. For now, let's say it this way: The right hiring decisions today will save you considerable headaches in the future.

Ensure Expectations for Performance Are Always Crystal Clear

How can you possibly tell me I missed my goals? ranted Malu. *You never gave me any!* Yes, this happens more often that we would like. Use your company's performance management system to set expectations each year. Include both the "whats" (quantitative goals) and the "hows" (behaviors/competencies). And, review them with employees regularly. Clear expectations equal fewer surprises! See Chapter 18 ("Performance Management") for more help.

Pinpoint the Situation

At the end of this chapter we included a handful of situations—with some familiar characters—you may encounter and some advice on how to prepare for each one. Use it as a starting point to plan your conversations. Handling an employee who has tuned out is often much different than dealing with an employee who offends others by being a constant know-it-all.

An Ounce of Planning Is Worth a Pound of Cure

Plan your approach and conversation in advance. If the situation is serious or is likely to involve formal consequences like probation or termination, seek guidance from your HR specialists. One thing you can count on—employees are likely to ask for specifics: *What did I do wrong?* Make sure you seek and use real data (see the sidebar coming up for more). And we cannot stress this enough: As you prepare to speak with them, you should review how you will use the Interaction Guidelines and Key Principles. Using these skills will remind you to speak to the person and not react to the problem.

All-Around Coaching

Coaching, as we covered in Chapter 14, is one of your most important leadership roles. When you coach *proactively*, by helping your team members do things right from the start, it not only builds their confidence, but it also helps to prevent problems from occurring in the first place—a far better place to be. Better to learn from success than failure. But when you must react to a team member gone astray, coach for improvement *sooner* rather than later.

Keep Notes

Don't rely on your memory. Discussions with problem employees should be documented for three reasons. First, documentation helps you and them keep track of your agreements over time. Second, it keeps you on track for your next (of many) coaching conversation. And third, it ensures that there will be no misinterpretation later about what you discussed. (*I never said that, I didn't agree to that, I never knew it was a serious problem.*) If problems become severe enough to lead to disciplinary action or even termination, documentation will become even more crucial. It might very well be used as part of a legal proceeding in some countries, should the employee accuse you of wrongful treatment.

Be Prepared for Multiple Conversations

It might take several coaching and feedback sessions to reverse the negative trend. If you take two steps forward and one step back, that's OK—it's still progress. Always schedule follow-up meetings to review where things stand and to clarify the process. Positive feedback is also critical. If (when) things begin to turn for the better, let the person know with sincere, positive feedback. One supervisor told us she had five different meetings with one of her team members over a period of two months. It was worth it! The person has become one of her top performers.

Don't Get Hooked Emotionally

Your commitment to good leadership is admirable. And it's not a bad sign that you care about the employee, or that you're nervous about giving feedback. But others' problems can quickly become your problems. And to make matters worse, some employees may attack you personally—*It's all your fault.* Many leaders stay awake all night blaming themselves for an employee's or team's poor behavior. But, that doesn't mean it's your fault! Besides feeling sorry for yourself, you might also feel like you and you alone are on the hook for solving the mess. Take a breath. Your *role* is to help the employee understand that something needs to change. Then your *job* is to help *him* come up with solutions. And, in most cases, it should be the employee's solution, not yours. Your *goal* is to provide support without removing the person's responsibility and accountability for addressing the issues.

Using Data

Lack of specific data can quickly cause a performance discussion to go awry. Look for the employee to challenge your facts: *Give me some examples.* It's impossible to expect improvement if you can't clearly define the problem with data to back you up. Quantitative data is relatively easy to find; you can cite the number of times a person came in late or how many deadlines they missed. Behavioral data is more difficult. That's where STAR feedback (see Chapter 15) comes in handy. It enables you to gather feedback around both positive and negative behaviors. In discussions of poor performance, it's important to include quantitative and behavioral data, particularly when temperatures are running hot. Here's an example of how you can employ STAR:

S/T (Situation/Task)—*You participated in a team meeting last week on a new software system.*

A (Action)—*You constantly interrupted the discussion and refused to listen to other ideas.*

R (Result)—*Everyone in the meeting shut down. Clearly, they had no desire to continue participating. To make matters worse, we never were able to agree on a course of action.*

So, What Happened?

Remember Judy and Sam at the start of this chapter? After a series of emotional conversations, Judy was able to be candid, and got help resolving some personal issues. She became a great team member again. Sam wasn't open to feedback and had some other issues. He ultimately left the company. Hey, it happens.

Approaching a challenging employee should be viewed as an opportunity to help the person address the problem and get back on track. And on the rare occasion it doesn't, you do the person no favors by allowing his bad behavior to continue and ruin his career prospects going forward. But the key to success lies in the skills you use in your many coaching and feedback conversations (see Chapters 14 and 15). You'll find these skills paramount to every conversation you'll have as a leader.

We've also developed a helpful, somewhat lighthearted, guide that depicts some common difficult situations you might encounter, along with some advice for handling them.

Your Guide to Handling Difficult Employee Situations

While we believe the best way to handle problem employees is to focus on the situation, not the person, sometimes descriptions and illustrations aid our understanding of the types of people and situations that may consistently present the same challenges over and over again. Each "What to do?" section provides practical tips for handling each respective employee situation.

THE INVISIBLES

 Their cubicles are still empty at 9:30 a.m., and at the end of the work day, you see them walking out the door earlier than everyone else. Invisibles accept meeting requests but find an excuse to decline at the last minute, and they never join any team or company events. When they make a rare appearance at a meeting, their eyes are glued to laptops and smartphones. You must follow up on tasks assigned to them at least three times before you can get anything completed—and you have to do it via email or voice mail because Invisibles are nowhere to be seen.

What to Do?

Collect details of their poor work habits and their impact on the team. Discuss by focusing on the facts, seeking input on solutions to improve work habits in the future, and agreeing on a workable plan. If there's still no improvement on their chronic tardiness and absenteeism, it might be time for a more formal warning.

THE ZOMBIES

Sometimes good performers suddenly drag their feet, stare through dull, lifeless eyes, and just go through the motions of work until it's time to shut down. Something must have switched them off—perhaps a poorly managed conflict or a dearth of new challenges. Completely apathetic and disengaged, Zombies can easily bite and turn peers into sleepwalkers or slackers like themselves. So, immediate action from you is necessary.

What to Do?

Start by maintaining self-esteem; remember, Zombies were once good performers. Openly discuss what is weighing them down and what, if anything, will bring them back. Listen and respond with empathy and determine immediate next steps to address concerns. It might be time for a new project or team, or a completely new role, to bring a Zombie back to life.

THE VOLCANOES

Volcanoes are unpredictable and volatile with constant mood swings. While they might seem calm and dormant most days, there are emotions bubbling beneath the surface. An eruption can happen any time—and usually unexpectedly—spewing fireballs and ash on you, the entire team, and worse, your customers. Peers tiptoe around Volcanoes, not knowing when an explosion will come next.

What to Do?

Provide feedback on how mood swings affect others unintentionally, yet significantly. Revisit recent eruptions and determine if there are specific triggers to be aware of and address. Ask for their help and ideas on how to keep things on a more even keel.

THE SELFIES

Attention-seeking Selfies take every opportunity to post about their latest activities or tasks in the hope of getting a million likes from everyone. They're people pleasers, yet are clueless that everyone rolls their eyes with every shameless self-promotion at yet another meeting. Selfies are ultracompetitive and feel entitled to get every perk and incentive available, including that promotion they're clearly not ready for. The bottom line? It's all about them!

What to Do?

Provide honest feedback that this self-centered behavior is turning others off and negatively affecting the self-image they're trying very hard to promote. Reassure them that their efforts are getting the appropriate attention. Refocus competition by reminding the Selfie that the real competition is outside your organization!

THE STATUES

Statues stand tall and smug on a pedestal, feeling far superior to the teammates they tower over. Statues have touted their strengths and convinced those in the higher ranks that they deserve all the praise and accolades. In reality, Statues are typically hollow and hardly move—or do any of the real work. Although Statues depend on others to get things done, they typically try to put down their peers so they can continue to be the most admired and respected people on the team.

What to Do?

Disclose and share the negative impact Statues have on others and on their own self-image. Reinforce the message that it's not all about them by showcasing the strengths other team members bring. To help them step off the pedestal, provide feedback on their development areas as well as concrete opportunities where they can work with their peers.

THE WALLFLOWERS

 Wallflowers shift their gaze and avoid eye contact, not wanting to cause a ripple. You know they have a good head on their shoulders, but there are hardly any comments or questions from them. And Wallflowers always wait to be approached or told what to do, almost as if they're embarrassed to contribute. When asked for their ideas or input, they simply shrug and say, *Whatever works for you* or *Whatever you want* to stay safe and avoid responsibility.

What to Do?

Remind Wallflowers that you don't have all the answers and that you expect all team members to bring their ideas and solutions to the team. Encourage Wallflowers to take independent action within their area of responsibility. Provide specific tasks they can do on their own or with others (and support without removing responsibility!), then reinforce successes to build confidence and initiative.

THE BLACK CLOUDS

 Black Clouds bring heaviness and bad blah vibes as they sulk, badmouth others, and whine. Black Clouds are classic victims and take every opportunity to brood and complain about the situation at hand instead of seeking more information. They have trouble seeing the good in others and spread suspicion, fear, and negativity in the workplace.

What to Do?

Clarify and seek to understand the root cause of discontent or fears, and identify concrete ways to address their concerns. Show empathy as appropriate and ask for their help and ideas on what needs to change or improve. Provide feedback on how their mood and disposition negatively affect others and the team's output.

Mastery and Leadership Skills
17 DELEGATION
Be a Delegator, Not a Dumper

Pre:Think

Have you ever had a boss who dumped a task on you, providing little or no instruction regarding requirements or coaching to help you succeed? How did that feel? How did you cope? How do **you** want to be thought of as a leader—as a delegator or as a dumper?

To Delegate or Not to Delegate, That Is the Question

Let's face it: All too often leaders hold onto tasks and activities that they clearly should let go. So, what holds *you* back? Do you:

- Keep tasks because you believe short-term results may suffer as the person you delegate to gains experience?

- Avoid delegating developmental assignments because of the time and effort required to ensure the person's success?

- Worry about becoming expendable if you delegate more tasks?

- Fall into the trap of delegating to the same people over and over again because you know they'll do the job?

- Avoid delegating to your team because you know each member is too busy?

- Keep tasks because you fear that people would do the work differently than the way you'd like to see it done?

If you're like many first-time leaders, you clearly don't have the time or capacity to do everything yourself. But delegating tasks can be daunting, particularly if you're reluctant to give up the kind of work you enjoy or are worried about losing momentum on a project if the delegated work isn't up to standard right away. It's tempting to do the math this way: *If I'm spending more time helping others than it would take to do the work myself, it's just not worth it.* But that math doesn't add up. Not only is it a fast track to burnout (yours), but it's a surefire way to get your team feeling bored, mistrusted, stifled, and unimportant. You'll end up getting less work done, not more. And by underdelegating, you ensure that your organization is staffed with individuals who aren't prepared to take on new challenges in the marketplace as they arise. Sure, you want to get work done, but you also want everyone to contribute to the company and grow their skills while they're at it. DDI's data bears this out. In our 360-assessments (your peers, boss, and direct reports), delegation is one of leaders' lowest-rated skills.[1] In other words, it ranks among the competencies with the highest percentage of development needs.[2]

We have a way of defining delegation that helps you avoid the mistakes that many leaders, new or established, make—and ensure that you're delegating, not dumping.

> **Delegation Defined:** *Continually looking for and following through on opportunities to achieve results and/or build capability by assigning task and decision-making responsibilities to individuals or teams with clear boundaries, support, and follow-up.*

Let's unpack this. Delegation is a critical leadership tool that allows you to free your time to focus on other key initiatives. At the same time, it's much more than just assigning tasks to people. Rather, it's a tool for ensuring that every member of your team is contributing to business results and continually developing new skills and expertise. Your job is to scan the landscape and look for opportunities to match the right people with the right tasks that can accomplish both. If you're successful, you'll unlock your time, skills, and abilities to yield the greatest benefits for everyone. It's good for you, your team, your company, and your customers. And looking for these opportunities should become second nature to you.

The process of delegating lies in "whats," "who's," and "hows." Ask yourself:

1. *What* should I delegate, and what should I keep? (Allocating work in the right way.)

2. How do I decide *who* gets what? (Giving the work to the right people.)

3. *How* do I effectively communicate the decision? (Addressing your team's personal and practical needs.)

4. *How* do I follow up? (Monitoring and coaching on the delegated tasks.)

Need a little coaching from Tacy? Her video will help you understand how to delegate with purpose—and confidence. Find it at our microsite.

What Should I Delegate, and What Should I Keep?

To think about how to allocate the work in the right way, it's important to understand *authority*. Specifically, the authority that the person receiving the task will have in three key areas: To *make decisions* about the work, to *utilize resources*, and to *solve problems*. You'll need to make some important decisions about what authority to give up, when, and why. There are four basic categories to consider:

Keep the Task

Hold onto the authority and responsibility for handling the task. You'll most likely keep a task when it is exclusively in your area of responsibility, such as a performance problem that can threaten the group's results. (Most things related to personnel issues probably should stay with you.) Additionally, you'll want to keep the task when others aren't qualified or can't meet the deadlines.

Delegate the Idea Generation

Assign responsibility for generating ideas or thinking through a situation. Delegating in this way is appropriate when you want the benefit of others' expertise or perspectives, or when you want to build commitment by involving people who will be affected by the ideas or decisions generated. Don't make this an empty exercise! If you're not prepared to accept the ideas that come up (within limits), you'll send the message that you don't trust your people. Not only is that demotivating, but you'll also lose credibility.

Delegate the Task

Assign responsibility for completing a well-defined task that involves little or no decision-making authority. In this case you, as the leader, retain the idea generation, but simply delegate the activity to complete the task. These are the kinds of tasks that must be done by the book but offer an opportunity for a team member to try something new. For example, if your business is heavily regulated, then you could use of this type of delegation, with clear guidelines, with a new team member over a few projects.

Delegate the Authority

Assign responsibility for completing a well-defined task that involves defined decision-making authority. This is a big one. When others are qualified to make bigger decisions or can perform the task with a bit of coaching, then this is a perfect opportunity to delegate authority for the entirety of the task. For example, instead of you on-boarding the new team member on project management, why not let your two senior project leaders do the training? Eventually, the new person would be working closely with these team leaders anyway, and it will help build their skills together.

Take a moment now to think about how you spend your time at work. What tasks or responsibilities could you delegate to achieve results faster and more effectively? What new roles are you taking on? Which ones can you delegate? What tasks can you delegate to free up more of your time to focus on top priority objectives? Use Tool 17.1 to help you.

DDI PRO TIP: Ask your peers what types of tasks and assignments they typically delegate, and then ask them to share any lessons learned and benefits they've realized.

What Should I Delegate?

Instructions: Reflect on the four categories described on the previous pages and write your tasks on the simple chart below. (Note: This is a great notebook exercise for you to repeat regularly.) When done, celebrate! You've created your delegation to-do list, full of what to keep and what to delegate to your team.

Keep the Task

❑ _____

❑ _____

❑ _____

Delegate the Idea Generation

❑ _____

❑ _____

❑ _____

Delegate the Task

❑ _____

❑ _____

❑ _____

Delegate the Authority

❑ _____

❑ _____

❑ _____

How Do I Decide Who Gets What?

Throughout this book, we've encouraged you to have lots of conversations with others. The pre-delegation conversations you'll have, especially as a new leader, will be the key to helping you figure out which person is right for what assignment. But these conversations shouldn't stop once you've been in your role for a while! If you're doing your job, your team's capabilities will be growing measurably right away. Rethink the possibilities each time you decide to delegate a task.

 DDI PRO TIP: Consider the impact that delegating a certain assignment to a team member will have on the rest of the team. Will some people be upset that they weren't chosen for the job? Will the new task hinder the team member's progress in other tasks? How will it affect the team's results?

The four questions below can help you identify the best candidate for each delegation from Tool 17.1. Engage the process, even if you think you already know the answers:

- **Abilities**—Does this person have the knowledge and skills needed to handle the task/responsibility?

- **Availability**—Does this person have time to take this on? Could his work be reprioritized?

- **Motivation**—Is this person motivated to handle this delegation?

- **Development Needs**—Does this person have a development need, or is this an opportunity to build the team's capability?

Let's explore the final question. It's crucial to understand that most delegations are developmental, meaning that they help people develop new skills while still meeting business goals. In fact, it's rare for one not to have some developmental aspect, even for experienced people. When you set someone on a path to learn by doing, which is what delegation often means, it will be important for you to make sure she has what she needs to succeed.

How Do I Effectively Communicate the Decision?

By now you should have a sense of how important communication is to your leadership career. The Key Principles and Interaction Guidelines are the bones upon which you can build an effective communication strategy for any priority. Use Figure 17.1 as a handy reference for how to optimize these interaction skills for a delegation discussion.

17.1 Conducting the Delegation Discussion

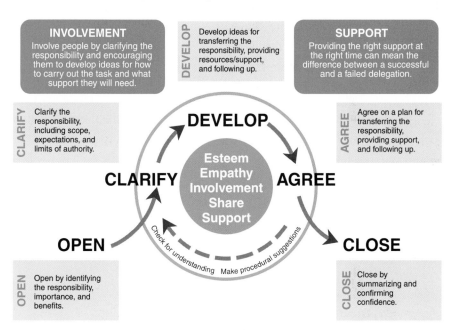

How Do I Follow Up (and Avoid Being a Dumper)?

In our Pre:Think, we asked you about dumping. We've all been there. Leaders typically dump out of desperation. Your manager may have needed something done and didn't have the time or energy, so she piled it onto your plate and let you deal with it entirely—only to expect it back complete with a bow on top.

Well, the rescue is here for these struggling, desperate leaders. Follow-up is the key to ensure you're never seen as a dumper! When it comes to follow-up, it's important to agree on how you'll *monitor* progress, coach when needed, and *measure* success. If you don't, you risk setting up people for failure.

Monitoring refers to the methods used to observe and track progress as the person carries out the delegated task. Monitoring methods allow you to make adjustments, if needed, before performance begins to slip. These methods also provide opportunities to reinforce performance when people make progress. For example, a leader could monitor a team member's progress by observing her initial meetings and then following up to provide performance feedback and ongoing coaching. You'll find that it's better to monitor closely at first. You can step back as the person gains experience.

Measuring refers to the performance outcomes, standards, or measures against which you, the person, and perhaps others will evaluate results of the delegated tasks. *Results measures* provide specific, objective targets—in terms of quality, quantity, cost, or timeliness—against which people can measure their outcomes. These targets also enable you and the person to gauge the impact of the delegation on key business results. It will ease your burden if you encourage people to gather feedback and other performance data as they handle the responsibility. This beats waiting for a formal report or feedback. Self-measurement is more empowering because it puts the responsibility for success squarely in the hands of the person doing the job.

Together you'll need to agree on monitoring and measurement methods that work for each person—methods that consider your needs and the experience and personal needs of your team member. But keep in mind that a leader who over-controls can demotivate someone pretty quickly. It's all about finding the right balance for your comfort level and theirs.

It's counterintuitive, but staying in touch with a delegated task is actually the means of letting go and ultimately empowering people to own the task, with you in a support role.

It's counterintuitive, but staying in touch with a delegated task is actually the means of letting go and ultimately empowering people to own the task, with you in a support role. And this is at the heart of the last Key Principle—provide support without removing responsibility. During your delegation conversation, be sure to clarify and agree on the level of support you'll provide as the leader. Or, in the situation mentioned earlier about on-boarding a new associate, that support would come from your team leaders, who would keep you informed of progress.

TECH TIP!! Sometimes a lightweight check-in is all someone needs to stay confident and motivated. Follow up using multiple communication channels. Impromptu check-ins can be done using virtually any method, including emails, texts, instant messaging, and so on: *Just noticed you hit your most recent deadline! Keep going! The next one might be tougher; ping if you need me.*

Additionally, you might want to consider flagging your delegations in your task list, or setting email reminders via any of the new apps available today. They help you, as a leader, to check back in at the appropriate time.

No! Don't Take the Monkey Back!

One of the hardest things for you to resist will be what we call *reverse delegation*, where you let someone who has hit a snag give back some (or all!) of the task to complete. (Even worse, you snatch it back as you get anxious.) Think back to the leader walking around with all of his monkeys (delegated tasks) on his shoulders from Chapter 7. Resist the impulse! Instead, recognize that these moments are a signal for you to provide more or different support.

To keep the task monkeys happily perched where they belong, you'll need to coach your team early and often. These ongoing coaching conversations will help you determine how things are going and get ahead of any obstacles. Your interactions can be either formal or informal, and might be as simple as a "How's it going?" text. But your job is to have the person effectively handle the task or responsibility on her own, from start to finish. So, delegation doesn't stop at the first handoff meeting. It's a journey that you take together.

> **Formal discussions** are planned milestone meetings to assess progress, provide feedback and coaching, address any concerns, and readjust the initial plan based on the person's progress.
>
> **Informal discussions** can happen at any time through impromptu conversations or quick check-ins. The goal is to proactively address any challenges or problems the person might encounter and to provide additional coaching and support.

When you have these conversations, be sure to ask open-ended questions, which help people evaluate their own progress and identify things that are worrying them. So, rather than plan for what you will tell the person, plan for what you will ask.

DDI PRO TIP: Don't assume that the person doesn't need help. People often are hesitant to ask for assistance because you have entrusted them to take on this task or responsibility. In their minds, asking for help may be perceived as a sign of weakness.

Finally, if you're really sensing trouble on the horizon, it might be wise to enlist other stakeholders as allies to give feedback and, if appropriate, to share suggestions and advice. If you feel you need to step in, step lightly! Emotions can run high when a project gets shaky. Revisit and adjust your plan for responsibility, authority, support, and follow-up based on the person's progress. And stay positive.

You live in an exciting time with ever-increasing demands on your company, team, family, and yourself. Preparing people to meet these demands is good for everyone. As a leader, you can't afford not to share the wealth that experience brings, and neither can your team.

Mastery and Leadership Skills
18 PERFORMANCE MANAGEMENT
An Ongoing Cycle, Not an Event

Pre:Think

Consider the following two questions. First: *Do you want your boss to tell you how you're doing at work?* And second: *Do you enjoy doing performance appraisals?* If you're like most people we've surveyed, the first answer is a resounding yes, and the second is an emphatic no. This is the paradox of performance management.

Beating the System

The simplest way to explain what good performance management should do is to help people—managers and individual contributors alike—understand how they're meeting their job's objectives and growing as professionals. And if you hover over its strategic purpose, performance management enables your company to execute on its business strategy by creating alignment of priorities up and down the organization and accountability toward these goals. So, if your company is like most, there's probably some sort of performance management system in place that you'll be asked to use. These systems are often computer based and provide consolidated reporting to senior management. You might need to use specific forms. The information you gather—the goals set, milestones achieved, and the like—is often used to generate a number or other rating that the company uses to evaluate each employee. The entire process can feel stressful and awkward and often shuts down, rather than encourages, meaningful discussion. But it doesn't have to!

Like many organizational systems, performance management is an *imperfect but necessary* component of today's complex businesses. And you shouldn't just pencil it in as an annual event. Performance management should be part of a larger cycle of performance thinking that takes place all year long. But you should make the system work for you. This chapter can help you redesign your existing performance management duties into a series of meaningful conversations that can enable your employees to feel more secure, engaged, and poised to grow. But before we move into the specifics of how to have these conversations, let's review two points that will help you understand the bigger picture of performance management.

It's Not about You

A number of years ago a direct report complained to Rich, *I have 10 people on my team. I don't have time to do all those performance reviews.* To which Rich (wisely) replied, *You don't have to do 10 reviews. You only need to do one—yours.* In other words, employees need to own their performance and the conversation about it. And you need to show them how.

Each of your direct reports should play the primary role of collecting performance data, summarizing results, and even suggesting preliminary ratings. Partly, this is a practical approach. You can't make people perform better. But you can coach, guide, and support them to better understand where they are in their own development journey. But there is a personal component here as well. People who track their own performance data are more likely to course-correct early if something goes wrong and are more engaged overall. Now, it might seem like you're giving up control of the conversation, but you're not. Your job is to manage the process—meeting timelines, ensuring that the right data is brought to the discussion, and using the right rating criteria—and, most importantly, manage the performance discussion. (We'll talk more about this shortly.)

 TECH TIP!! Encourage your team members to use email to ask key people—including you!—for feedback during and after big accomplishments like presentations, meetings, or project milestones. Have them identify a specific project or skill. A quick note—*I'm trying to improve my work on data visualizations. What did you think of the graphics in the presentation? What could have gone better?*—helps them track progress during the year and gives them rich data to discuss with you at performance review time.

Be a Coach, Not a Judge

Many performance management systems (and common perceptions of the boss) set up the leader as an appraiser or evaluator of the employee. Part of it is by design: Many of the systems you'll be using generate a number (or series of numbers) that grade people on their performance. Most people dread this, and with good reason. David Rock and the NeuroLeadership Institute suggest that judging conversations about what you did or didn't do well last year puts the brain in a fear state that limits our ability as humans to absorb information.[1] It's a fairly big design flaw, and it can get in the way of real moments of insight about your performance.

You can hack the system easily by framing the performance management process as a series of coaching conversations instead of a single review discussion. And, how do you deliver on that promise? You coach and develop people every week throughout the year and use periodic reviews (at least one at midyear). In this way, the end-of-year discussion is more of that ongoing coach/review cycle than an appraisal.

As the team's leader, you'll need to know each person's performance and development goals and be ready to proactively provide coaching and feedback—and, you should be documenting results along the way. So, when the midyear or year-end review comes along, you and your direct report will summarize the results and agree on a rating. Figure 18.1 shows how coaching and performance are closely linked. It's your job to keep them linked.

FIG 18.1 The Performance Cycle: A Guide for Leaders

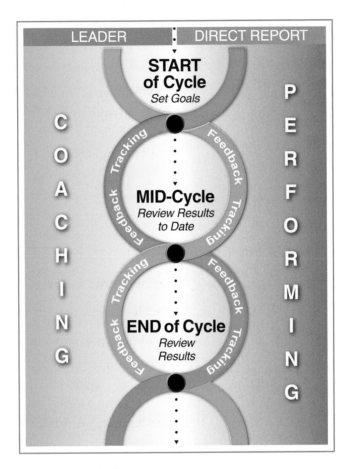

Setting Goals

Each performance cycle (usually a year in length) starts with goal setting. There are two types of equally important goals: Performance and behavioral. Think of it this way: Performance goals describe "what" a person should do, and behavioral goals describe "how" they should do it. You've probably worked with someone who was good at getting things done—while alienating his coworkers. And it's likely that you worked with someone who was easy to get along with, but didn't perform well. Your job is to coach and develop both the whats and the hows. Let's start with the whats.

Making Performance Goals SMART (the "Whats")

Most organizations advocate writing performance goals that meet certain criteria. We call them SMART goals; your organization might use another formula that is similar. Well-written SMART goals are your anchor for coaching and performance discussions.

If you're not familiar with how to write SMART goals, look at the following short tutorial. Here is an important tip: Don't skip any parts of SMART, or you'll pay for it in the review, especially if the person is underperforming. One missing component can lead to misunderstanding or even arguments: *I thought the deadline was February. You can't change it now.*

Criteria for Well-Written Goals

SMART stands for:

Specific—defines specific results to be achieved.

Measurable—defines quantity, cost, or quality metrics to determine progress.

Attainable—allows for a challenging, yet achievable, goal.

Relevant—supports the achievement of team or organizational goals.

Time bound—specifies a due date, time frame, or frequency rate.

Tips for Writing SMART Goals

- Start each goal with an action verb (for example, "increase," "complete," "attain").

- Define quantity, cost, timeliness, and/or quality as well as any due dates or time frames.

- Avoid writing all-or-nothing goals. For example, "Train everyone in the department on the new software system by the end of the third quarter" is a goal that's either met or it's not. Instead, provide flexibility, such as a range, to make the goal more attainable: "Train 95 to 100 percent of the department . . ."

- Don't mistake tasks or activities for performance goals. For example, "Poll service representatives to find out if they're seeing certain trends in product usage" might be one of many tasks to be completed to achieve a performance goal.

- Make sure each goal is observable. The results of the person's efforts need to be evident to you and others who will provide feedback on performance.

- Limit the number of goals to between one and three for each major output of the job. This makes the overall performance plan realistic. You always can add or modify as needed.

- Ask the direct report: *Does this goal benefit you, our team, and the organization?* If not, consider rewriting it.

Formula for Writing SMART Goals

You and your direct reports can use this three-part formula to write performance goals that meet the SMART criteria.

Start with an **action verb**, such as:	Include a **measurement**, such as:	Include a **due date, time frame, or frequency rate**, such as:
Increase . . .	How much	Phase 1 by end of second quarter
Complete . . .	How many	End of fiscal year
Attain . . .	How much better	Daily
Achieve . . .	How much faster	Weekly
Reduce . . .	Costing how much less	As scheduled

Examples:

Action Verb	Measurement	Due Date

Decrease shipping errors by **3 to 5 percent** by the end of the third quarter.

Achieve an **average minimum rating of 3 on a 5-point scale** in each quarterly customer satisfaction audit.

Reduce patient wait time to **20 minutes** by the end of the fiscal year.

Behavioral Expectations (the "Hows")

Behavioral goals describe the expectations for *how* the person will accomplish the performance goals. We've talked a lot about behavior in this book, and this is one reason why. Sometimes we see organizations use the terms "competencies," "values," or even "roles" to describe the *how*. You don't need a behavioral goal for every performance goal; in fact five to seven competencies are usually enough for each person's job. For example, to perform effectively, a frontline service provider likely needs to have a real handle on customer service, contributing to team success, quality orientation, and adaptability. Part of your role as leader is to identify the most important *hows* in the person's plan and link them to the related performance goals.

Gathering data on behaviors is a bit trickier than the often-quantitative SMART goals. Using the STAR technique (Chapter 15) is a good way to do this. Both you and your team members should gather STARs throughout the performance cycle. Encourage your direct reports to not only prepare their own STARs, but to also seek them from others (e.g., peers, customers, suppliers, and so on).

> Competencies are clusters of related behaviors that are associated with success or failure in a job.

Guiding Performance Conversations

Unfortunately, most performance management systems draw attention away from the most important thing—the goal-setting and performance review discussions and all the coaching conversations you'll have with your team members in between. Leaders (and employees) focus too much on completing the form and generating performance ratings; they speed through what's needed most—a candid, transparent, two-way discussion of expected versus actual performance. (In fact, we suspect that too many leaders use the form and the system as a way to *avoid* a frank discussion.)

As we saw at the top of this chapter, people want to know where they stand and how they're doing; this is your chance to have them tell you. Yes, you read that correctly. Because people own their performance, they should own the performance discussion, which means they should have the most air time. You can encourage and reinforce this by guiding the conversation: *So, what do you have for the next goal?* and *Given the data you've collected, how would you rate performance on this goal—"below," "above," or "meets expectations"?*

Most leaders fear that employees will talk only about the positives, ignore negative feedback, and overrate their performance. However, we've found the opposite to be true—especially if you've been having coaching discussions throughout the performance cycle. Most people will talk candidly about their successes and areas where they came up short. And more often, they'll underrate their performance rather than overrate it. Either way, it's important to let the employee go first and find out how she views her performance before you either agree and reinforce the rating, or disagree and start a discussion around why.

The Boss Is Still the Boss

We've avoided (even rejected) the term *boss* so far, but it applies here. Relative to performance management, you are responsible for the final judgment on performance ratings. If, after an honest discussion of performance, you disagree with a direct report, it's your rating, as the boss, that goes into the system. Most performance management systems provide an opportunity for employee comments, and you should encourage the person to express any disagreements there, but in the end, the organization expects you to be the boss. And that's the really good news.

If you break up performance management conversations into small, lighter-weight, but meaningful, chunks throughout the year, the review at the end isn't something for either of you to dread. Instead, it becomes an opportunity to celebrate everything that's been accomplished, even to relive some of the wonderful *We did it!* stories that people who work together should share more often. Any serious problems that may have occurred have already been surfaced in previous conversations, so there are no surprises. And if any problems persist, there are plans in place to address them. This kind of performance review helps you find out what's really going on with your team, and helps team members find their best fit in the organization.

If you can master this, not only will your performance review system be good for your team and the organization, but it will also transform you into a leader whom people trust and admire.

Mastery and Leadership Skills
19 YOU AND YOUR NETWORK
Nurture Your Business Relationships

Pre:Think

If you had a problem in your life, to whom would you reach out for advice? Why? Make a list of at least five names. Now, who in your personal life reaches out to you for help? Why? Make a list of at least five names.

It *Is* Who You Know

The idea of a belonging to a network intimidates many people. There are many reasons for this—all of them perfectly reasonable. For many of us, networking feels like a cringe-inducing chore, filled with awkward conversations with people who can't really help you anyway. Is networking even a real thing? What's the point?

This feeling has only gotten more profound as the world has gone digital. Today, social networks now define information overload. Our online lives can seem like an always-on fire hose of data with the good stuff you might need for work wedged in between checking Instagram and taking lunchtime selfies. Even if you're sold on the idea of a network, it's hard to know how to build a good one or if your efforts are paying off. Maybe you just hate asking other people for things, like help. Or, maybe you aren't really a people person. Humans can be challenging, we agree.

We've talked a great deal in this book about leadership as a human endeavor, and a deeply rewarding one at that. And we promise you this: You'll find fewer areas that provide as much benefit in your leadership career than your network. And yes, you do already have one. All around you in your organization (and in your life) there are people who can share valuable information about how you can be better at your job and become a happier, more relaxed leader. You're a resource for others as well! When nurtured, these relationships blossom into partnerships you can lean on to navigate even the most difficult work situations. A strong network is a valuable resource to guide you through the complexity of work today.

A strong network is a valuable resource to guide you through the complexity of work today.

You've heard us talk about the matrix in previous chapters. Today, nobody works as an island, alone. That's part of what we mean by *complexity*. Your job depends on getting work done through people who may or may not report to you, who may not work anywhere near you, and whose lives you may know little about. They might be more senior than you in the organization, or not. And information no longer comes only from the guy in the corner office who deals out the marching orders. Information about everything—from customer needs and product changes, to developments at your company, to best practices in your field—now bombards you from all angles. You might not even see your boss very much anyway! You can't Google the really important stuff, like how to get along with specific people and remove institutional roadblocks.

To be able to do your job more quickly and efficiently, it really *is* who you know. But unlike social networking, this is not about who will *follow you*. It's about who will *respond* to you. And that requires developing personal connections, even if you're not a people person.

Not all networks are equal. The type of goal you want to achieve will dictate which network you'll reach out to. Every leader needs five kinds of networks[1]:

- An *idea network* to spark innovation and offer advice on new ways to solve problems.

- A *development network* of individuals who are invested in your growth.

- A *social network* of close relationships from which to seek advice and support.

- An *influence network* of colleagues who can help you harness resources and information to get things done.

- A *career network* of people you can tap for career advice within and outside your company.

> I think networking and finding somebody to help champion you is critical to your career success — whether that is your boss, upper management, or a mentor. New leaders should make an effort to go to lunch with folks that they work with and network with them to develop relationships. To be successful you'll need these relationships in the future. At some point or another, you may be applying for a position, or there may be a reorganization going on and someone's going to ask your boss or other people that you work with, "What kind of person is Kathy, and can she do this job?" That's your networking paying off!
>
> **—Sales Director**, US chemical company

In this chapter we scrap the stereotypical concept of networking at a cocktail party and embrace a new definition.

Purposeful Networking Defined: *Proactively forming key business relationships for the purpose of exchanging useful information that helps you do your job.*

We'll share some tips to help you establish a diverse network populated by people who differ from you in terms of job function, work experience, time at the company, or even future goals. This will add interesting angles to your own thinking about your job and broaden your understanding of how your organization functions. Not only that, but it will make for a more lively, interesting life! Cultivating a purposeful network is a skill that will serve you well throughout your leadership career. And, yes, more people probably will show up to your company birthday party, which is an extra added bonus.

Alone we can do so little; together we can do so much.

–Helen Keller

Where Do You Stand on the Value Ladder?

Networking relationships, as we define them, only work when the value flows both ways. They flourish when you are seen as a person who gives as much as you receive. Networks don't just bloom overnight; it takes time for people to get to know and trust you. And even though you might be new at your job, you have plenty to contribute. Consider the people you listed in the Pre:Think exercise who seek you out for help. You already are someone people choose to count on. Now it's time to become someone people want to partner with.

Remember Marian, the university communications specialist we introduced you to in Chapter 2? She had been thrust into a leadership position after her deeply unpopular boss was abruptly fired. But the politics of the university were difficult to navigate. She had to wait six months before the administration would make a formal announcement of her new job. During that interim, the information vacuum made everybody nervous. Who was accountable? *We provide publishing services for every department in the university,* she explained. *Annual reports, website updates, news. It wasn't just about us. Everyone was going to be affected.*

Marian took the courageous step of introducing herself to every department head and showing up at the industry functions she usually skipped as a lowly team member. In an informal way, she let them know that she would have a role to play as a leader in her department. That opened doors right away. She also sought out several key people in a variety of production functions—like the printers and web professionals—who understood her new role better than she did. *I wanted to give them a chance to get to know me, but I also needed to learn about how they worked.*

She got creative. *I started hanging around and casually joined meetings that were starting after mine finished,* she laughed. She began offering helpful advice to anyone with communication needs that fell outside her current range of projects. *Nobody minded that I stuck around. People liked it!* She made some new friends and reached out in new ways—like informally mentoring other working mothers at the university.

Her new network really came through: They helped her identify the power players—and their quirks. *I knew who was abrupt and grumpy, and not to take it personally.* And, in every department she met people who had problems with her predecessor. *I could address their concerns before they happened again,* she said. She also got a handle on all the basic production issues that caused constant delays. By the time she officially took over her team, all members were able to handle their assignments more quickly and smoothly than ever before. *If I hadn't reached out to those people, it would have been impossible for me.*

Three Ways to Think about Your Network Now

You'll want to build a network that helps you do your job better, both day-to-day and in your development as a leader. But you'll also want to gather deeper insights that might help you see around corners to changes that are coming. Or find ways to help your team be more innovative. Or brainstorm new ways to keep your people engaged and happy. And we cannot stress this enough: Networking is about sharing information and value. So, you'll want to be able to contribute these things to your network as well.

Start by thinking of the three arenas, or subsets, of networks as shown in Figure 19.1, and how you can best play a role in them. And remember—the goal of building a network is to establish valuable connections before you need to ask for help.

FIG **19.1** The Three Arenas

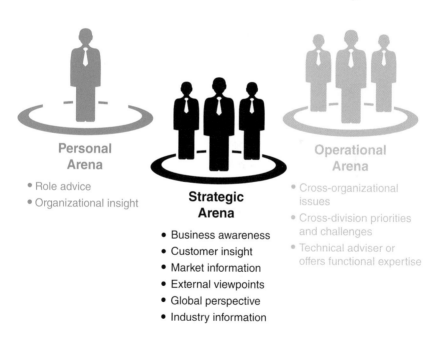

Personal Arena
- Role advice
- Organizational insight

Strategic Arena
- Business awareness
- Customer insight
- Market information
- External viewpoints
- Global perspective
- Industry information

Operational Arena
- Cross-organizational issues
- Cross-division priorities and challenges
- Technical adviser or offers functional expertise

The Four Practices of Networking

To build the kind of network that touches all three arenas, you'll need a strategy. We call this strategy the *Four Practices*, because they offer practical ways to handle your network as it grows (see Figure 19.2).

FIG **19.2** The Four Practices

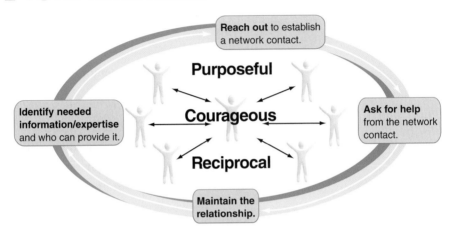

To help you discover where you're already strong and where your networking skills might need a little work, head to the microsite for a self-assessment around the Four Practices. This will give you a handy road map for your next steps.

Want to earn extra networking points right out of the gate? Reach out to the best networker in your new network—preferably someone you'd like to get to know better. (Maybe even your new boss.) Show him your self-assessment results and explain your goal of growing a network. If the person is as good as you think, he'll be happy to help!

Let's explore how to establish and maintain purposeful business networks via the Four Practices.

1. **Identify needed information/expertise** and who can provide it.

This action is often the starting point in purposeful networking—identifying *information, knowledge, skills,* or *support* that will help you do your job more effectively and identifying the people who can help you acquire it. For example:

- Technical and other job-specific information or expertise.

- Coaching on how to handle a challenging situation or task.

- Knowledge of a group's functions, processes, or procedures.

- Perspectives on the organization's culture or unwritten rules.

- Candid performance feedback.

- Advice on career opportunities.

- Warnings and alerts on emerging issues and opportunities, the rationale for decisions, and the implications of decisions.

- Goals/Expectations for a role, responsibility, or task.

- Advice on how to work effectively with a new boss or senior leader.

2. Reach out to establish a network contact.

Many people fear that their efforts to build a networking relationship will be rejected. While this fear is grounded in human nature, experienced networkers know that it's largely unfounded. Still, for many people, making the initial contact requires a *courageous* act. Most people will be more receptive to your attempts to reach out than you might think. Rarely does anyone turn down a phone call from someone who is looking for help. For example: *I've just taken over the ABC project, and I'm trying to get to know people who . . .*

The goal in reaching out to establish a networking contact is to become memorable in a good way. In this initial and usually brief contact, you need to create the feeling that you're someone worth knowing and sharing information with regularly. People who effectively establish network contacts consistently use the Three Ps. They make a:

- Positive impression.

- Personal connection.

- Purposeful case for making a follow-up contact.

Let's face it—most people would admit they don't enjoy trying to connect with others in a new and unfamiliar setting, such as a conference. But there are some personality styles that make networking almost second nature. Specifically, extroverts find it quite easy to make contacts, and they are comfortable inserting themselves into activities or events that provide more opportunities to network.

This is not to say that people who are introverts cannot be incredibly effective networkers. They most certainly can! While they might need to practice the social aspect of networking, they often become more comfortable when talking about the business and retrieving information. In our experience, introverts are more likely to ask questions that will reveal useful information.

And regardless of personality type, many people just feel more comfortable reaching out to a network contact when the interaction is not face-to-face. Networking will never be easy for some people. Yet, it is a skill—and like any skill, you can get better at it with practice.

Reflection Point

How does your personality help or hinder your ability to network?

3. **Ask for help** from the network contact.

Research confirms that asking for help is a behavior tied to job success. In fact, it's difficult to conclude otherwise. If you don't ask for help, you might not have all the information you need. You might propose an idea you think is sound, not knowing that it has been tried before and failed.

But asking for help can be difficult. Start by identifying something you really need help with, like managing a poor performer or handling a challenging project. Then, find someone with whom you've already established a relationship, and has the insight you need. Also, choose someone who's likely to respond. Has she responded before? Does she enjoy being tapped for her expertise?

One good way to manage any anxiety you may feel about asking your network for help is by making a point to provide support for others as part of your leadership brand. (See Chapter 5 for more.) When you look for opportunities to be helpful, people will spread the word. Your contacts also will see you as worth their time, because you reciprocate by offering valuable information that helps them with their work or their passions.

DDI PRO TIP: If you're looking for ways to gain expertise or insights from others, use open-ended questions: *What is the most important thing I need to know about____? or How do you usually handle this type of situation? or This is my situation. Why is it happening? How might I respond?*

4. Maintain the relationship.

Maintaining the relationship is where the true value of networking is realized. People who do this effectively keep up their end of the networking bargain by *reciprocating* with their partners—giving information and support as well as seeking it. They also *proactively* provide support and pass along information that will be valuable to a partner.

WE ASKED,
YOU ANSWERED via LinkedIn

Q: What's your best advice for building your network?

Susan McPherson:

I had a really successful networking experience in my first leadership job. There were people in 35 offices around the world, and we mostly communicated online—before social networking. I developed a habit of emailing to introduce myself to people in similar roles to me, learning what other people were working on and how my department could be of value to them. There is nothing like getting an email like that when you're drowning, I promise you! I made friends and allies. But it was the voice I had to master: friendly but through a business lens.

I also developed a habit of regularly sharing information that I thought was relevant to their jobs or the company, sharing the work that I was doing and more importantly, sharing the news when I thought other people were doing good work. In the end, we all became advocates for each other. It's an important part of networking—you want people outside of your circle talking about you and the work that you're doing. I'm sure I got my next job because of it.

It's much easier to build relationships this way today, and it's almost imperative to have a few hours a week dedicated to networking now.

Connecting the Dots

We believe that the power of leadership—and building relationships—is in the conversations you have with the people around you. And, ironically, this is what often trips people up. Starting a conversation can be hard anyway, and if you have a networking goal in mind, it can feel forced and transactional, as if you're talking to someone only because you want something from them.

Now would be a good time to remember our favorite touchstone, the Key Principles. Networking is about conversations, which are prime opportunities to use the Key Principles, which have kindness, empathy, and respect for others baked right in. If you rely on the Key Principles throughout your conversations with others, things won't feel forced or selfish. You can be truly present with people and appreciate them for who they are.

Five Easy Ways to Get Started TODAY

1. **Start with 10.**
   Identify 10 people for your new network as being able to help you do your job now. Introduce yourself, either by email or in person, and let them know that you're looking forward to getting to know more about how they work and how you can help them. Do you have any connections in common? Mention them! Afterward, connect on LinkedIn with a personal note that references the conversation. Follow them on Twitter, but skip Facebook—that's for actual friends.

2. **Leverage the power networkers.**
   Deepen your relationships and leverage network contacts that serve as hubs or central connectors. These people always seem to know where to start, and if they don't, they can connect you to someone who does. Use these power networkers to find information or other strategic contacts. Also, use the high-value contacts to help spread your ideas or information to others in their network database.

TECH TIP!! *Your network is your net worth. In a digital world, your contacts and connections are more important than the sleek curve of your expensive business card. Think before you hit Enter—always. Everything you place online today is searchable by a potential employer or client. What lasting digital memory or impression do you wish to leave?*

When sharing information such as articles or videos, be choosy. For open feeds like LinkedIn or internal collaboration platforms like Yammer, share what is generally going to be the most helpful or surprising to your network, and that is relevant to them. (Think industry trends, news, leadership tips, or innovations that impact your field.) Limit yourself to one or two posts a day, unless part of your job is to be an information source for others.

If you uncover something that might be of immediate help to a specific person—like information about a competitor or a development that relates to a project they are working on—send it to them privately, via text message or email. Include a short note as to why you thought it would help.

Skip controversial subjects! This is a business network, not a personal venting platform. If it's not going to help someone do their job, don't share it.

—**Luke Wyckoff**,
Chief Visionary Officer at Social Media Energy

3. Take five, as often as you can.

In-person meetings (either face-to-face or voice-to-voice) are crucial to building relationships. But who has time? Look for opportunities to help those around you in small but meaningful ways. When you see an opportunity to be helpful, consider scheduling a five-minute conversation. Yes, just five minutes! You might send an email like this: *I notice you have a meeting with Samir next week. I have some information that should help. Do you want to meet for five minutes before your final prep?*

4. Congratulations are in order.

Your network members may be reaching new goals, winning awards, or accomplishing a big project. Take a few minutes to acknowledge them. A few sincere, kind words go a long way. And, it's a good network partner who reaches out when times are rough as well (e.g., accidents, illness, layoff).

5. Put your network on your calendar.
It's important to schedule time to think about how your network is developing. Is it meeting your needs? Use the Four Practices as a guide to develop a weekly to-do list—people to meet, information to gather and share, meetings to schedule.

Want to Join Our Network?

To start an ongoing conversation with DDI as your career grows, join our network via:

| LinkedIn | Twitter | Facebook | Blog | You Tube | Google+ |

Mastery and Leadership Skills
20 INFLUENCE
Look Up, Down, and Across

Pre:Think
Think about the people in your life who have influenced you to take a risk. It might be someone you know, like a teacher who encouraged you to try a new course or discipline. Or it might be a person—like a political, religious, or community leader—whose life story inspired you to join a cause you believed in. What got you to take the leap?

Inspiration can be an exhilarating feeling.

Especially when it takes life or work in exciting new directions. You might feel that part of your job is to inspire people around you to embrace new ideas and new business prospects when they arise. And that is certainly true. But we think about the mechanism behind that inspiration in a very precise way. We call it *influence*, which is a skill that can be learned, measured, and applied in your daily life. We define influence as moving people toward a commitment that supports a specific business outcome. Easy to define? Yes. Easy to do? Not always. But today, more than ever, it's an essential skill.

We define influence as moving people toward a commitment that supports a specific business outcome.

Consider these examples:

- A pharmaceutical sales rep wants to influence physicians to flag medical records for their breast cancer research drug.

- A lead engineer needs the commitment of people, resources, and time throughout her company to update an existing process manual.

- A marketing manager at a national nonprofit wants to influence the CEO to use social media to spread a positive vision for their organization.

Influencing Takes Personal Power

Decades ago, organizations tended to have more traditional structures, with top-level leaders issuing orders down the line to workers below. Leaders were expected to have all the information at their disposal to make good business decisions. And they expected others to do what they were told. This is what we refer to as *position power*. When your boss says, *I know you're busy, but by first thing tomorrow, I need you to draft a project implementation plan for our new client,* you do it, right? Because the boss asked, of course you do. But, depending on your perspective, your hands may do it, but your heart may not be in it. In extreme cases, people who feel told, coerced, or pressured may ultimately sabotage a project or assignment. Position power might feel like the most efficient way to operate, but in fact, it's the least effective way to encourage people to move toward a commitment that's good for the business and everyone involved.

But what we learned then is even more true now that companies are flatter, more agile, and more global: To do their jobs, leaders need to work effectively with people in other parts of their organization, most of whom don't fall directly under their authority in any way. Frontline leaders have been telling us for years that they were uncovering issues that they simply didn't know how to fix or finding potential value that they didn't know how to unlock. Today, you'd be hard-pressed to find a leader whose job didn't depend on, at least to some degree, his ability to get work done through a network of people he rarely sees and might never have even met.

> **Influence = Personal Power:** *Influence is the skill that helps you work effectively with people over whom you have no* position *power by opening their eyes to an idea or opportunity and getting them to commit to it and you. It's about you expressing your personal* power. *And we hear from people all the time how much of a love/hate relationship they have with this new reality.*

Not only do leaders need to work effectively with other people in other parts of their organization, but they often see—before their own bosses do—opportunities that, if addressed, could make the entire organization better. We're talking about unexplored business opportunities, better ways of sharing information, or even new ways to meet customer needs. These are excellent chances to make a lasting impact. (We get into this in a bit more detail in the Innovation chapter on the microsite.) Today's new matrix organizations raise the stakes for everyone to collaborate across teams, across disciplines, and even across time zones more effectively.

But having ideas is not enough. Neither is identifying people who can help you meet your goals. The human part of how to get people to commit to a new direction is the very heart of what influencing is. And for that, you'll need to make a good case.

I find it pretty stressful. On one hand, we can really have a bigger reach. But I feel like I have to do a lot of detective work to figure out how everything works, because we're moving so fast and growing so quickly. I'm only responsible for one physical product. There is shipping, marketing, finance ... then we have outside customers — we all relate to each other but in these weird, informal ways. Being able to find the key people in charge of things is one thing. But getting everyone on board with any of my manufacturing issues ... I felt it was really beyond me.

—**Mario**, manufacturing lead for an organic products company

Reflection Point

Your influence opportunity:

1. What idea, alternative, or opportunity requires you to influence others to take action?

2. How does your idea support the organization's goals, values, and objectives?

3. Who are the key stakeholders you need to influence, and why do you need their commitment?

4. What challenges do you anticipate, and what support do you need?

Developing an Influence Strategy

Your influence strategy is simply an action plan to organize your thoughts before you begin calling meetings, writing emails or having conversations with people. Your strategy needs to incorporate real evidence—data, reports, statistics, expert opinions—that help make your case. (Many people like to skip this step; *don't*.) Think of your influence strategy as your personal persuasive compass. You need to be confident before you talk to people that you're pointing them in the right direction. Ask yourself, *Does what I'm asking make sense? Are my data and the assumptions I've drawn from it correct? Do I sound manipulative, or are these truly shared goals? Am I really giving people a chance to understand my thinking?* And most importantly, *Am I gaining commitment—winning their hearts—or just telling them what to do?*

> What really motivates people at Facebook is doing stuff they're proud of.
>
> —**Mark Zuckerberg**, cofounder and CEO of Facebook

Figure 20.1 depicts seven steps we've identified that will help you shape an influence strategy that works. We also provide some examples to spark your thinking about how you might make these strategies your own.

FIG 20.1 Influencing Strategies

Advocate Benefits Showing others how an idea benefits the organization can help them see things in a new light. It is important to first ensure that the idea reflects the organization's goals, values, and direction. Link the benefits to people's interests and beliefs so they can better relate to what you are saying.

In explaining her idea for an updated customer interface, Monique cited its increased functionality and higher level of usability. She tied these benefits directly to the organization's objective to reduce customer service calls.

Jim plans to request new safety equipment for his team and needs approval for funds and training. To support his request, he will provide safety data from other organizations that have purchased and used the equipment and expert opinions citing reduced injuries.

Collect Evidence Presenting evidence that supports your idea can make all the difference. Gather solid supporting data to make your case, confirmed by statistics, reports, literature, and expert opinions that will be meaningful to those you need to influence.

Consider Environment Factors The culture within your organization may determine how you present an idea. Before broaching a topic, consider your organization's goals, values, and objectives; current events; and communication methods. Established protocols as well as unspoken rules also are important.

Chris noticed that requests made near the start of a budget cycle were more likely to be approved. She began to time her requests to stakeholders around these cycles to maximize her chance of receiving approval.

Influencing Strategies *cont'd*

Earlier this year, Roberto supported Julie when she proposed a process improvement to her manager. His support was instrumental to gaining the manager's commitment. Julie would be happy to return the favor if Roberto needed her support.

Establishing trust and credibility with key players is good common practice and can help to facilitate an influencing opportunity. Build short- and long-term relationships with people on whom you can rely and allow them to rely on you.

Create and Nurture Your Business Network

Encourage Experiences

Allow people you are trying to influence to see an idea in action. Create opportunities for them to experience the impact, importance, and practicality of the idea.

Maya wants to implement a new plan for distributing patient medications. She sets up a simulation that allows her leader to see how her idea would simplify the process and eliminate distractions and interruptions.

Marcus, a computer programmer, met opposition when he proposed using a new work flow. He solicited the endorsement of a well-respected colleague from another group who had used the same process successfully.

Ask for help. A subject matter expert, a customer, or your manager can provide opinions, perspective, and personal experiences to help you influence others.

Enlist Third-Party Involvement

Plan Small Wins

Gradual but steady progress, or a series of small wins, can be more effective in influencing others than relying on one interaction. Identifying how to achieve these wins while continuously monitoring progress will help to fuel motivation and move you toward gaining others' commitment.

Jennifer thought Tony would resist her proposal to replace a key vendor, based on his reaction to similar requests. To get a small win, she recommended and asked him to try a new vendor for one upcoming job. He agreed to try the vendor and revisit her request if this was successful.

These types of conversations can be challenging to start. In our experience, people hoping to influence others struggle in two primary ways: First, they're sensitive about asking for things because they don't want to hurt an existing relationship. So, they often don't make their case at all. They're *thinking too much* about the other person. Second, people can be too assertive, prompting others to perceive them as pushy or insensitive. They *aren't thinking enough* about the other person.

Consider a third, more balanced, approach that acknowledges everyone right up front: *You and I have similar needs in some ways, different in others.* This helps the person you're attempting to influence feel understood and respected. It also shows that you see her as a potential solution, and not an obstacle. The person will be more likely to give you honest feedback, which will help you find out where she falls on the commitment spectrum. Is she on board? How far? Why?

Use Packaging to Engage Hearts and Minds

Influencing others, as we are talking about it here, can take time. Indeed, it can be a project unto itself! You might have one conversation or many, and find yourself writing emails, scheduling meetings, giving presentations, or even making a prototype. It's all part of your job. You'll find over time that as you practice your influencing behaviors, they'll become your natural way of operating in the world.

We've said you need to use real data to present your ideas—and you should. But we also encourage you to think about packaging your ideas. That is, framing your thoughts in ways that are most likely to persuade, surprise, or delight whomever you're speaking with. You can accomplish this by using metaphors, stories, and visuals that not only tell your story well, but that people may want to share with others. (This is especially true for meetings and presentations, but also effective in one-on-one conversations and emails.) Packaging your ideas with some care and flair utilizes some fairly basic marketing principles of generating understanding and awareness—like we all do on social media *every day*—and can help you influence colleagues and team members within your company. Ask yourself:

- What metaphor or analogy can provide a new insight or simplify a complex issue?

- How effectively do people use stories in my organization?

- How can I convert data into simple, memorable pictures?

- What types of visuals (slide presentations, and so on) do I find most effective?

What if someone were to give you feedback after a presentation saying, *Your content was good, but you served it up in such a dry format. I'm afraid it wasn't memorable to the audience and won't move them to action.* You'd be devastated, right? Well, this is exactly why we need to help you package your message in a compelling way, using vivid images, powerful questions, and even an element of surprise to help you engage both the hearts and minds of those you need to influence and have a greater impact.

Following are three packaging techniques to help capture attention and engage your audience mentally and emotionally.

Paint the Picture: Metaphors, analogies, stories, humor, and strong visuals can *build vision* and leave a *memorable* impression.

- **Metaphor**—A figure of speech in which a word or phrase denoting one object or idea is used in place of another to suggest a likeness between them.
  - *Camille's suggestions for spicing up the proposal process are just the extra pinch we need if we're going to create an irresistible package.*
  - *Let's clear the air on this issue before continuing.*
- **Analogy**—Comparing different items by relating what is unknown to what is known.
  - *Working through this process is like driving through a city for the first time: Lots of wrong turns and trips the wrong way down one-way streets, but eventually you get to your destination.*

The Unexpected: Wisely used, the element of surprise can catapult people out of their comfort zones, causing them to consider new ideas or changes *thoughtfully.*

The Power of Questions: Questions have the power to elicit input, control the discussion flow, and evoke emotion.

- **Open**—Cannot be answered with one word; encourages discussion.
  - *How does this change affect your current process?*
- **Closed**—Requires a definitive answer; focuses the conversation.
  - *Have we agreed to begin on Monday?*
- **Provocative**—Gets to the core of an issue; exposes consequences; provokes emotion; drives choices.
  - *Can our business survive if we don't take action to be more innovative?*

Reflection Point

Take a moment-in-time, mental snapshot of your influence opportunity. Then use the images or visual relationships that you envisioned. Remember, keep it simple. If it cannot be shared simply, an image might not be the right packaging technique to use!

Gauge Readiness and Gain Commitment to Act

You've now created a master strategy for your influence opportunity and planned how to package it in a way that's memorable and will move people to action. Your next step is to gain your stakeholders' commitment. How can you do that?

Begin by gauging their readiness—assessing when people need more time, or if they're ready to move forward and commit to action. There are three possible actions to take.

- **Confirm and Close**—When you need an immediate response or you're confident the person is on board. *Tip:* Don't hesitate to ask for verbal or written commitment. A "public" commitment is most effective to ensuring that others follow through.

- **Seek and Develop**—The person is unconvinced or remains neutral or skeptical. *Tip:* Be ready to use a suitable decision-making tool and technique, especially when you use this step in a group interaction.

- **Step Back**—Skeptics are emotional, confrontational, or unwilling to move forward. *Tip:* Don't drop the issue. Schedule a time to reconvene. Consider whether you truly need this person's commitment or if you could proceed without it.

Then you need to agree on next steps. The true measure of commitment is action. Whether confirming significant commitment or incremental steps toward the final goal, be sure the appropriate follow-up action is agreed upon, including specific responsibilities, time frames, and tracking methods.

Ready, Set, Influence!

By now you should have a pretty good sense of what influence can mean in your career. You should also see how some of the material in other chapters in this Mastery section, like networking (Chapter 19), managing change (on the microsite), and coaching (Chapter 14), will help you master the social skills necessary to frame your influence conversations for maximum impact.

Mastery and Leadership Skills
21 A WOMAN'S FIRST LEADERSHIP JOB
Own the Moment

Pre:Think

Take a moment to notice what your body language is when you join in a meeting. Do you slip in late? Take a seat away from the table? Do you walk in quietly? Or, instead strike a power pose? Ask a trusted peer to tell you how you appear to others.

A Make-or-Break Point

More than any other moment in a woman's professional life, her first leadership role marks a make-or-break point that can shape her choices for the rest of her career. This chapter features practical advice from Tacy on how to be—or support—a successful female first-time leader.

Erika didn't just lean in and pursue her ambitions; she took control. *I'm a technical analyst, but had always wanted to move into management,* she said. For software engineers making the leap, that typically meant working with a company for a long time, paying your dues and proving yourself. She had been inching her way up the ladder by lobbying for and winning increasingly high-profile projects for eight years. Everything was going according to plan! Her manager was supportive. There was a job for her in the works, and her life was falling into perfect order. *Once I mastered my new position,* she thought, *we were going to have a kid. Because it's almost impossible to do both at the same time.* And that's when things got dicey. Out of the blue, her husband got a promotion they couldn't pass up. Their move, which took her from Atlanta to New Jersey, uprooted her carefully designed life plan. *To get on the management track, I had to start all over somewhere else.*

What Erika did next was a tour de force of goal setting, personal development, and sheer grit. Just weeks into a new job, she decided to jam as much career growth into as short a time as humanly possible. First, she decided to sweeten her resume with a new, and highly regarded, technical credential. *I found a course online* [in India] *that because of the time zone difference would let me take the certification course during nights and weekends so I could take on new projects at work.* Even though she was already working double time, she persuaded her manager to give her stretch opportunities that helped her learn how her new company operated. *He worked with me to get projects done, so any mistakes I made wouldn't be a problem.* And with a flair for planning that reaches far beyond the scope of this book, she managed to finish her studies and pass her certification exam early in her first trimester. She literally heaved her way to the finish line. *I was really, really, really sick! But the hard work was behind me.* Again, all according to plan. She had reached her goal in less than two years and stepped into her first solo management role as a happy new mom when she returned from maternity leave.

And that, of course, is when things went crazy wrong.

Earlier in this book we pointed out that what makes you a successful leader may have nothing to do with what made you successful in the past. The challenges you face as a leader are much different—and they can be extra tough. But for women, the life-planning super heroics associated with landing leadership roles are not enough. *I hadn't thought about how hard it would be to actually lead the team,* Erika said. For all of her accomplishments, she had cultivated few skills necessary to manage a group of experienced engineers, all of whom had more impressive credentials and all of whom were men. And the company's leadership culture took her completely by surprise. *They wouldn't even accept my meeting requests,* she recalled. As she failed to meet benchmark after benchmark, Erika knew her plan was in trouble. She was living in a new community, with a new job, and her son was barely a toddler. *I was exhausted,* she said. *All the time.*

The Glass Ceiling Is Alive and Well

Although women are making real and steady gains in higher education and earning entry-level jobs in fields previously dominated by men, they have made few inroads into upper-leadership positions. A quick look at the numbers shows that the glass ceiling is alive and well: Women comprise 53 percent of entry-level workers, 40 percent of managers, 35 percent of directors, 27 percent of vice presidents, 24 percent of senior vice presidents, and 19 percent of C-suite execs.[1] Female Fortune 500 CEOs? About 5 percent.[2] The rise of women to senior leadership positions, whether as executives, board members, venture-backed entrepreneurs, or in government, simply has not happened.

At the same time, the business case for gender diversity has never been stronger. DDI and The Conference Board's *Global Leadership Forecast (GLF)* found that organizations with more women consistently perform better financially. As shown in Figure 21.1, companies in the bottom 20 percent of financial performance have only 19 percent women in all leadership positions; companies in the top 20 percent have 37 percent—almost twice as many.[3]

FIG 21.1 More Women Leaders = Better Company Performance

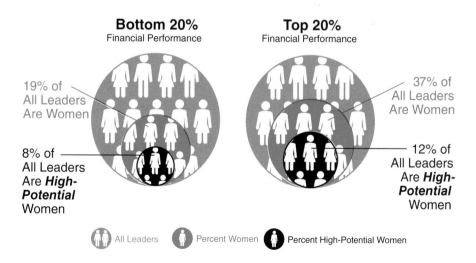

Organizations with Better Financial Performance Have More Women in Leadership Roles

Bottom 20%
Financial Performance

Top 20%
Financial Performance

19% of All Leaders Are Women

37% of All Leaders Are Women

8% of All Leaders Are *High-Potential* Women

12% of All Leaders Are *High-Potential* Women

All Leaders   Percent Women   Percent High-Potential Women

So, why are women falling off the management ladder? Here's one possible answer: Female talent opts out after their first experience at the frontline level.

Business culture remains an issue. With a diminishing number of available female leaders seeking to advance, there are fewer women to observe as role models. This means fewer opportunities to influence an organization to embrace the real benefits of true diversity. And, it would seem, fewer people to advocate for women coming up the ranks. *I thought the whole "do business over golf thing" was a cliché,* one young banker said. *It wasn't. And by the second time I was passed over for a promotion, I got the message. I can't fit in here.*

In 2008 Hewlett Packard conducted an internal study to learn why more women weren't applying for senior leadership jobs. It seems to be a pretty cut-and-dried case of male versus female personalities at work. Men apply for a job when they meet only 60 percent of the stated job qualifications.[4] Women apply only if they can show they meet 100 percent. This has offered only the latest evidence that there's a personality gap holding women back. If only we were more confident! Well, yes and no.

> Men apply for a job when they meet only 60 percent of the stated job qualifications. Women apply only if they can show they meet 100 percent.

Research clearly shows that there is no real difference between genders in terms of leadership ability. And women know this. According to the *GLF* 2014–2015, female leaders rated themselves as effective as males on an entire array of competencies, the important skills that make leaders truly effective.[5] Multiple other studies show that female leaders are every bit as competent as their male counterparts. In fact, DDI's own testing and assessment processes—which measure real behavior, not survey data—show little difference in leadership ability when it comes to gender. More on that shortly.

So, what's holding women back? Women polled in the *GLF* study cited a lack of opportunities to lead teams and gain global leadership experience. These experiences, rich with potential, are important proving grounds for career advancement. Additionally, they provide a strong boost to leaders' capabilities and confidence. And this is where we women can do ourselves—and the women leaders we supervise—some real good. We need to proactively identify key leadership development assignments and ensure that our best-laid plans become realities.

Developmental opportunities have absolutely impacted my career. I'm being sought out as a trainer, advocate, go-to person, and subject matter expert because of my training. My people skills are strong, I get better results from those I interact with, my responsibilities continue to increase, and my value is evident.

—Regional manager, consumer products industry

As a consequence, denying women equal access to development can quickly lead to feelings of resentment.

Encouraging gender diversity in your organization's leadership pool means greater diversity of thought, which, in turn, leads to improved problem solving and greater business benefits (see Figure 21.1). But, bottom line, it's especially important to ensure that women have equal access to development experiences. This, in turn, ensures that they are equally qualified and ready now for the next promotion opportunity. Women must ensure (or demand) equal treatment by gender for these transformative development experiences.

Males were able to go to more seminars and conferences. When it came to the female executives, it was a real tight pick-and-choose. And if you did get to go, it was only once every other year.

—Director, health care organization

After asking female leaders what would boost their effectiveness, the consensus was this: Organizations need to start creating more transparency, paying more attention to promoting women in leadership roles, and cultivating an atmosphere in which everyone has a chance to be a leader.

Is It a Matter of Confidence?

So, what could hold you back? Are you worried about the travel requirements associated with a global leadership experience and the impact on your real or future family? Or do you simply lack confidence to stretch into a larger role with more responsibility? According to *The Confidence Code* by Claire Shipman and Katty Kay—both prominent broadcasters—confidence is a key differentiator.[6] To sum up the situation, men think they can and women think they can't. Our own *GLF* research on gender differences (see Figure 21.2) echoes this theme, with women tending to self-evaluate themselves as less-effective leaders than their male peers. In other words, we have a paradox—based on this survey data, women perceive themselves to be *less effective* as leaders than men but at the same time are *slightly more effective* in *leadership skills*. So, is it a matter of confidence?

FIG **21.2** Where Are the Gender Differences?

Where are the Gender **Differences**?

Are prepared to meet business challenges	
Are effective in leadership skills	
Have had developmental assignment opportunities	
Are confident in ability to meet management challenges	
Have received information about the competencies/skill areas needed to succeed as a leader	
Have a written an up-to-date development plan	
Consider self to be a more effective leader compared to peers	
Lead people in different countries and continents	
Have completed one or more international assignments	
Lead geographically dispersed teams	

Favors Women   No Significant Difference   Favors Men

Another possible interpretation comes from author Tara Sopher Mohr in a post for *Harvard Business Review*.[7] After surveying over a thousand men and women, she discovered that the primary reason both genders cited for not applying for a job for which they lacked some of the qualifications was, *I didn't think they would hire me, and I didn't want to waste my time.* While lack of confidence can hold women back in the workplace, so, too, might a failure to understand just how the workplace systems actually operate. That is, applying for jobs with just some of the stated credentials is actually how it's done. For the inside track on how your company operates, particularly for women leaders, you'll have to tap into your own network (see Chapter 19). And that, of course, takes a good bit of confidence.

Tacy's Wake-Up Call

I've suffered from a lack of confidence myself. A few years ago, I took on a fairly significant leadership leap. I was chosen to transform one suite of our company's offerings from individually customized training products to a series of technologically driven, scalable ones that could reach many, many more clients. I led the research and development of nine courses, working with an interdisciplinary team that executed beautifully on the product vision. But when it came time to name an overall product leader—the "face" of these new products, if you will—I wasn't even considered. The role would oversee R&D (which I currently ran), marketing, public relations, field education, and rainmaker sales role.

I was about to be passed over for that leadership position without even realizing I was competing for it. Another candidate, a man, had begun to aggressively lobby with the executive team for the product leader title. Decision makers favored him, in part because he appeared hungrier for the role and I was busy getting the day-to-day work done. In other words, I thought it was a given, baked into the work I was doing, and that I had earned it.

Wake-up call!

> It's what we don't know about how business works that also holds us back. And we can do something about that every day.

And that's when I came to an important realization that has served me, and the young women I mentor. It's what we don't know about how business works that also holds us back. And we can do something about that every day.

How did I handle it? I called a meeting of our president and another senior leader and declared my interest in the position. But I didn't focus on what I had already done. Instead, I focused on the extensive experiences I already had from tangential products, wisdom I could leverage from previous product launches, my knowledge of the organization, and the how to get things done that would guarantee the new product's future success. They may have overlooked me for a variety of reasons, but it was my responsibility to bring myself—and my talents—back to their attention.

They gave me the job. Fast-forward to my performance review two years later. The solution had become the fastest-growing product in DDI history, and I received the favorite compliment of my career. The president said, "No one could have executed for DDI on this new venture the way you did, Tacy. I count the fact that I gave you this job as one of the best decisions I have made in my career."

Once I realized I needed to, I declared myself to my bosses. Notice I said "declare," not defend. I needed to make the case for why I was the right person for the job and the tasks that were on the horizon.

Declare Yourself Early and Often

While everyone needs to declare their readiness for the next step up, women often miss cues such as when and how often to remind people what we *can do* now and what we *want* to do in the future. And as conscientious rule followers, women might miss the point that merely following instructions is not enough to win the day.

> Women often miss the cues as to when and how often we need to remind people what we can do.

For women, the declarative conversation carries real weight. This call to action applies to all women—single, married, working moms, blended-family moms. Any woman who is balancing it all needs to step away from the fray and daily struggles of being her best, keeping her head above water, and getting things done to focus on the future, *her* future as a leader, and declare herself.

Rethink Mentorship

Finding a good mentor is like winning the lottery for any new professional. And DDI research shows that if you find a good candidate and ask for his or her sponsorship, the person will likely say yes.[8] But finding the right person is no easy chore. And many young women resist asking. It feels needy, like you're asking someone to like you. And your career may languish in the meantime.

Our best advice? Look for *micromentors*—people who can give you feedback about your career as it evolves, particularly if you're facing a stretch assignment, like delivering an important presentation or bringing a new business unit online. It's less about your overall career, and more about finding an expert who can help you now. And don't ask just women! Because there are fewer women in leadership ranks as you go up, why limit yourself? Female mentors can provide advice based on the wisdom gleaned from their career paths. Male mentors can advise you on how you're coming across to others in the workplace. Both can help you enhance your political savvy. This opportunity provides you with a good excuse to expand your network without feeling like you're asking someone to go steady with you forever.

Kelly Hoey agrees. She is an angel investor, start-up adviser, and a former corporate attorney who works with early-stage companies with female founders. *In some ways I wish that women would stop focusing on mentorship entirely*, she says.

When women fail to find one, or worse, when one doesn't magically appear, women tend to give up. It's likely that potential micromentors are all around you. *I always tell women, "Look at the landscape. Look at who is giving you work. Look at who is observing your work, or is talking about what you're doing. That person is willing to help you. That person is willing to spend political capital to help you advance."* Those people are the ideal people to ask for short-term mentorship or coaching. *Those are the ones who speak up for you when you're not in the room. Give them a reason to know what you're capable of.*

DDI PRO TIP: Create your own three-person affinity group. Take it upon yourself to find one promising woman one step below you in your organization and another who is one step above you. Create a small networking and support group that helps each of you grow as professionals and navigate the specifics of your company.

Needed: An Attitude Change

The September 2014 *Real Simple/Time* Magazine Success Poll surveyed 1,000 women on how they define success, how much importance they attach to it, and the risks they've taken to achieve it. Their polls found that only 8 percent of women consider themselves a success all the time. And, 36 percent of women often feel people at work think they're more qualified than they actually think they are.[9]

So, what we women need is an attitude change. Or a different voice in our head guiding the way. A great voice is Sheryl Sandberg, who said, *Women need to shift from thinking "I'm not ready to do that" to thinking "I want to do that—and I'll learn by doing it."*[10] Admittedly, learning on the job takes courage, but the risks are worth it.

The Wisdom of Women (Including Madonna)

Rich and Tacy started up a conversation—four dozen conversations to be precise—with top women leaders around the globe who are ahead of their game. The following advice and personal wisdom comes from these women, who are climbing the ladder themselves.

Don't Settle for a Ho-Hum Work Life

The women we spoke to consistently demonstrated passion for their roles. It was passion that helped them face obstacles head-on. Passion that allowed them to address the complex challenges that came their way. One woman leader said, *When I'm happy at work, it makes everything else in life hum.* They also spoke of the importance of *having a connection to an underlying purpose, needing value alignment,* and, ultimately, choosing a job and career that you actually want to devote your energies to. According to one, *I'm a true believer that if you enjoy what you do, your performance will be higher and you will be more successful.*

When you find your passion, you can inspire yourself and your team to greater levels of performance.

Fail Often, Fail Well

Know and understand what is important to you, and be very clear about the goals you want to achieve. However, don't be afraid to fail along the way. *Success is about working out what you want to do, not necessarily driving for the name or title, but more about the richness of what you're doing,* one of our female senior leaders said. In other words, failure is not about failure; it's about learning.

And that's not all. Failure provides opportunity to recalibrate our internal report-card listing areas of personal strength and understanding our weaknesses. Failure is often described as key to innovation and real breakthroughs as leaders.[11] The senior women we interviewed would coach others to not miss opportunities for reflection, self-insight, and learning. According to one, *You need to understand yourself and what is right for you, not what the organisation thinks is right for you.* As another leader said, *There's no obstacle that can't end up being a stepping stone to something greater if you can work out how to get over it.*

Find People Who Believe in You Even More Than You Believe in Yourself

The comments made earlier to rethink mentorship is advice echoed by our panel of senior women. Mentors and sponsors will be able to provide you with insight, guidance, and advice, even with challenges you haven't yet encountered. *Make yourself meet these people, and continue to meet them within the organization,* because if you choose the right ones, they'll back you when you need it most.

In addition to organizational resources, these highly successful female senior leaders also had support systems beyond work. Many told us about the importance of personal relationships with friends and family—*an unspoken support that is without much acknowledgement,* but one that is of great value in buffering both stress and pressure at work. For many of them, success is defined by balancing work-life priorities, as this allows you to *give yourself some purpose in life other than work.* I now recognize that this is a secret to my personal success as I have a core group of powerful female friends, who serve as my executive advisory board. We're always on call to cheer each other on or hash through the big life issues when they arise. So, I encourage you to find your girl posse and lean on them.

Show Your Value; Stand Out

Think back to my wake-up call. Do you have your own personal wake-up call? I hope you heed my advice and declare yourself. Be sure to demonstrate results and make them visible. Because remember that doing a good job is not defined by long hours, but rather, by the outcomes you deliver. *Earning respect and doing a good job of what you do gets you a long way.*

And, finally:

Be Madonna-Like and Vogue

What did your Pre:Think exercise reveal? Are you shrinking into a corner, or are you striding into a meeting looking ready to take charge? I challenge you to channel your inner rock star—in this case, Madonna. One of the talents that Madonna (and performers of all types) master is to seize the stage with an air of confidence. Were they born this way, or did they develop this skill? It's likely that the confidence they project to the audience was developed over time. As a young singer, Madonna most likely was scared silly on the inside, but didn't let those emotions show on the outside. Even now, after performing for over 30 years, Madonna admits that she still gets nervous before a show.

But, she marches forth anyway, taking on new challenges (like a Super Bowl halftime show).[12]

But this advice is not just for rock stars. Wearing a mantle of fearlessness, backing yourself, and having the tenacity to get back on the horse when you fall off were all cited by our women leaders as critical characteristics in their move up the ladder. In fact, one savvy leader offered the following advice when women do hold themselves back from that next opportunity: *When you feel envy, question why you haven't gone for it yourself.*

When you feel envy, question why you haven't gone for it yourself.

How do we become Madonna-like? Well, this is a bit of a cheat, but it works: If you strike a power pose before an important meeting or conversation, you will feel more powerful. Get pumped! Every meeting is an opportunity. Join the 8 percent of women leaders who strike a power pose to get pumped for a meeting.[13]

#LeadLikeAGirl

In 2014, a new video redefined the phrase "like a girl," as something strong and powerful. It was part of the larger #LikeAGirl campaign by Always, the feminine hygiene brand owned by Procter & Gamble. In the video, a cast of men and women of all ages were asked to describe what they think the phrase "like a girl" means. The result was troubling. Waving hands and flipping hair, the participants pretended to run "like a girl" and throw "like a girl." Everyone—except, notably, the young girls—demonstrated that "just like a girl" is often perceived as an insult. Yet the young girls demonstrated purposeful, athletic motions.

So, in closing, we've confirmed that organizations with more women consistently perform better financially. In other words, it's good to #LeadLikeAGirl. And, perhaps you didn't need your own personal wake-up call, but I hope we, and the senior leaders who lent their insights, have inspired you to take a chance, seek a mentor, and strike a pose, like Madonna in her "Vogue" video. Others will see you as poised, credible, and confident. And, in turn you'll build your own inner confidence to stretch, grow, sometimes fail, and learn.

A woman is like a tea bag. You never know how strong she is until she gets in hot water.

–Eleanor Roosevelt

240

We have a responsibility to our family and our community to give back to others and use our leadership skills in our day-to-day lives beyond work.

22 LEADERSHIP CHANGES THE WORLD
The Difference Is You

In the course of writing this book, we've spent quite a bit of time—separately and together—thinking about what leadership really means to people today. We've made the case, we believe, for the deep science behind leadership development. But we hope you'll also take the time to celebrate the profoundly human part of what you're doing by pursuing a leadership career: helping yourself and others grow. This growth will pay off for everyone involved, including your business and your customers. And your leadership skills can help your keep your career on track even if your industry is in turmoil, and even if the economy is bad.

At some point, you may have started to notice that a different you is emerging: one who is more certain about the future, one who has a deeper understanding of and connection to the people around you. This is your leadership voice gaining strength. Use it! Hand that inner you the microphone as often as you can. It's good for you, your company, and for the world as a whole.

You'll find value in these leadership skills beyond the 40 or 50 (okay, 60) hours you spend at work. Remember back in Chapter 8, when we shared the story of the leader who used the Discussion Planner as the emotional roadmap for a really tough conversation with his son? That was his leadership voice making a difference in his family. Tacy loves the story that a new leader shared with her. Right after he completed his training, he returned home to find his wife in tears. She had abruptly lost her job. Instead of reacting, he listened. Asked questions. In between hugs and tissues, he used the Key Principles to help her move from distress to next steps. The best part? *She asked me, "What happened at that training session? You've come home a whole new person!"* he told Tacy. Maybe. Or maybe it's just that his new skills helped him be his more authentic self when the person he loved needed him.

At DDI we view leadership as a service to others that rises above how we even think about ourselves. We believe we have a responsibility to our family and our community to give back to others and use our leadership skills in our day-to-day lives beyond work. DDI has instituted a program where all associates can take a day off to share the science of our leadership skills in the community. We've had associates take the Key Principles into their children's middle schools. (Think about the power of teaching bossy, know-it-all teenagers how to maintain self-esteem, use empathy, and involve others!) Others have helped women transitioning back into the workforce hone their presentation skills. Our associates were able to help the Teach for Malaysia program, an education nonprofit that trains teachers to serve in Malaysia's poorest communities, to reduce teacher turnover by training them in world-class interviewing skills. Before the training, if a poor hiring decision resulted in a teacher leaving, students found themselves without a teacher for up to six weeks. With the stakes that high, leadership skills are a game changer. We feel confident that you will find ways to apply your skills to make all your causes and relationships better.

To learn more about how people have been able to apply our science to better the world—and how you can too!—head to our microsite for a free copy of the digital book *Spark!* There you will find true stories of how leaders like you have made a difference in some inspiring and surprising ways.

It's Time to View Leadership as a Profession (and a Confession)

So, given all the benefits of leadership we've shared with you, why isn't "leadership" a thing?

A rock pile ceases to be a rock pile the moment a single man contemplates it, bearing within him the image of a cathedral.

—**Antoine de Saint-Exupery**, *The Little Prince*

Here's an example of what we mean. Those who have travelled internationally will be familiar with the arrival and departure cards that you complete as you pass through immigration. On a recent overseas trip, Tacy got to chatting to the traveller next to her.

He was a senior leader in a global mining organization. As they talked, she shared a bit about DDI and the work she does in the leadership field. The man challenged her with a question: *So, what do you write in the occupation field of your departure card?* He had appropriately (and diplomatically) put her on the spot. And no, "leader" wasn't it. (The answer: HR consultant.)

Why?

Rich recently expressed something similar in a blog that it's time for leadership to be viewed as a genuine profession. In this post, he reflected that in 30-plus years of traveling the world, not once has somebody introduced themselves to him as a leader. He raised several key questions. Are leaders in roles because they choose to be, or because they want to be? Are they passionate about mobilizing a workforce, driving organizational change, or being a positive role model for an organization's culture? Do leaders stop and think about what they represent and how others look to them for guidance, support, confidence, and growth?

So, now it's confession time. Do you?

We believe that if leadership is viewed and embraced as a true profession, the impact on an organization, its people, and the world will be enormous. And so we end this book with a challenge: When people ask you what you do for a living, tell them you're a leader. And mean it.

> We end this book with a challenge: When people ask you what you do for a living, tell them you're a leader.

We believe that leadership is a craft that is perfected through the focused dedication of time, attention, and self-awareness—not unlike a chef, artist, or surgeon. When you become a leader, whatever your level or industry, it becomes your profession. We believe that you have an obligation to invest the time and effort to become the best leader you can be.

Part 3: Bonus Chapters and Tools

At last! Your journey is nearly complete. But, don't worry—we're still here to guide you. We've created a rich microsite featuring more research than you can shake a stick at, along with tips, tools, videos, and even a simulation that will help you practice your newly acquired leadership skills.

The microsite also includes three bonus chapters and a useful checklist:

Change: It's about People
It's no surprise that 70 percent of workplace change initiatives fail. This chapter helps you turn resistance into commitment and inspire team members to take ownership of change. It also helps you create an agile work environment where people are more open to change.

Innovation: Be Prepared to Fail Early and Often
The pressure to find new and creative solutions can be intense. To drive a culture of innovation, you'll need to push your and your team's thinking. This chapter prompts you to do that with tips and techniques to generate new ideas and add value to your organization.

Your Next Career Move and Next Adventure: Reflect, Envision, Engage
This chapter is about taking what you've discovered about yourself and using it to explore your career options as you map out your future direction—be it upward, across, or an enriched current role.

New Leader Checklist: Navigating Your First Six Months
This user-friendly, month-by-month checklist helps you successfully navigate through your transition. It calls out key administrative activities, suggests development activities for you and your team, points out areas you should clarify with your boss, and provides suggestions for creating an optimal cultural/social environment.

Be sure to bookmark the site and return to it often as you continue your leadership journey.

www.YourFirstLeadershipJob.com

Citations

Chapter 1: Now You're a Leader

1. Matt Paese and Simon Mitchell, *Leaders in Transition: Stepping Up, Not Off* (Pittsburgh: Development Dimensions International, 2007).

Chapter 2: Boss or Catalyst?

1. Pete Weaver and Simon Mitchell, *Lessons for Leaders from the People Who Matter,* Trend Research (Pittsburgh: Development Dimensions International, 2012), 12.

2. Ibid., 14.

Chapter 3: Navigating the Transition to Leadership

1. Evan Sinar and Matt Paese, *Leaders in Transition: Progressing along a Precarious Path* (Pittsburgh: Development Dimensions International, 2014), 10–11.

2. Ibid., 5.

3. Ibid., 7.

Chapter 4: Your Leadership Brand, Part 1

1. Morgan W. McCall, "Identifying Leadership Potential in Future International Executives: Developing a Concept," *Consulting Psychology Journal: Practice and Research* 46, no. 1 (1994): 49–63, doi:10.1037//1061-4087.46.1.49; Morgan W. McCall, *High Flyers: Developing the Next Generation of Leaders* (Boston: Harvard Business School Press, 1998); Jim Collins, "Level 5 Leadership," *Harvard Business Review* 79, no. 1 (January 2001): 66–76; Doug Bray and Ann Howard, "The AT&T Longitudinal Studies of Managers," in *Longitudinal Studies of Adult Psychological Development,* ed. Klaus Warner Schaie (New York: Guilford Press, 1983); Brent Roberts and Robert Hogan, *Personality Psychology in the Workplace* (Washington, DC: American Psychological Association, 2001).

2. Ursula Burns, interviewed by Ellen McGirt, *Fast Company,* New York, November 19, 2011.

3. Jim Collins, *Good to Great: Why Some Companies Make the Leap—and Others Don't* (New York: HarperBusiness, 2001).

Chapter 5: Your Leadership Brand, Part 2

1. Douglas McGregor, *The Human Side of Enterprise* (New York: McGraw-Hill, 1960).

2. "Top 10 Business Bestsellers of the Decade," *Hartford Courant*, January 10, 2000.

3. William C. Byham and Jeff Cox, *Zapp!® The Lightning of Empowerment: How to Improve Productivity, Quality, and Employee Satisfaction* (New York: Harmony Books, 1988/1991).

4 Mary L. Tracy and Matt Paese, "Two Perspectives on Identifying Potential," *DDI GO Magazine*, Spring 2005, 22.

5 Morgan W. McCall, "Identifying Leadership Potential in Future International Executives: Developing a Concept," *Consulting Psychology Journal: Practice and Research* 46, no. 1 (1994): 49–63, doi:10.1037//1061-4087.46.1.49; Morgan W. McCall, *High Flyers: Developing the Next Generation of Leaders* (Boston: Harvard Business School Press, 1998); Jim Collins, "Level 5 Leadership," *Harvard Business Review* 79, no. 1 (January 2001): 66–76; Brent Roberts and Robert Hogan, *Personality Psychology in the Workplace* (Washington, DC: American Psychological Association, 2001); Doug Bray and Ann Howard, "The AT&T Longitudinal Studies of Managers," in *Longitudinal Studies of Adult Psychological Development*, ed. Klaus Warner Schaie (New York: Guilford Press, 1983).

6 Mary L. Tracy and Matt Paese, "Two Perspectives on Identifying Potential," *DDI GO Magazine*, Spring 2005, 22–23.

7 John Zenger and Joseph Folkman, "Feedback—You Need It, Your Employees Want It!" *Zenger Folkman's Monthly Webinar Series,* webinar, February 20, 2014, slide 8.

8 Ibid., slide 13.

Chapter 6: Leadership Is a Conversation, Part 1

1 Eric Matson and Laurence Prusak, "Boosting the Productivity of Knowledge Workers," *McKinsey Quarterly,* September 2010.

2 A. H. Maslow, "A Theory of Human Motivation," *Psychological Review* 50, no. 4 (1943): 370–396.

3 "It's Better to Give Than to Receive, Even If We Don't Realise It," *PR Newswire US*, November 5, 2014, *Business Source Corporate Plus*, EBSCOhost (accessed December 9, 2014); Katherine Nelson et al., "'It's up to You': Experimentally Manipulated Autonomy Support for Prosocial Behavior Improves Well-Being in Two Cultures over Six Weeks," *The Journal of Positive Psychology* (in press); Sonja Lyubomirsky, *The How of Happiness: A New Approach to Getting the Life You Want* (New York: Penguin Press, 2008); Stephanie L. Brown et al., "Providing Social Support May Be More Beneficial Than Receiving It: Results from a Prospective Study of Mortality," *Psychological Science* (Wiley-Blackwell) 14, no. 4 (July 2003): 320–327, *Business Source Corporate Plus*, EBSCOhost (accessed December 14, 2014).

4 Steven Stowell, "Coaching: A Commitment to Leadership," *Training & Development Journal* 42, no. 6 (1988): 34.

5 Akira Ikemi and Shinya Kubota, "Humanistic Psychology in Japanese Corporations: Listening and the Small Steps of Change," *Journal of Humanistic Psychology* 36, no. 1 (Winter 1996): 104–121.

6 Marcus Cauchi, "The 70/30 Rule: Which Side Are You?" *Paul Simister's Business Coaching Blog* (blog), October 8, 2008, http://businesscoaching.typepad.com/; Neil Rackham and Terry Morgan, *Behaviour Analysis in Training* (London: McGraw-Hill, 1977).

7 Development Dimensions International, "Manager Ready Behavior Performance," accessed September 24, 2014, Manager Ready database.

8 Mark Busine et al., *Driving Workplace Performance through High-Quality Conversations* (Pittsburgh: Development Dimensions International, 2013), 9.

Chapter 7: Leadership Is a Conversation, Part 2

1 Neil Rackham, *SPIN Selling* (New York: McGraw-Hill, 1988); Neil Rackham, *Major Account Sales Strategy* (New York: McGraw-Hill, 1989).

2 William Oncken Jr. and Donald L. Wass, "Management Time: Who's Got the Monkey?" *Harvard Business Review* 52, no. 6 (November 1974): 75.

3 Pete Weaver and Simon Mitchell, *Lessons for Leaders from the People Who Matter: How Employees around the World View Their Leaders* (Pittsburgh: Development Dimensions International, 2012).

Chapter 8: Your Five-Step Conversation Road Map

1 Development Dimensions International, "Manager Ready Behavior Performance," accessed September 24, 2014, Manager Ready database.

2 Malcolm Gladwell, *Outliers: The Story of Success* (New York: Little, Brown and Co., 2008).

3 Daniel Goleman, *Emotional Intelligence: Why it Can Matter More Than IQ* (New York: Bantam Books, 2005).

Chapter 9: Nothing Else Matters Unless You Get Results

1 Tim Maly, "Should You Send That Email? Here's a Flowchart for Deciding," *Fast Company,* February 22, 2012, www.fastcodesign.com/1669094/should-you-send-that-email-heres-a-flowchart-for-deciding.

Mastery and Leadership Skills

Chapter 10: Hiring and Selecting the Best

1 Peter F. Drucker, "How to Make People Decisions," *Harvard Business Review* 63, no. 4 (July 1985): 22–25.

2 Brad Remillard, "What Are the Total Costs of a Bad Hire?" *IMPACT Hiring Solutions* (blog), 2010, www.impacthiringsolutions.com/blog/what-are-the-total-costs-of-a-bad-hire/.

3 Scott Erker and Kelli Buczynski, *Are You Failing The Interview?* (Pittsburgh: Development Dimensions International, 2009), 4, 9.

4 Tom Janz et al., *Behavior Description Interviewing: New, Accurate, Cost Effective* (Upper Saddle River, NJ: Prentice Hall, 1985); Robert W. Eder and Gerald R. Ferris, *The Employment Interview: Theory, Research, and Practice* (Newbury Park, CA: SAGE Publications, 1989).

5 Erker and Buczynski, *Are You Failing The Interview?,* 13–14.

Chapter 11: What Your Boss Really Wants from You

1 Richard Wellins et al., *Be Better Than Average: A Study on the State of Frontline Leadership*, Trend Research (Pittsburgh: Development Dimensions International, 2013), 3.

2 Tom Rath and James K. Harter, *Wellbeing: The Five Essential Elements* (New York: Gallup Press, 2010), 133.

3 Anna Nyberg et al., "Managerial Leadership and Ischaemic Heart Disease among Employees: The Swedish WOLF Study," *Occupational and Environmental Medicine* 66, no. 1 (2009): 51–55.

⁴ Steve Arneson, "Introduction" in *What Your Boss Really Wants from You: 15 Insights to Improve Your Relationship* (San Francisco: Berrett-Koehler Publishers, 2014), OverDrive Read.

Chapter 12: Engagement and Retention

¹ Gallup Consulting, *State of the Global Workplace: A Worldwide Study of Employee Engagement and Wellbeing,* Trend Research (Washington, DC: Gallup Consulting, 2013), 99.

² Richard S. Wellins et al., *Employee Engagement: The Key to Realizing Competitive Advantage,* Monograph (Pittsburgh: Development Dimensions International, 2011).

³ Mark C. Crowley, "The Sharp Drop-Off in Worker Happiness—and What Your Company Can Do about It," *Leadership* (blog), April 30, 2012, www.fastcompany.com/1835578/sharp-drop-worker-happiness-and-what-your-company-can-do-about-it.

⁴ Randall Beck and Jim Harter, "To Win with Natural Talent, Go for Additive Effects," *Gallup Business Journal,* June 2014, 1, *Business Source Corporate Plus,* EBSCOhost (accessed December 19, 2014).

⁵ Jennifer Robison, "Turning around Employee Turnover: Costly Churn Can Be Reduced If Managers Know What to Look for—and They Usually Don't," *Gallup Management Journal Online,* May 8, 2008, 1–6, *Business Source Corporate Plus,* EBSCOhost (accessed December 19, 2014).

Chapter 13: Meetings

¹ "Wasted Time in Meetings Costs the UK Economy £26 Billion," *Business Matters Magazine* (May 20, 2012), www.bmmagazine.co.uk/in-business/6795/wasted-time-in-meetings-costs-the-uk-economy-26-billion/.

² Patrick R. Laughlin et al., "Groups Perform Better Than the Best Individuals on Letters-to-Numbers Problems: Effects of Group Size," *Journal of Personality & Social Psychology* 90, no. 4 (April 2006): 644–651; Gary Charness and Matthias Sutter, "Groups Make Better Self-Interested Decisions," *Journal of Economic Perspectives* 26, no. 3 (Summer 2012): 157–176; M. E. Shaw, "Comparison of Individuals and Small Groups in the Rational Solution of Complex Problems," *American Journal of Psychology* 44 (July 1932); D. W. Taylor and W. L. Faust, "Twenty Questions: Efficiency in Problem-Solving as a Function of Size of Group," *Journal of Experimental Psychology*, 44 (November 1952); G. B. Watson, "Do Groups Think More Efficiently than Individuals?" *Journal of Abnormal and Social Psychology*, 23 (October 1928).

Chapter 14: Coaching

¹ Pete Weaver and Simon Mitchell, *Lessons for Leaders from the People Who Matter,* Trend Research (Pittsburgh: Development Dimensions International, 2012), 9.

Chapter 15: Feedback Fundamentals

¹ Jack Welch 2003 presentation, The Conference Board, New York.

² Evan Sinar and Matt Paese, *Leaders in Transition: Progressing along a Precarious Path* (Pittsburgh: Development Dimensions International, 2014), 7.

³ James Clevenger, "The SOP for Workplace Interactions," *Talent Management Intelligence* (blog), August 8, 2014, www.ddiworld.com/blog/tmi/august-2014/the-sop-for-workplace-interactions; James Clevenger, "Guidance from Above: The Manager's Role in Driving Lean," *Talent Management Intelligence* (blog), November 19, 2014, www.ddiworld.com/blog/tmi/november-2014/the-managers-role-in-driving-lean.; James Clevenger, "Eliminating the 9th Form

of Waste," *Talent Management Intelligence* (blog), July 23, 2014,
www.ddiworld.com/blog/tmi/july-2014/eliminating-the-9th-form-of-waste.

4   Adecco, *2013 State of the Economy and Employment Survey* (Melville, NY: Adecco
    Employment Services, 2013).

5   Accenture, *How Leading Manufacturers Thrive in a World of Ongoing Volatility and Uncertainty*
    (Chicago: Accenture Inc.), 20.

Chapter 17: Delegation

1   Development Dimensions International, "Leadership Mirror Performance Ratings,"
    accessed December 10, 2014, Leadership Mirror database.

2   Development Dimensions International, "Manager Ready Behavior Performance,"
    accessed September 24, 2014, Manager Ready database.

Chapter 18: Performance Management

1   David Rock, "SCARF: A Brain-Based Model for Collaborating with and Influencing Others,"
    NeuroLeadership Journal no. 1 (2008), www.your-brain-at-work.com/files/NLJ_SCARFUS.pdf.

Chapter 19: You and Your Network

1   Daniel Hallak, "Five Networks to Accelerate Your Career," *TD: Talent Development* 68, no. 10
    (October 2014): 104–105.

Chapter 21: A Woman's First Leadership Job

1   Joanna Barsh and Lareina Yee, *Unlocking the Full Potential of Women at Work*
    (New York: McKinsey & Company, 2011), 3.

2   Catalyst, *Catalyst Census: Fortune 500 Appendix 1 — Methodology*, Catalyst Census
    (New York: Catalyst, 2013).

3   DDI and The Conference Board, *Ready-Now Leaders: Meeting Tomorrow's Business
    Challenges, Global Leadership Forecast* (Pittsburgh: Development Dimensions International,
    2014), 40.

4   Georges Desvaux et al., "A business case for women," *The McKinsey Quarterly* no. 4 (2008):
    26–33.

5   DDI and The Conference Board, *Ready-Now Leaders: Meeting Tomorrow's Business
    Challenges, Global Leadership Forecast* (Pittsburgh: Development Dimensions International,
    2014), 41.

6   Katty Kay and Claire Shipman, *The Confidence Code: The Science and Art of
    Self-Assurance — What Women Should Know* (New York: HarperBusiness, 2014).

7   Tara Mohr, "Why Women Don't Apply for Jobs Unless They're 100% Qualified,"
    Harvard Business Review, last modified 2014, accessed December 17, 2014,
    https://hbr.org/2014/08/why-women-dont-apply-for-jobs-unless-theyre-100-qualified.

8   Stephanie Neal et al., *Women as Mentors: Does She or Doesn't She? A Global Study of
    Businesswomen and Mentoring* (Pittsburgh: Development Dimensions International, 2013), 7.

9   "Work & Money," *Real Simple,* September 01, 2014, 196, 198.

10 Sheryl Sandberg, "It's a Jungle Gym, Not a Ladder" in *Lean in: Women, Work, and the Will to Lead* (New York: Knopf, 2013), OverDrive Read.

11 "Failure Issue," *Harvard Business Review* 89, no. 4 (2011).

12 "Madonna Is 'So Nervous' about Super Bowl Performance," *People.com,* last modified 2014, accessed December 17, 2014, www.people.com/people/article/0,,20565802,00.html.

13 "Work & Money," *Real Simple*, September 01, 2014, 198.

Acknowledgments

We (Rich and Tacy) owe tremendous thanks to many people who have helped us shape our vision for *Your First Leadership Job* into reality. We are indebted to the wisdom of over ten million leaders in 26 countries, who have used DDI's teachings to become catalyst leaders. They've sparked action in themselves, their teams, and their companies and, on behalf of DDI, we are thrilled to have made an impact. We also want to thank the more than 20,000 facilitators/instructors who have become certified instructors, master trainers, and overall ambassadors for DDI's interaction skills. You people are black belts and our heroes. Thank you for your stories, your spirit, and your passion to push us beyond where we thought we could go.

For their review, insight, edits, and gentle shaping over this past year, we specifically thank:

- Ellen McGirt, our behind-the-scenes writer, who helped us transform our HR speak into readable stories. We know we've all grown together through this process. Ellen, your encouraging voice will forever ring in our heads every time we write!

- Jim Concelman for his content guidance on every single competency-based skill development in our Mastery and Leadership Skill chapters. Thank you for being our beacon of frontline leadership development.

- To the multiple generations—spanning over four decades—of DDI's instructional designers, product managers, and consultants for their vision and for creating DDI's learning systems for frontline leader development.

- Nikki Dy-Liacco for her reviews and guidance on social media aspects of the book and for coining #LeadLikeAGirl, Tacy's new personal motto.

- Bob Rogers and Bill Byham for their review and support through every chapter. Thank you for enhancing (and maintaining) our self-esteem with your focused feedback.

- Evan Sinar and Aaron Stehura for their leadership analytics and data/research from our rich database.

Acknowledgments *cont'd*

- Jill George, Stephanie Morris, Jim Concelman, Annamarie Lang, and Nikki Dy-Liacco for sharing their wisdom throughout the new leader checklist.

- John Verdone, king of teaching the Key Principles and Interaction Guidelines, for his down-to-earth style, which helped shaped our foundational chapters.

- Nikki Dy-Liacco (again—we kept her busy!) and Brad Thomas, who described and illustrated the caricatures of difficult employees.

- Nancy Guarino and Sandy Eby for keeping us on track. Without you, we both would have been lost, and Rich would have lost his shoes, we are sure!

- Bill Proudfoot, the editorial eagle eye. Thank goodness you were the master of the "minkey" throughout this final push to publication.

- Stacy Infantozzi for her beautiful layout and formatting. We're honored to have had your immense talents for this book. Also, Patrice Andres and Lisa Weyandt for their graphic support.

- Liz Hogan and Elaine Bardzil for keeping us squeaky-clean and honest in our citations.

- Richard Narramore, our editor at Wiley, for his support and guidance.

- Finally, the dozens of leaders around the globe whom we interviewed for this book. Thank you for generously sharing your personal stories and leadership challenges: Alex Badenoch, Joe Bergen, Cathy Boysko, TJ Carey, Gary Cass, Mabel Chan, Hilary Crowe, Michael Daley, Louise Doyle, Kate Eastoe, Fiona Fleming, The Hon. Patricia Forsythe, Michelle Gibson, Colleen Harris, Jason Henningsen, Jude Hollings, Cathrin Kalbfell-Rolfe, Rushikesh Kasture, Ehrrin Keenan, Christian Lang, Stephen Lee, Joy Linton, Yang Liu, Trisha McEwan, Christine McLoughlin, Cathy Manolios, Jo Mithen, Rilla Moore, Helen Newall, Anne O'Keefe, Leanne Plenty, Amiya Kanta Rath, Kirstin Schneider, Qian Shi, Mark Slootmaker, Maria Tassone, Trish Unwin, Sylvie Vanasse.

About DDI

Who We Are. Development Dimensions International, Inc., or DDI, is a leading talent management consultancy. Forty-five years ago, we pioneered the field; today we remain its chief innovator.

What We Do. We help companies transform the way they hire, promote, and develop their leaders and workforces. The outcome? Leaders like you who are ready to inspire, understand, and execute business strategy, and address challenges head-on.

How We Do It. If you have ever had a leader you revered, or marveled at how quickly a new hire came up to speed, you might very well be experiencing DDI at work. Annually, we develop 250,000 leaders worldwide. Often, we are behind the scenes, creating custom training or assessment that clients can roll out on their own. Other times, we are more visible, helping clients drive big changes in their organizations. Always, we use the latest methods, based on science and the test of time.

Who We Do It With. Our clients are some of the world's most successful companies. They are Fortune 500s and multinationals, doing business across a vast array of industries, from Shanghai to San Francisco and everywhere in between. We serve clients from 42 DDI-owned or closely affiliated offices. Visit www.ddiworld.com for more information.

Why We Do It. The principles and skills we teach don't just make people better employees; they are at the heart of what makes for happier and more fulfilled human beings—better family members, better neighbors, better friends.

About the Author

Tacy M. Byham, PhD

Tacy was named CEO of Development Dimensions International, Inc. (DDI) in 2014. She began her career there in the early 1980s as an intern in the video productions department and computer/technology groups. After graduate school she worked as a trainer in Europe and an assessor for tech clients in the United States. She helped develop innovations and eventually used her experiences to build DDI's fast-growing executive development business.

An expert in creative, custom solutions to address talent management challenges, Tacy's clients include Keurig Green Mountain, ADP, BNY Mellon, and Texas Children's Hospital. Her writing has been featured in *The Conference Board Review, CLO* magazine, *People Matters* (India), and *The ASTD Leadership Handbooks* (2010 and 2014). She is also a frequent presenter for the Conference Board and ATD (formerly ASTD), where she speaks on topics ranging from innovation, to women and leadership, to mid-level leadership.

Tacy grew up in the home of a thought leader and entrepreneur. Her father, Bill Byham, founded DDI in 1970, and Tacy's own perspective on leadership was developed over a lifetime of dinner conversations with her family about what makes people better stewards of the things that matter to them. She was immersed in the science of human possibility from day one as well as the importance of community service (her mother is a retired politician and community volunteer). *We traveled the world as DDI grew,* Tacy says of her early access to leaders and management thinkers. *I had a bird's eye view of how things actually worked and could work better. I was inspired. And, after working for a few bad bosses in the tech industry, I wanted to join DDI to work with our fascinating clients and help solve their people challenges.*

On reflection, it's not what you get, but what you give. Well, recently, one of Tacy's teammates left DDI to pursue his life's passion. In a parting note he wrote, *I could write pages on how thankful I am to have worked for you. I really appreciate your genuine care and concern for me . . . for all of us!*

Tacy holds an MA in Mathematics/Computer Science from Mt. Holyoke College and a PhD in Industrial/Organizational Psychology from the University of Akron.

@TacyByham

About the Author

Richard S. Wellins, PhD

Rich currently serves as head of worldwide research and marketing for DDI. He has loved every minute of being a leader (well, almost every minute). Since joining DDI more than 30 years ago, he's held various leadership roles, including positions in sales, R&D, and marketing. Rich earned his PhD in Social/Industrial Psychology from American University. Prior to DDI, he served as a professor of psychology at Western Connecticut State University and as a research psychologist for the US Department of Defense.

This is Rich's fifth book on leadership, including a best seller, *Empowered Teams*. He has worked with dozens of clients on leadership assessment and development projects, including Toyota, AXA, Nissan, Colgate, A.T. Cross, and Sunrise Living. He has presented dozens of conference keynotes on his research around the world, including the Society for Human Resource Management (SHRM), The Conference Board, Association for Talent Development, HRoot (China), and People Matters (India). He currently serves as a judge for CNBC's Asia Business Leaders of the Year Award (ABLA), interviewing the top-performing CEOs throughout Asia. Rich also spearheads DDI's biennial *Global Leadership Forecast,* which features data on best leadership practices collected from over 75,000 leaders. His work has been featured in *Forbes,* the *New York Times,* National Public Radio, CNBC, *Fortune,* and the *Wall Street Journal*.

Rich's interest in leadership came from two life-changing experiences. The first: *My father owned two drug stores, and my mother worked with him running the cosmetics counter,* he recalled. As a teen, Rich was assigned every dirty job there was, from running deliveries to cleaning restrooms. *My dad wanted to make sure that nobody thought I got better treatment than anyone else.* One of the stores served a neighborhood in New Britain, Connecticut, with a high poverty rate. His dad sent him on almost all the deliveries in the community to individuals who relied on the supplies he delivered. *His objective was to teach me, and I'm grateful,* Rich said. *All of these were valuable lessons in leadership, sharing, and accountability.*

His second leadership learning experience was with the Department of Defense as a research psychologist. He spent time on field exercises with the 101st Airborne, working with first lieutenants. As Rich likes to say, *If you can do well as a military first-line leader, the rest of your leadership positions will be a lot easier.*

@RichWellins

Index

Page numbers followed by *f* refer to figures.

A

Ability:
  delegation based on, 196
  gender differences in leadership,
    232, 234*f*
Absenteeism, 187–188
Accountability, 106–107
  ensuring, 107
  joint, 107
  and responsibility, 106
  self-assessment of, 91
  for solving problems with difficult
    employees, 186
  and strategy execution, 90*f*
Acknowledgment. *See also* Recognition
  of contact's successes, 219
  of needs, 225–226
Advice, from women leaders,
  238–240
Age, feedback seeking and, 43
Agendas, meeting, 155–156
Agree (Interaction Guideline):
  in coaching conversations, 169*f*
  in Discussion Planner, 86
  example of, 79
  and leadership interaction styles, 82
  and other Guidelines, 76, 77, 78*f*
Alignment:
  of leader's role and organization's
    expectations, 24–26

  of priorities within organizations,
    201
Applicants:
  conveying positive impression of
    organization to, 119, 128
  misinterpreting information from,
    117
Arrogance, 13
Asking Behavioral Questions (tool),
  122–123
Asking for help:
  from bosses, 134
  and delegation, 200
  from network contacts, 214*f*,
    216–217
Asking questions:
  about applicant's behavior, 121–124
  about delegation, 195
  after poorly run meetings, 154
  in engagement conversations,
    140*f*, 142*f*
  to gain expertise and insights, 217
  in presentations, 227
Assenters, 82
Attitudes, of women leaders, 237
Authenticity, 32–34

B

BadBosses.com, 9
Balanced feedback, 177, 179

Behavior(s):
  asking applicants about, 121–124
  of authentic vs. inauthentic leaders,
    32–33
  of best leaders, 74, 74*f*
  of best vs. worst bosses, 15
  of catalyst leaders, 11*f*, 12
  of coaches, 164*f*, 167
  of difficult employees, 181–184
  of leaders in effective conversations, 63
  of perfect coaches, 167
  as predictor of future behavior, 121
  reasons to address problem,
    183–184
Behavioral questions, 121–124
Boss(es), 130–134
  assessing your, 130
  attributes of good vs. bad, 131
  behaviors of best vs. worst, 15
  catalyst leaders vs., 9–11
  improving relationships with,
    131–134
Brand, leadership, *see* Leadership brand
Bringing out the best in people,
  35–37
Byham, Bill, 35–36

C
Career(s):
  leadership roles in women's,
    229–230
  and meeting quality, 150–151
Catalyst leader(s), 9–16
  behaviors and beliefs of, 11*f*, 12
  bosses vs., 9–11
  characteristics of, 11
  conversations of, 47
  defined, xiii, 1
  and motivation/productivity of
    employees, 15

ownership building by, 72
and success factors for frontline
  leaders, 13*f*, 14,
Clarify (Interaction Guideline):
  in coaching conversations,
    169, 169*f*
  in Discussion Planner, 85
  example of, 78
  and leadership interaction styles,
    81, 82
  and other Guidelines, 76, 77, 78*f*
Close (Interaction Guideline), 76–79
  in coaching conversations, 169*f*
  in Discussion Planner, 86
  example of, 79
  and other Guidelines, 76, 77, 78*f*
Coaching, 161–172
  assessing impact of individual
    performers before, 165–166
  demonstrating empathy in, 59
  and employee engagement, 137
  improving accountability with, 107
  improving team functioning with,
    185
  Interaction Guidelines for, 168–169
  Key Principles for, 169–171
  and performance management,
    203, 204*f*
  and personal/practical needs of direct
    reports, 168
  practicing skills related to, 172
  proactive, 162–167, 164*f*, 170, 185
  reactive, 162–167, 170
Collaboration, 36–37
Communication. *See also*
  Conversations, effective
  about accountability, 107
  in delegation, 193, 197–199
  with networks, 219
  sharing feelings to improve, 69

Communication skills, 60, 83–84
Competencies:
  and behavioral goals, 207
  as focus of interview, 120
  selecting applicants based on, 117
  in Success Profile^SM, 13, 14
Confidence, 34, 232–235
Contacts, network:
  asking for help from, 214f,
    216–217
  maintaining relationships with,
    214f, 217
  reaching out to establish, 214f,
    215–216
  tips for increasing number of,
    218–220
Continuous learning, 126
Conversations, effective, 46–74.
    See also Interaction Guidelines
  asking for help and encouraging
    involvement in, 62–65
  coaching, 166–171
  delegation, 197–199, 199f
  with difficult employees, 185–187
  on employee engagement, 139f,
    140–143
  with good leaders, 47–48
  for influencing others, 224, 225
  Key Principles in, 49
  listening and responding with
    empathy in, 56–60
  maintaining/enhancing self-esteem
    in, 50–56
  performance management, 207–208
  planning, 83–86
  practical and personal needs of
    others in, 48–49
  providing support without removing
    responsibility in, 72–73
  retention, 146–148

  sharing thoughts, feelings, and
    rationale in, 66–71
Culture, 89, 232
Customer focus, 122, 126

D
DDI, see Development Dimensions
    International
Decisions, rationale for, 66–69, 71
Decision-making authority, 193, 194
Delegation, 191–200
  authority associated with, 193–195
  avoiding reverse, 199–200
  as challenge for leaders, 22
  defined, 192
  effective communication about,
    197–199
  and employee engagement, 137
  reasons leaders avoid, 191–192
Develop (Interaction Guideline):
  in coaching conversations, 169f
  and leadership interaction styles, 81, 82
Developmental feedback, 174, 177–179
Development Dimensions
    International (DDI), 3, 7, 32, 47,
    48, 63, 80, 99, 126, 145, 192, 220,
    231, 232, 236, 242
Discussion Planner, 83, 85–86, 241
Disengaged employees, 137, 188

E
Effective conversations,
    see Conversations, effective
Effort, recognizing, 144–145
Emotions, 3, 6, 60, 160
Emotional intelligence, 83
Empathy Key Principle, 56–60
  in coaching conversations, 170
  for detached leaders, 82
  with family members, 58

Empathy Key Principle (*continued*)
  and giving feedback, 176
  identifying facts and feelings with, 59–60
  and importance of listening as communication skill, 60
Employee engagement, 135–148
  benefits of, 135–136
  conversations about, 143
  creating environments for, 136–137
  drivers of, 138–139
  energy associated with, 137
  improving, 140*f*–142*f*
  and Interaction Guidelines, 80*f*
  and praise, 144–145
  and retention conversations, 146–148
  starting conversations about, 140–142
Empowerment, 35–37
Esteem Key Principle, 49–56
  in coaching conversations, 170
  enhancing self-esteem, 50, 52–55
  and giving feedback, 176
  maintaining self-esteem, 50–52, 55
Execution of strategy, *see* Strategy execution
Extroverts, 215

F
Failing forward, 40
Failure:
  learning from, 161, 162
  of strategies, 90
  women leaders on, 238–239
Family members:
  effective conversations with, 48
  listening and responding with empathy to, 58
  support from, 239
  using leadership skills with, 241–242

Feedback, 173–180
  and accountability, 107
  asking for, 40–41, 202
  being receptive to, 39–43
  complete vs. incomplete, 179
  for difficult employees, 185
  from direct reports, 5, 41
  effective, 173–174, 177
  from peers, 145
  STAR approach to delivering, 176–180
Feelings, sharing, 66–71, 171.
Female first-time leaders, *see* Women leaders
First-time leader(s), 7
Following up:
  for accountability, 107
  on delegated tasks, 193, 197–198
  with difficult employees, 185
Frontline leader(s):
  defined, 7
  success factors for, 13–14, 13*f*,
Frontline Leadership Success Profile, 14

G
Getting-to-know-you conversations:
  with direct reports, 38–39
  with key stakeholders, 24–26
Glass ceiling, 231–233
Global Leadership Forecast (GLF), 231–234
Goals:
  behavioral, 204, 207
  measuring progress against, 99
  and performance management, 204–208
  prioritizing, 94
  SMART, 205–206

H

Heart disease, poor leadership and, 131
Help, asking for, 62–65, 134, 214*f*, 216–217
Hierarchy of needs, 51
Hiring, 115–129
    conducting interviews for, 120–129
    costs of mistakes in, 115–116
    improving team functioning with, 184
    and mistakes with applicant selection, 117–119

I

Identifying Your Top Priorities (tool), 95
Identify Talent to Retain (tool), 147
Individual contributor(s):
    assessing impact of, 165–166
    deciding to remain a, 27
    mind-set of, 19
    success for leaders vs., 88–89
Influence, 139, 221–228
    as challenge for leaders, 23–24
    examples of, 221–222
    packaging messages for greater, 226–228
    and personal power, 222–223
    social skills needed for, 228
    and stakeholder commitment, 228
    strategies to improve, 224–225
Influencing strategies, 224–225, 224*f*
Interaction Guidelines, 75–86. *See also* specific guidelines
    for coaching, 168–169
    for conversations about employee engagement, 139
    in conversations with difficult employees, 185
    in delegation discussions, 197, 197*f*

    and employee engagement, 80*f*
    and Key Principles, 79, 80*f*
    meeting practical needs with, 49, 75–76
    in meetings, 76–79
    planning for conversations involving, 83–86
    results of using, 80*f*
Interaction skills, xiii
    for coaching, 168–171
    in engagement conversations, 139
    for facilitating meetings, 157–160
Interaction styles, leadership, 80–82
Interviews, with job applicants, 120–129
Introverts, 215–216
Involvement:
    encouraging, 62–65
    personal need for, 170
Involvement Key Principle, 62–65
    in coaching conversations, 170
    for the Interrogator, 81
    and other Key Principles, 49
    and time spent listening vs. speaking, 62–64

J

Job satisfaction, 5, 18, 126
Joint accountability, 107

K

Key Principles. *See also* specific principles
    and behaviors of best leaders, 74, 74*f*
    for coaching, 169–171
    in conversations about employee engagement, 139
    in conversations with difficult employees, 185
    in delegation discussions, 197, 197*f*

Key Principles (*continued*)
    and Interaction Guidelines, 79, 80*f*
    and leadership interaction styles, 81
    meeting personal needs with, 49
    in networking, 218

L
Leaders:
    avoidance of delegation by,
        191–192
    behaviors of best, 74, 74*f*
    benefits of addressing problem
        behaviors for, 183
    conversations with good, 47–48
    roles of, 24–26, 229–230
Leader-like activities, time spent on,
    99
Leadership:
    legacy of, 43–45
    and life skills, 241–242
    as profession, 242–243
    as science, 7
Leadership brand, 1, 28–45
    authenticity in, 32–34
    and being receptive to feedback,
        39–43
    and bringing out the best in people,
        35–37
    and leadership differentiators, 30
    as legacy of leadership, 43–45
    and making a good first impression,
        29–30
    mistakes that damage, 28–29
Leadership development, for women,
    232–233
Leadership interaction styles, 80–82
Leadership Pipeline, 21, 21*f*
Leadership skills, 241–242
#LeadLikeAGirl, 240
Legacy, leadership, 43–45

Legal issues:
    in candidate selection, 128–129
    with difficult employees, 183
#LikeAGirl campaign, 240
Listening:
    authentic, 171
    with empathy, 56–61
    time spent speaking vs., 62–65

M
Management:
    and interacting vs. managing, 96, 96*f*
    need for measurement in, 99
Managers, 25, 41, 111. *See also* Senior
    management
Measurement, 99–105
    assessing your use of, 92
    for delegated tasks, 198
    with outcome vs. progress measures,
        100–105
    prompts associated with, 105
    selecting activities for, 99
    of SMART goals, 206
    and strategy execution, 90*f*
Meetings, 149–160
    anticipating and preventing
        problems in, 157
    attention at, 151
    costs associated with, 149
    Interaction Skills in, 76–79,
        157–160
    "one down" and "two down," xii
    tips on conducting, 155–157
    virtual technology for, 153
Mentorship, 236–237, 239
Micromanagers, 35, 87
Motivation:
    of delegation candidates, 196
    of employees working for catalyst
        leaders, 13

of job applicants, 118, 125–126
for pursuing leadership position, 18

N

Network(s), 209–220
  types of, 210–211
Networking:
  activities for, 218–220
  benefits of, 211
  as challenge for leaders, 23
  conversations for, 218
New Leader Checklist, 245
Nonverbal communication, 140*f*

O

Open (Interaction Guideline):
  in coaching conversations, 169*f*
  example of, 78
  and leadership interaction styles, 81
  and other Guidelines, 76, 77, 78*f*
Ownership, building, 72–73

P

Partnership building, 122
Performance:
  discussing, with difficult employees,
    186
  expectations for, 184
  self-esteem and, 51
Performance appraisals, 201, 203
Performance management, 201–208
  and coaching, 203, 204*f*
  conversations for, 207–208
  purpose of, 201–202
  setting goals in, 204–207
Personal needs:
  addressing, in coaching, 168
  considering others', 48–49
  defined, 49
  and employee engagement, 139

meeting others', 75. *See also* Key
  Principles
Planning:
  for conversations with difficult
    employees, 184–185
  with influencing strategies, 24*f*,
    224–225
Position power, 222
Positive feedback, 174, 177, 179, 185
Power, personal vs. position,
  222–223
Practical needs:
  addressing, in coaching, 168
  considering others', 48–49
  defined, 49
  and employee engagement, 139
  meeting others', 49, 75–79
Praise, 52–55, 144–145
Priorities, 93–99
  identifying your, 94–95
  performance management for
    alignment of, 201
  for retention efforts, 146
  time spent on critical, 93, 96–99
Proactive coaching, 162–167
  behaviors associated with, 164f
  defined, 162
  to improve team functioning, 185
  Involvement Key Principle in, 170
  reactive vs., 166
Profession, leadership as, 242–243

R

Rationale, for decisions, 66–69, 71,
  137, 171
Reactive coaching, 162–167
  defined, 162, 163
  and personal needs of team
    members, 170
  proactive vs., 166

Readiness to lead, 19, 234, 237

Receptivity to feedback, 39–43

Recognition, 50, 126, 144–145

Reference checks, 127

Relationship building, 48, 218

Results measures, 198

Retention, employee, 135, 138–139, 146–148

S

Self-centered behavior, 189

Self-esteem. *See also* Esteem Key Principle

  in coaching conversations, 170

  enhancing, 50, 52–55

  maintaining, 50–52, 55, 176

Senior management:

  feedback-seeking behavior by, 43

  importance of authenticity to, 33

  informing, of direct reports' accomplishments, 145

  performance management reports for, 201

  women leaders in, 231–233

Share Key Principle, 66–71

  and benefits of sharing rationale, 68–69

  examples of sharing thoughts, 69

  and leadership interaction styles, 81, 82

  sharing feelings appropriately, 69–70

SMART goals, 205–206

SPARK! How the Science Behind DDI Transforms Lives In and Out of the Workplace (Dy-Liacco, Fox, and Rogers), 242

Stakeholders:

  commitment from, 228

  reaching out to, 25–26

STAR approach:

  to asking behavioral questions, 123–124

  to conducting performance discussions, 186

  to delivering feedback, 176–180

Strategy execution, 87–112

  and accountability, 90*f*, 106–107

  as challenge for leaders, 23–24

  and defining success in terms of the team, 88–89

  elements of, 89–92

  and focus, 90*f*, 93–99

  and measurement, 90*f*, 99–105

Stress:

  and strategy execution, 87–88

  with transition to leadership position, 3–4, 17

Success Profile^SM, 13, 13*f*, 14

Support:

  identifying needed, 214–215, 214*f*

  for network contacts, 216, 217

  and responsibility, 72–73

  for women leaders, 239

Support Key Principle, 72–73

  in coaching, 172

  in delegation discussions, 198

  and leadership interaction styles, 81

  and taking over direct reports' problems, 72–73

T

Team(s):

  benefits of addressing problem behaviors for, 183

  candidate selection by, 127

  delegation's effect on, 196

  improving functioning of, 184–186

success in terms of, 88–89

task ownership by, 72

Team members:

  letting, do their jobs, 172

  nonviable solutions from, 64–65

  one-on-one meetings with, 38–39

  practical and personal needs of, 48–49

  selecting, for delegation, 193, 196

Technology:

  for coaching, 165, 171

  for communicating with networks, 219

Transitions, Leadership Pipeline, 21, 21f

Transition to a leadership position, 17–27

  alignment of your role and organization's expectations in, 24–26

  challenges associated with, 3–4, 22–24

  key activities during first six months of, 27, 133

  in Leadership Pipeline, 21, 21f

  and motivation for pursuing position, 18

  reaching out to stakeholders in, 25–26

  stressors in, 17

Trust:

  gaining, xii, 32–33

  and Share Key Principle, 66–71

Turnover, 80f

U

Using Interaction Skills to Solve Meeting Problems (tool), 158–160

V

Verification reference checks, 127

Virtual meetings, 153

W

Well-being, 131

Women leaders, 229–240

  advice from, 238–240

  confidence of, 232–235

  declarative conversations for, 236

  effects of leadership roles on careers of, 229–230

  and "leading like a girl," 240

  mentorship for, 236–237

  in senior leadership positions, 231–233

Wyckoff, Luke, 219

Y

"Your First Leadership Job" microsite, 8, 11, 48, 108, 133, 145, 223, 245

Z

Zapp! The Lightning of Empowerment (Byham), 35–36